COMMUNICATION AS CULTURE

Media and Popular Culture
A Series of Critical Books

SERIES EDITOR
David Thorburn
*Director of Film and Media Studies and Professor
of Literature,
Massachusetts Institute of Technology*

In recent years a new, interdisciplinary scholarship devoted to popular culture and modern communications media has appeared. This emerging intellectual field aims to move beyond inherited conceptions of "mass society" by recognizing the complexity and diversity of the so-called mass audience and its characteristic cultural experiences. The new scholarship on media and popular culture conceives communication as a complex, ritualized experience in which "meaning" or significance is constituted by an intricate, contested collaboration among institutional, ideological, and cultural forces.

Intended for students and scholars as well as the serious general reader, **Media and Popular Culture** will publish original interpretive studies devoted to various forms of contemporary culture, with emphasis on media texts, audiences, and institutions. Aiming to create a fruitful dialogue between recent strains of feminist, semiotic, and marxist cultural study and older forms of humanistic and social-scientific scholarship, the series will be open to many methods and theories and committed to a discourse that is intellectually rigorous yet accessible and lucid.

Communication as Culture

ESSAYS ON MEDIA AND SOCIETY

JAMES W. CAREY

Boston

UNWIN HYMAN

London   Sydney   Wellington

Unwin Hyman, Inc.
955 Massachusetts Avenue, Cambridge, Mass. 02139, USA

Published by the Academic Division of
Unwin Hyman, Ltd,
15/17 Broadwick Street, London W1V 1FP, UK

Allen & Unwin Australia Pty Ltd,
8 Napier Street, North Sydney, NSW 2060, Australia

Allen & Unwin (New Zealand) Ltd,
in association with the Port Nicholson Press Ltd,
Compusales Building, 75 Ghuznee Street, Wellington 1, New Zealand

First published 1989
Second impression 1990

Library of Congress Cataloging-in-Publication Data

Carey, James W.
 Communication as culture : essays on media and society /
James W. Carey
  p. cm. — (Media and popular culture : 1)
  Bibliography: p.
  Includes index.
  ISBN 0-04-445062-1. ISBN 0-04-445064-8 (pbk.)
  1. Mass media. 2. Culture. 3. Communication—
Technological innovations.   I. Title.   II. Series.
P91.C33 1988   88–14390
302.2'34—dc19   CIP

British Library Cataloguing in Publication Data

Carey, James W.
 Communication as culture : essays on media
 and society — (Media and popular culture)
 1. Society. Role of mass media
 I. Title II. Series
302.2'34
ISBN 0–04–445062–1
ISBN 0–04–445064–8 pbk

Set in 10 on 12 point Palatino
Printed in Great Britain by
Billing and Sons, Ltd, London and Worcester

Contents

Series Editor's Introduction

In their unrevised form as articles and lectures, the essays gathered in this book helped to establish the ground for cultural approaches to the study of communications and modern technology. On reading in *The American Scholar* the first version of "The Mythos of the Electronic Revolution" (chapter 5), Marshall McLuhan wrote Carey a letter hailing him as a "fearless character," who was taking "his academic life in his hands."

McLuhan had a keen awareness of the embedded institutional power of the "mass communications" establishment in the decades following World War II and an equally strong sense of its intellectual inadequacy, its narrow empirical and behaviorist notions of people and cultural institutions. He recognized how bold and in its own way how radical is Carey's ambition—it was McLuhan's as well, of course—to put in question our inherited mythologies of "communication" and "mass media" and the "electronic revolution."

Yet in the theoretically self-conscious and ideologically attuned discourse that dominates cultural interpretation of all sorts as we begin this last decade of the twentieth century, Carey's fearlessness might be said to reside in nearly opposite virtues. His voice is distinctive and important in our current scholarly climate, that is, in part for its very refusal to yield entirely to a vocabulary of power, for its resistance to the privileging of "ideological" as against "mythic" or "ritual" or "anthropological" elements in the description and interpretation of cultural formations.

Mediating and ambivalent, the essays collected here insist on the ideological/political dimensions of media theory and practice, but they do so in a moderating, pluralist, and citizenly spirit. Culture is not a one-way process, so runs Carey's continuing subtext. A domination model of social experience must oversimplify cultural transactions, which always contain elements of collaboration, of dialogue, of ritualized sharing or interaction. A "progress" model is similarly reductive, masking a rationale for established power and established ways of thinking and also underestimating the individual and communal, the interactive dimensions of culture.

This book itself embodies the virtues of dialogue and intellectual collaboration, of course. The pluralist American philosophers John Dewey and William James are shaping spirits here; and I imagine

ix

that Carey's nonspecialist use of these thinkers and his generous, lucid accounts of such contemporaries as Clifford Geertz, Raymond Williams, and Harold Innis will be helpful for many readers. Still more, I hope that Carey's flexible spirit, his hostility to terminologies, his pluralist and democratic notions of culture will reach a wide new audience of teachers and scholars and reader-citizens.

—David Thorburn

Acknowledgments

In the course of composing the essays collected herein, I acquired a large and cosmopolitan set of obligations, and now is the time to discharge a few of them.

The National Endowment for the Humanities provided a year's respite from administrative duties to work on three of the essays. Likewise, the Institute of Advanced Study at the University of Illinois underwrote some leisure for time at the typewriter and in the library. The Gannett Center for Media Studies at Columbia University granted me five months as an Inaugural Fellow for research, writing, and revision. Finally, I passed a happy season at the University of Georgia in its School of Journalism, undistracted, as a visiting professor celebrating the bicentennial of our first public university. To those institutions—and to Everette Dennis, Daniel Alpert, and Thomas Russell—I am greatly indebted.

My largest obligation is to John J. Quirk of Chicago, with whom I wrote two of the essays and from whom I learned much. David Thorburn's energy and interest brought the collection together. Many others helped along the way, often in forms they would scarcely recognize. Here are a few with instant apologies to those I have omitted: Gail Crotts, Norman Sims, Douglas Birkhead, Roxanne Zimmer, Jacqueline Cartier, John Pauly, Roberta Astroff, Keya Ganguly, and Robert Fortner.

I have been blessed with membership on the faculty of two fine institutions: briefly at the University of Iowa and over a considerable period at the University of Illinois at Urbana-Champaign. Much help and companionship came from people in both places: Lary Belman, John Erickson, Hanno Hardt, Charlotte Jones, Howard Maclay, Kim Rotzoll, Chuck Whitney, Ellen Wartella, Wick Rowland, Howard Ziff, Rita Simon, Larry Grossberg, and Cliff Christians. Barbara Welch has been a unique friend sharing her talents and affections generously. Albert Kreiling's thought traces, even when it makes him unhappy, many of the sentences. Bill Alfeld has taught me more than anyone else over thirty happy years. Ted Peterson has tried valiantly to untangle the prose along with the thought. Jay Jensen has always been a particular inspiration. Joli Jensen edited an early version and then shared her unparalleled gift for friendship. Eleanor Blum has been a consummate librarian to a generation of us at Illinois and, so much the better, a person of special affection. Much of everything unfolded in long walks and long talks with my friend and indispensable companion, Julian Simon.

These essays are reprinted largely as they originally appeared. In every chapter I yielded to the temptation to update a reference or two, alter a word here and there, and rebuild an occasional paragraph. I did merge together a few essays that at one time had an independent existence. That resulted in considerable revision, particularly in chapters two, four and six. Despite those alterations, the outlook and specifics remain true to the original publication, even when in hindsight I wanted to alter more than a few judgments. The original sources, with thanks and acknowledgment, are as follows:

Chapter 1 appeared in *Communication*, Volume 2, No. 2, published by Gordon and Breach Ltd. (1975). Copyright © Gordon and Breach Science Publishers S.A.)

Chapter 2 appeared in *Mass Communication and Society*, James Curran et al., eds. (London: Edward Arnold Ltd., 1977). As revised, it incorporates material I originally wrote for an essay with Albert L. Kreiling in *The Uses of Mass Communication*, Jay G. Blumler and Elihu Katz, eds. (Beverly Hills: Sage Publications, 1975). Reprinted by permission of Sage Publications, Inc.

Chapter 3 appeared as "Mass Media: The Critical View," in *Communications Yearbook V* (Beverly Hills: Sage Publications, 1982). Reprinted by permission of Sage Publications, Inc.

Chapter 4 appeared in the *Mass Communication Review Yearbook*, Vol. 5 (Beverly Hills: Sage Publications, 1986). Reprinted by permission of Sage Publications, Inc.

Chapter 5 written with John J. Quirk appeared in *The American Scholar*, Volume 39, No. 2 (Spring 1970), and is reprinted as it appeared without the customary scholarly apparatus. It contains a number of "new" paragraphs I have added and incorporates some material contained in what was a second part of the original piece. That appeared in *The American Scholar*, Volume 39, No. 3 (Summer 1970). (Both articles copyright © by the United Chapters of Phi Beta Kappa.)

Chapter 6 was originally published as "Culture, Geography and Communications: The Work of Harold Innis in an American Context," in *Culture, Communication and Dependency*, W. Melody et al, eds. (Norwood, NJ: Ablex Publishing, 1981). As revised, it incorporates material from "Canadian Communication Theory," in *Studies in Canadian Communications*, edited by Gertrude Joch Robinson and Donald Theall (Montreal: McGill University Studies in Communications, 1975).

ACKNOWLEDGEMENTS

Chapter 7 written with John J. Quirk appeared in *Communications Technology: Impact and Policy* edited by George Gerbner et al, New York: John Wiley, 1973. Reprinted by permission of John Wiley & Sonsm Inc. I have added an "afterword" to the essay.

Chapter 8 appeared in *Prospects: The Annual of the American Studies Association*, Vol. 8 (Cambridge: Cambridge University Press, 1983).

Nena Richards patiently and generously reassembled and retyped the manuscript; Juanita Craven and before her, Zerla Young and Lorraine Selander kept life together.

Work composed over an extended period amid the usual demands of classes, administration, and family could not be sustained except through the goodness of all those mentioned earlier. Goodness we cannot repay, but we can at least exonerate it. Beyond such forgiveness are the deeper gifts: Bill, Tim, Matt, and Dan. The work, as the life, is dedicated to them and, most of all, to Bette: always present. And my Father: always present, although absent.

Introduction

In *Democracy and Its Discontents,* Daniel Boorstin summarized his version of American history with the comment that "perhaps the most important single change in human consciousness in the last century, and especially in the American consciousness, has been the multiplying of the means and forms of what we call 'communication'" (1974: 7). Boorstin's wavering conclusion is common enough, even unexceptional, though it remains largely uninvestigated. But is it true?

Certainly until recent times most ordinary men and women stood outside of and were inaccessible to and uninterested in communications that were mechanically reproduced beyond the circle of village and kin. Ordinary people could not be easily gathered together, held still, and sat down for an appeal, advertisement, advice, or admonition. To reach them one had to work through elaborate networks of personal relations: churches, political parties, neighborhoods, ethnic societies. The instruments of communication were expensive and distant and, for most people, uninteresting and irrelevant. The impression is too often left in our histories that in the nineteenth century people sat around waiting for the news from Washington or entertainment from the metropolis. Waiting at the post for a letter from home is an old habit enlarged by the great democratic migrations; waiting for the newspaper or waiting at the television set are modern ones enlarged by the great urban and suburban migrations of the more recent past. Today the mass media are inescapable and people feel slightly less alive when unhooked from long lines of news and entertainment. James Leo Herlihy describes the protagonist of *Midnight Cowboy,* Joe Buck, as never being far from a television set and of not being sure that life was continuing when the flickering image was not present. There is necessary license here, but the insight is sound: modern communications have drastically altered the ordinary terms

1

of experience and consciousness, the ordinary structures of interest and feeling, the normal sense of being alive, of having a social relation.

Still, a melodramatic modernism or postmodernism, one that underscores the revolutions and ruptures that come with electronic communication, is not particularly helpful and is pretty much based on an illusion. In many of the essays that follow I attempt to puncture this view, to deconstruct the satanic and angelic images that have surrounded, justified, and denigrated the media of communications. We are dealing with an old story rather than a new one. Although the computer and satellite have reduced time to a picosecond, an instantaneous present, and the globe to a point where everyone is in the same place, this is simply the latest chapter in an old tale. The habits of mind and structures of thought that seem characteristic of our age, particularly the talk of a communications revolution and exalted hopes and equally exaggerated fears of the media, are repetitions so predictable as to suggest undeviating corridors of thought.

If we yield to a useful ethnocentrism, we can see that the "multiplying of the means and forms of communication" and their peculiar social role is a central feature of American history from the outset. One need not erect complex metaphors of a "virgin land" or the "first new nation" to recognize that we were a creation, in significant ways, of an attempt to revolutionize the conditions under which culture was made and disseminated: to dislodge culture from the villages in which it was created, to resettle it at a distance, to readapt it to uncongenial surroundings. But this technological extension and resettlement could never unload the instincts and necessities of an ancient past outside history. We remained possessed by that which we no longer quite possessed: rituals and narratives that are in the strict sense anthropological.

The United States was, to flirt with more deterministic language, the product of literacy, cheap paper, rapid and inexpensive transportation, and the mechanical reproduction of words—the capacity, in short, to transport not only people but a complex culture and civilization from one place to another, indeed between places that were radically dissimilar in geography, social conditions, economy, and very often climate. This was an undertaking understood as the eclipsing of time and space. But neither could be eclipsed. Grafting ancient European cultures onto new material conditions created strange but identifiable scar tissue. The need to ritualize and stabilize experience in the new world had to be accomplished with resources carried from elsewhere.

A different and more congenial way of putting it is that the United States was created at a moment when a historical void was opened up—a space in between the oral and written traditions. This was a moment when ancient forms of association, politics, and entertainment conducted by speech and storytelling were overlaid with newer habits of literacy: reading and writing. The older oral tradition depended on certain habits and capacities. However, it did not travel well unless stabilized by writing and reinforced by printing. The new written tradition cultivated distinctive habits and practices—spending a lot of time alone, conversing over distances, composing in private, maintaining introspective records, keeping up with the news—that were at odds with the oral tradition. Moreover, both traditions were substantively empty until they were reciprocally filled: until the characteristic tales of the oral tradition were translated into a printed register; until the characteristic habits and outlooks of printing filtered through speech and discourse. The entire transmigration is a complicated one, but the political side of the story, though well known, warrants a brief recounting.

Until the end of the eighteenth century there was a broad consensus in political philosophy stretching from Plato and Aristotle through Rousseau and Montesquieu that there were natural limits to democracy, limits of both geography and population. The geographic model of democracy was taken from the Greek city-states, states that were quite small, varying in size from ten by ten up to seventy by seventy kilometers according to some estimates. These were political units so small that any citizen could travel on foot from the most remote point in a city-state to its political center and return in one day. What was true of geography was likewise true of population. Robert Dahl in *Size and Democracy* (1973) reminds us that Plato calculated the optimal number of citizens in a democracy as 5,040. The number displays the fallacy of misplaced concreteness, but it expresses the democratic desire for universal participation. Greater numbers would make democratic debate and discussion impossible. Democracies or republics were limited, then, by the range of the foot and the power of the tongue.

It is a truism that political organization is limited by prevailing modes of transportation and communication and changes with improvements in these technologies. But Greek democracy turned limitations into virtues. Democracies, or so the theory goes, had to be large enough to be self-sufficient but small enough that citizens could know one another's character. Democracies had to be large enough to be autonomous but small enough to share the roles that constituted self-government: no permanent bureaucracy, please. This was an oral democracy based upon practices of assembly, debate, disputation, and talk and not on the mere transmission of orders, instructions, and responses. Debate provided the model for decision making, but it also provided for the cultivation of the arts of rhetoric and disputation and the related feats of memory that were central to Greek ideals of character, education, and political life.

Bruce Smith in *Politics and Remembrance* argues that republics are mnemonic structures; they are erected "upon the injunction: remember" (1985: 7). The primordial memory is that republics have concrete historical beginnings and therefore can have concrete historical endings. When Aristotle defines man as a "political animal," he means both more and less than we do by the phrase. Man's natural place was in the polis, but this place was defined through speech, through an oral tradition, which cultivated the resources of remembrance: remembrance of the achievement and fragility of republican politics. Republics, then, are a tissue of relations in space and time, relations expressed in the basic terms of republican existence—citizen and patriot.

To be a citizen is to assume a relation in space to one's contemporaries: to all, irrespective of class and kin, who exist in the same place under the canopy of politics as fellow citizens. To be a patriot is to assume a relation in time to the republican tradition: to the predecessors with whom one shares a patrimony. These are relations that are wide and deep but marked, in J. G. A. Pocock's useful phrase, by radical finitude.

The federal union, as embodied in the Constitution and the Federalist Papers, both affirmed the republican tradition and attempted to transcend and contradict it. Jefferson's notion of perpetual revolution isolated each political generation within the stream of history and telescoped time to the dimension of a lifetime. The Constitution proposed a republic on a scale never before imagined or thought possible: continental in its geography, virtually unlimited in its population. The problems of space and size were reinforced by formidable barriers of terrain: mountain ranges and scarcely navigable north-south rivers. Geography suggested a pattern of unity that did not follow the political development of the colonial period: outside of the militarily vulnerable Atlantic shipping corridor, movement north to south was slow and hazardous and the internal system of natural waterways cut patterns that did not fit the natural flows of population and information. Perhaps geography, or so some thought, would overwhelm the republic before it began.

How was this continental nation to be held together, to function effectively, to avoid declension into faction or tyranny or chaos? How were we, to use a phrase of that day, "to cement the union"? To make it all too simple, the answer was sought in the word and the wheel, in transportation and transmission, in the power of printing and civil engineering to bind a vast distance and a large population into cultural unity or, as the less optimistic would have it, into cultural hegemony. This required placing enormous emphasis upon literacy, the press, and education. It required isolating, to some degree, local life from national life and created the problem of maintaining equilibrium between them, which has preoccupied us ever since. If republican unity was to be technologically achieved by way of the space-binding potential of communication, republican character and virtue was to be achieved by the time-binding power of oral speech and discourse.

For much of the eighteenth and nineteenth centuries American society did, here and there, approximate the Greek ideal and hence the continuing imaginative pull of the New England town meeting. The dense political units of the eastern states were organized around the mobility of the horse rather than the foot. Moreover, the life of the citizen was situated in and preoccupied by, our federal histories notwithstanding, the activity of the local community: distance and terrain led to an emphasis that reached a somewhat romantic flowering in Jefferson's ideal of a democracy of the middle landscape.

But the point is this: from the outset a key discourse of American life has entertained different and contradictory notions of the practice of communication—one that derives from modern advances in the printing press and transportation and one that is situated within the ancient theory and practice of the voice. The contradiction is symbolized, though hardly resolved, by the uneasy juxtaposition of assembly, speech, and press in the First Amendment.

The Federalist Papers are, among other things, a running argument with Montesquieu and inherited political theory: an attempt to resolve the contradictions that the geography and population of this continent presented to received theory. In two of the most worked-over of the essays, numbers 10 and 14, Madison argued that improvements in communications would efface distance and facilitate continental democracy: "The Communication between the western and atlantic districts and between different parts of each will be rendered more and more easy, by those numerous canals which art finds it so little difficult to connect and complete" (*The Federalist*, 1961: 87). Moreover, Madison argued that geography would assist rather than hinder union. The problem of continental democracy was to be solved by the press and the art of transportation engineering. A constitutionally protected technology would amplify the debate of democracy and serve as a check on government. Engineering and communication would bind the nation together, collect representatives to public functions and disperse them to constituencies, and give a vivid presence to a continent-wide public discourse.

This solution, what I call a transmission or transportation solution, was embodied in that ambiguous phrase, "the communication between east and west." In Jefferson's mind one of the functions of the central government, a notion that seems so apposite to his commitment to agrarian democracy, was the building of roads and canals and the education necessary to turn these instruments into channels of national information and intelligence. Alan Trachtenberg in *Brooklyn Bridge: Fact and Symbol* (1965) elegantly retells this part of the story, and I here paraphrase. In 1806, Jefferson announced an ambitious program for the "progress of improvement" to bring the highway to the country, which, more than anything else, brought the country to the city. Henry Adams pointed out that this plan contained the crown of Jefferson's hopes for republican government in America: a national system of public higher education and a national system of roads commensurate "with the majesty of the country." The roads would guarantee the Union: "New channels of communication will be opened between the states, the lines of separation will disappear, their interests will be identified and their union cemented by new and indestructible ties" (Jefferson, 1854: 11).

Jefferson's secretary of the Treasury, Albert Gallatin, issued a report in 1808 recommending that internal improvements should be federally controlled because their benefits were national.

> Good roads and canals will shorten distances; facilitate commercial and personal intercourse; and unite by a still more intimate community of interests the most remote quarters of the United States. No other single operation within the power of government can more effectively tend to strengthen and perpetuate that union which secures external independence, domestic peace and internal liberty (Jefferson, 1854: 11).

The consequences of this policy were ambiguous, securing some of the benefits Jefferson and Gallatin sought but frustrating some of their more precious hopes, particularly the dream of an agrarian republic. But most important, the episode established a particular creed recited at each new advance in technology: the technology of transport and communication would make it possible to erect the vivid democracy of the Greek city-state on a continental scale. In North America technology is not only artifact but actor; or, as I put it later, it is machines that have teleological insight. The latest in technology is always the occasion of metaphysical voyages outward in space but backward in time: a journey of restoration as much as of progress.

In this fragile society technology and communication, then, created the hope of economic, political, and cultural unity. Small markets thinly spread in space could be integrated into one large market capable of efficient exploitation. Small political units thinly dispersed in space could be collected into one political organism. Small cultural enclaves thinly dispersed over a continent could be collected into one great community. But the same technology and geography that inspired the hope stimulated the fear: the entire experiment could descend into factionalism or, worse, contagions of demogogic enthusiasm. The lines of communication that transmitted a common culture and cemented the union could be run backward: a nervous system in reverse might collect antidemocratic energies, mass movements, and primitive enthusiasms in the provinces and concentrate them in the capitals. The hope and fear are the systolic and diastolic beats of the culture.

Madison labored to show that "extent of territory" would allow us to have one without the other, the hope without the fear:

> Extend the sphere and you take in a greater variety of parties and interests; you make it less probable that a majority of the whole will have a common motive to invade the rights of other citizens; or, if such a common motive exists, it will be more difficult for all who feel it to discover their own strength, and to act in unison with each other (*The Federalist*, 1961: 64).

Garry Wills in *Explaining America* warns against too literal a reading of Madison's notion that "extent of territory" would provide a "logistical block to evil combinations" such that bad roads would give us both political unity and human virtue (1981: 220). That interpretation, he suggests, would expose Madison's argument to refutation by the telegraph.

But that, of course, is precisely the refutation that many read into electronic communication and the rise of the great illiterate media of film and broadcasting.

I share those hopes and fears and live with rather than try to escape the contradictions and ambiguities of the culture. But my attitude toward them is one suggested by George Bernard Shaw. Mulling over some hopes, fears, and contradictions of his own, Shaw commented that "if you can't get the skeleton out of the closet you might as well make it dance." The essays that follow do not attempt to exorcise the contradictions in communications and technology or the ambiguities of American culture. Rather, they attempt to use the contradictions and ambiguities as a resource; to exploit them in order that we might, in a happy phrase of Clifford Geertz, "increase the precision with which we vex one another." In part I, I explore the notion of culture and cultural studies and outline attitudes toward communication and technology that I hope take us beyond happy pastorals of progress or grim narratives of power and domination. If culture and technology are opposed at the outset, twin actors in one kind of intellectual drama, they are joined in the second part of this book in narratives we tell ourselves about ourselves. Stories about technology, as I have already suggested, play a distinctive role in our understanding of ourselves and our common history. Technology, the hardest of material artifacts, is thoroughly cultural from the outset: an expression and creation of the very outlooks and aspirations we pretend it merely demonstrates. Finally, then, these essays aim collectively to demonstrate how media of communication are not merely instruments of will and purpose but definite forms of life: organisms, so to say, that reproduce in miniature the contradictions in our thought, action, and social relations.

I promise more than I deliver, for these essays originated as speeches and seminars given over the last eighteen years. Composed episodically, the essays are sometimes in an irritable counterpoint to one another, more a running argument and an extended conversation than a neatly articulated structure. But in that they mirror the pulse and texture of the culture that is their underlying subject.

9

PART I

Communication and Culture

CHAPTER 1

A Cultural Approach to Communication

I

When I decided some years ago to read seriously the literature of communications, a wise man suggested I begin with
John Dewey. It was advice I have never regretted accepting.
Although there are limitations to Dewey—his literary style
was described by William James as damnable—there is a
depth to his work, a natural excess common to seminal
minds, that offers permanent complexities, and paradoxes
over which to puzzle—surely something absent from most
of our literature.

Dewey opens an important chapter in *Experience and Nature*
with the seemingly preposterous claim that "of all things
communication is the most wonderful" (1939: 385). What
could he have meant by that? If we interpret the sentence
literally, it must be either false or mundane. Surely most
of the news and entertainment we receive through the
mass media are of the order that Thoreau predicted for
the international telegraph: "the intelligence that Princess
Adelaide had the whooping cough." A daily visit with
the New York *Times* is not quite so trivial, though it is
an experience more depressing than wonderful. Moreover,
most of one's encounters with others are wonderful only
in moments of excessive masochism. Dewey's sentence,
by any reasonable interpretation, is either false to everyday
experience or simply mundane if he means only that on some
occasions communication is satisfying and rewarding.

In another place Dewey offers an equally enigmatic
comment on communication: "Society exists not only by

13

transmission, by communication, but it may fairly be said to exist in transmission, in communication" (Dewey, 1916: 5). What is the significance of the shift in prepositions?[1] Is Dewey claiming that societies distribute information, to speak rather too anthropomorphically, and that by such transactions and the channels of communication peculiar to them society is made possible? That is certainly a reasonable claim, but we hardly need social scientists and philosophers to tell us so. It reminds me of Robert Nisbet's acid remark that if you need sociologists to inform you whether or not you have a ruling class, you surely don't. But if this transparent interpretation is rejected, are there any guarantees that after peeling away layers of semantic complexity anything more substantial will be revealed?

I think there are, for the body of Dewey's work reveals a substantial rather than a pedestrian intelligence. Rather than quoting him ritualistically (for the lines I have cited regularly appear without comment or interpretation in the literature of communications), we would be better advised to untangle this underlying complexity for the light it might cast upon contemporary studies. I think this complexity derives from Dewey's use of communication in two quite different senses. He understood better than most of us that communication has had two contrasting definitions in the history of Western thought, and he used the conflict between these definitions as a source of creative tension in his work. This same conflict led him, not surprisingly, into some of his characteristic errors. Rather than blissfully repeating his insights or unconsciously duplicating his errors, we might extend his thought by seizing upon the same contradiction he perceived in our use of the term "communication" and use it in turn as a device for vivifying our studies.

Two alternative conceptions of communication have been alive in American culture since this term entered common discourse in the nineteenth century. Both definitions derive, as with much in secular culture, from religious origins, though they refer to somewhat different regions of religious experience. We might label these descriptions, if only to provide handy pegs upon which to hang our thought, a transmission view of communication and a ritual view of communication.

The transmission view of communication is the commonest in our culture—perhaps in all industrial cultures—and dominates contemporary dictionary entries under the term. It is defined by terms such as "imparting," "sending," "transmitting," or "giving information to others." It is formed from a metaphor of geography or transportation. In the nineteenth century but to a lesser extent today, the movement of goods or people and the movement of information were seen as essentially identical processes and both were described by the common noun "communication." The center of this idea of communication is the transmission of signals or messages over distance for the purpose of control. It is a view of communication that derives from one of the most ancient of human dreams: the desire to increase the speed and effect of messages as they travel in space. From the time upper and lower Egypt were unified under the First Dynasty down through the invention of the telegraph, transportation and communication were inseparably linked. Although messages might be centrally produced and controlled, through monopolization of writing or the rapid production of print, these messages, carried in the hands of a messenger or between the bindings of a book, still had to be distributed, if they were to have their desired effect, by rapid transportation. The telegraph ended the identity but did not destroy the metaphor. Our basic orientation to communication remains grounded, at the deepest roots of our thinking, in the idea of transmission: communication is a process whereby messages are transmitted and distributed in space for the control of distance and people.[2]

I said this view originated in religion, though the foregoing sentences seem more indebted to politics, economics, and technology. Nonetheless, the roots of the transmission view of communication, in our culture at least, lie in essentially religious attitudes. I can illustrate this by a devious though, in detail, inadequate path.

In its modern dress the transmission view of communication arises, as the *Oxford English Dictionary* will attest, at the onset of the age of exploration and discovery. We have

15

been reminded rather too often that the motives behind this vast movement in space were political and mercantilistic. Certainly those motives were present, but their importance should not obscure the equally compelling fact that a major motive behind this movement in space, particularly as evidenced by the Dutch Reformed Church in South Africa or the Puritans in New England, was religious. The desire to escape the boundaries of Europe, to create a new life, to found new communities, to carve a New Jerusalem out of the woods of Massachusetts, were primary motives behind the unprecedented movement of white European civilization over virtually the entire globe. The vast and, for the first time, democratic migration in space was above all an attempt to trade an old world for a new and represented the profound belief that movement in space could be in itself a redemptive act. It is a belief Americans have never quite escaped.

Transportation, particularly when it brought the Christian community of Europe into contact with the heathen community of the Americas, was seen as a form of communication with profoundly religious implications. This movement in space was an attempt to establish and extend the kingdom of God, to create the conditions under which godly understanding might be realized, to produce a heavenly though still terrestrial city.

The moral meaning of transportation, then, was the establishment and extension of God's kingdom on earth. The moral meaning of communication was the same. By the middle of the nineteenth century the telegraph broke the identity of communication and transportation but also led a preacher of the era, Gardner Spring, to exclaim that we were on the "border of a spiritual harvest because thought now travels by steam and magnetic wires" (Miller, 1965: 48). Similarly, in 1848 "James L. Batchelder could declare that the Almighty himself had constructed the railroad for missionary purposes and, as Samuel Morse prophesied with the first telegraphic message, the purpose of the invention was not to spread the price of pork but to ask the question 'What Hath God Wrought?'" (Miller, 1965: 52). This new technology entered American discussions not as a mundane fact but as

16

divinely inspired for the purposes of spreading the Christian message farther and faster, eclipsing time and transcending space, saving the heathen, bringing closer and making more probable the day of salvation. As the century wore on and religious thought was increasingly tied to applied science, the new technology of communication came to be seen as the ideal device for the conquest of space and populations. Our most distinguished student of these matters, Perry Miller, has commented:

> The unanimity (among Protestant sects), which might at first sight seem wholly supernatural, was wrought by the telegraph and the press. These conveyed and published "the thrill of Christian sympathy, with the tidings of abounding grace, from multitudes in every city simultaneously assembled, in effect almost bringing a nation together in one praying intercourse." Nor could it be only fortuitous that the movement should coincide with the Atlantic Cable, for both were harbingers "of that which is the forerunner of ultimate spiritual victory . . . ." The awakening of 1858 first made vital for the American imagination a realizable program of a Christianized technology. (Miller, 1965: 91)

Soon, as the forces of science and secularization gained ground, the obvious religious metaphors fell away and the technology of communication itself moved to the center of thought. Moreover, the superiority of communication over transportation was assured by the observation of one nineteenth century commentator that the telegraph was important because it involved not the mere "modification of matter but the transmission of thought." Communication was viewed as a process and a technology that would, sometimes for religious purposes, spread, transmit, and disseminate knowledge, ideas, and information farther and faster with the goal of controlling space and people.

There were dissenters, of course, and I have already quoted Thoreau's disenchanted remark on the telegraph. More pessimistically, John C. Calhoun saw the "subjugation of electricity to the mechanical necessities of man . . . (as) the last era in human civilization" (quoted in Miller, 1965: 307). But the dissenters were few, and the transmission

17

view of communication, albeit in increasingly secularized and scientific form, has dominated our thought and culture since that time. Moreover, as can be seen in contemporary popular commentary and even in technical discussions of new communications technology, the historic religious undercurrent has never been eliminated from our thought. From the telegraph to the computer the same sense of profound possibility for moral improvement is present whenever these machines are invoked. And we need not be reminded of the regularity with which improved communication is invoked by an army of teachers, preachers, and columnists as the talisman of all our troubles. More controversially, the same root attitudes, as I can only assert here rather than demonstrate, are at work in most of our scientifically sophisticated views of communication.

The ritual view of communication, though a minor thread in our national thought, is by far the older of those views—old enough in fact for dictionaries to list it under "Archaic." In a ritual definition, communication is linked to terms such as "sharing," "participation," "association," "fellowship," and "the possession of a common faith." This definition exploits the ancient identity and common roots of the terms "commonness," "communion," "community," and "communication." A ritual view of communication is directed not toward the extension of messages in space but toward the maintenance of society in time; not the act of imparting information but the representation of shared beliefs.

If the archetypal case of communication under a transmission view is the extension of messages across geography for the purpose of control, the archetypal case under a ritual view is the sacred ceremony that draws persons together in fellowship and commonality.

The indebtedness of the ritual view of communication to religion is apparent in the name chosen to label it. Moreover, it derives from a view of religion that downplays the role of the sermon, the instruction and admonition, in order to highlight the role of the prayer, the chant, and the ceremony. It sees the original or highest manifestation of communication not in the transmission of intelligent information but in the construction and maintenance of an ordered, meaningful cultural world that can serve as a control and container for human action.

This view has also been shorn of its explicitly religious origins, but it has never completely escaped its metaphoric root. Writers in this tradition often trace their heritage, in part, to Durkheim's *Elementary Forms of Religious Life* and to the argument stated elsewhere that "society substitutes for the world revealed to our senses a different world that is a projection of the ideals created by the community" (1953: 95). This projection of community ideals and their embodiment in material form—dance, plays, architecture, news stories, strings of speech—creates an artificial though nonetheless real symbolic order that operates to provide not information but confirmation, not to alter attitudes or change minds but to represent an underlying order of things, not to perform functions but to manifest an ongoing and fragile social process.

The ritual view of communication has not been a dominant motif in American scholarship. Our thought and work have been glued to a transmission view of communication because this view is congenial with the underlying wellsprings of American culture, sources that feed into our scientific life as well as our common, public understandings. There is an irony in this. We have not explored the ritual view of communication because the concept of culture is such a weak and evanescent notion in American social thought. We understand that other people have culture in the anthropological sense and we regularly record it—often mischievously and patronizingly. But when we turn critical attention to American culture the concept dissolves into a residual category useful only when psychological and sociological data are exhausted. We realize that the underprivileged live in a culture of poverty, use the notion of middle-class culture as an epithet, and occasionally applaud our high and generally scientific culture. But the notion of culture is not a hard-edged term of intellectual discourse for domestic purposes. This intellectual aversion to the idea of culture derives in part from our obsessive individualism, which makes psychological life the paramount reality; from our Puritanism, which leads to disdain for the significance of human activity that is not practical and work oriented; and from our isolation of science from culture: science provides culture-free truth whereas culture provides ethnocentric error.

Consequently, when looking for scholarship that emphasizes the central role of culture and a ritual view of communication, one must rely heavily on European sources or upon Americans deeply influenced by European scholarship. As a result the opportunities for misunderstanding are great. Perhaps, then, some of the difference between a transmission and a ritual view of communication can be grasped by briefly looking at alternative conceptions of the role of the newspaper in social life.

If one examines a newspaper under a transmission view of communication, one sees the medium as an instrument for disseminating news and knowledge, sometimes *divertissement*, in larger and larger packages over greater distances. Questions arise as to the effects of this on audiences: news as enlightening or obscuring reality, as changing or hardening attitudes, as breeding credibility or doubt. Questions also are raised concerning the functions of news and the newspaper: Does it maintain the integration of society or its maladaptation? Does it function or misfunction to maintain stability or promote the instability of personalities? Some such mechanical analysis normally accompanies a "transmission" argument.

A ritual view of communication will focus on a different range of problems in examining a newspaper. It will, for example, view reading a newspaper less as sending or gaining information and more as attending a mass, a situation in which nothing new is learned but in which a particular view of the world is portrayed and confirmed. News reading, and writing, is a ritual act and moreover a dramatic one. What is arrayed before the reader is not pure information but a portrayal of the contending forces in the world. Moreover, as readers make their way through the paper, they engage in a continual shift of roles or of dramatic focus. A story on the monetary crisis salutes them as American patriots fighting those ancient enemies Germany and Japan; a story on the meeting of a women's political caucus casts them into the liberation movement as supporter or opponent; a tale of violence on the campus evokes their class antagonisms and resentments. The model here is not that of information acquisition, though such acquisition occurs, but of dramatic action in which the reader joins a world of contending forces as an observer at a play. We do not encounter questions about the effect or functions of messages as such, but the role of presentation and involvement in the structuring of the reader's life and time. We recognize, as with religious rituals, that news changes little and yet is intrinsically satisfying; it performs few functions yet is habitually consumed. Newspapers do not operate as a source of effects or functions but as dramatically satisfying, which is not to say pleasing, presentations of what the world at root is. And it is in this role—that of a text—that a newspaper is seen; like a Balinese cockfight, a Dickens novel, an Elizabethan drama, a student rally, it is a presentation of reality that gives life an overall form, order, and tone.

Moreover, news is a historic reality. It is a form of culture invented by a particular class at a particular point of history—in this case by the middle class largely in the eighteenth century. Like any invented cultural form, news both forms and reflects a particular "hunger for experience," a desire to do away with the epic, heroic, and traditional in favor of the unique, original, novel, new—news. This "hunger" itself has a history grounded in the changing style and fortunes of the middle class and as such does not represent a universal taste or necessarily legitimate form of knowledge (Park, 1955: 71-88) but an invention in historical time, that like most other human inventions, will dissolve when the class that sponsors it and its possibility of having significance for us evaporates.

Under a ritual view, then, news is not information but drama. It does not describe the world but portrays an arena of dramatic forces and action; it exists solely in historical time; and it invites our participation on the basis of our assuming, often vicariously, social roles within it.[3]

Neither of these counterposed views of communication necessarily denies what the other affirms. A ritual view does not exclude the processes of information transmission or attitude change. It merely contends that one cannot understand

21

these processes aright except insofar as they are cast within an essentially ritualistic view of communication and social order. Similarly, even writers indissolubly wedded to the transmission view of communication must include some notion, such as Malinowski's phatic communion, to attest however tardily to the place of ritual action in social life. Nonetheless, in intellectual matters origins determine endings, and the exact point at which one attempts to unhinge the problem of communication largely determines the path the analysis can follow.

The power of Dewey's work derives from his working over these counterpoised views of communication. Communication is "the most wonderful" because it is the basis of human fellowship; it produces the social bonds, bogus or not, that tie men together and make associated life possible. Society is possible because of the binding forces of shared information circulating in an organic system. The following quotation reveals this tension and Dewey's final emphasis on a ritual view of communication:

> There is more than a verbal tie between the words common, community, and communication. Men live in a community in virtue of the things which they have in common; and communication is the way in which they come to possess things in common. What they must have in common . . . are aims, beliefs, aspirations, knowledge—a common understanding—likemindedness as sociologists say. Such things cannot be passed physically from one to another like bricks; they cannot be shared as persons would share a pie by dividing it into physical pieces . . . . Consensus demands communication (Dewey, 1916: 5-6).

Dewey was, like the rest of us, often untrue to his own thought. His hopes for the future often overwhelmed the impact of his analysis. Ah! "the wish is father to the thought." He came to overvalue scientific information and communication technology as a solvent to social problems and a source of social bonds. Nonetheless, the tension between these views can still open a range of significant problems in communication for they not only represent different conceptions of communication but correspond to particular historical periods, technologies, and forms of social order.[4]

The transmission view of communication has dominated American thought since the 1920s. When I first came into this field I felt that this view of communication, expressed in behavioral and functional terms, was exhausted. It had become academic: a repetition of past achievement, a demonstration of the indubitable. Although it led to solid achievement, it could no longer go forward without disastrous intellectual and social consequences. I felt it was necessary to reopen the analysis, to reinvigorate it with the tension found in Dewey's work and, above all, to go elsewhere into biology, theology, anthropology, and literature for some intellectual material with which we might escape the treadmill we were running.

II

But where does one turn, even provisionally, for the resources with which to get a fresh perspective on communication? For me at least the resources were found by going back to the work of Weber, Durkheim, de Tocqueville, and Huizinga, as well as by utilizing contemporaries such as Kenneth Burke, Hugh Duncan, Adolph Portman, Thomas Kuhn, Peter Berger, and Clifford Geertz. Basically, however, the most viable though still inadequate tradition of social thought on communication comes from those colleagues and descendants of Dewey in the Chicago School: from Mead and Cooley through Robert Park and on to Erving Goffman.

From such sources one can draw a definition of communication of disarming simplicity yet, I think, of some intellectual power and scope: communication is a symbolic process whereby reality is produced, maintained, repaired, and transformed.

Let me attempt to unpack that long first clause emphasizing the symbolic production of reality.

One of the major problems one encounters in talking about communication is that the noun refers to the most common, mundane human experience. There is truth in Marshall McLuhan's assertion that the one thing of which the fish is unaware is water, the very medium that forms its ambience and supports its existence. Similarly, communication, through language and other symbolic forms, comprises the ambience of human existence. The activities we collectively call communication—having conversations, giving instructions, imparting knowledge, sharing significant ideas, seeking information, entertaining and being entertained—are so ordinary and mundane that it is difficult for them to arrest our attention. Moreover, when we intellectually visit this process, we often focus on the trivial and unproblematic, so inured are we to the mysterious and awesome in communication.

A wise man once defined the purpose of art as "making the phenomenon strange." Things can become so familiar that we no longer perceive them at all. Art, however, can take the sound of the sea, the intonation of a voice, the texture of a fabric, the design of a face, the play of light upon a landscape, and wrench these ordinary phenomena out of the backdrop of existence and force them into the foreground of consideration. When Scott Fitzgerald described Daisy Buchanan as having "a voice full of money" he moves us, if we are open to the experience, to hear again that ordinary thing, the sound of a voice, and to contemplate what it portends. He arrests our apprehension and focuses it on the mystery of character as revealed in sound.

Similarly, the social sciences can take the most obvious yet background facts of social life and force them into the foreground of wonderment. They can make us contemplate the particular miracles of social life that have become for us just there, plain and unproblematic for the eye to see. When he comments that communication is the most wonderful among things, surely Dewey is trying just that: to induce in us a capacity for wonder and awe regarding this commonplace activity. Dewey knew that knowledge most effectively grew at the point when things became problematic, when we experience an "information gap" between what circumstances impelled us toward doing and what we needed to know in order to act at all. This information gap, this sense of the problematic, often can be induced only by divesting life of its mundane trappings and exposing our common sense or scientific assumptions to an ironic light that makes the phenomenon strange.

To a certain though inadequate degree, my first clause attempts just that. Both our common sense and scientific realism attest to the fact that there is, first, a real world of objects, events, and processes that we observe. Second, there is language or symbols that name these events in the real world and create more or less adequate descriptions of them. There is reality and then, after the fact, our accounts of it. We insist there is a distinction between reality and fantasy; we insist that our terms stand in relation to this world as shadow and substance. While language often distorts, obfuscates, and confuses our perception of this external world, we rarely dispute this matter-of-fact realism. We peel away semantic layers of terms and meanings to uncover this more substantial domain of existence. Language stands to reality as secondary stands to primary in the old Galilean paradigm from which this view derives.

By the first clause I mean to invert this relationship, not to make any large metaphysical claims but rather, by reordering the relation of communication to reality, to render communication a far more problematic activity than it ordinarily seems.

I want to suggest, to play on the Gospel of St. John, that in the beginning was the word; words are not the names for things but, to steal a line from Kenneth Burke, things are the signs of words. Reality is not given, not humanly existent, independent of language and toward which language stands as a pale refraction. Rather, reality is brought into existence, is produced, by communication—by, in short, the construction, apprehension, and utilization of symbolic forms.[5] Reality, while not a mere function of symbolic forms, is produced by terministic systems—or by humans who produce such systems—that focus its existence in specific terms.

Under the sway of realism we ordinarily assume there is an order to existence that the human mind through some

25

faculty may discover and describe. I am suggesting that reality is not there to discover in any significant detail. The world is entropic—that is, not strictly ordered—though its variety is constrained enough that the mind can grasp its outline and implant an order over and within the broad and elastic constraints of nature. To put it colloquially, there are no lines of latitude and longitude in nature, but by overlaying the globe with this particular, though not exclusively correct, symbolic organization, order is imposed on spatial organization and certain, limited human purposes served.

Whatever reality might be on the mind of Bishop Berkeley's God, whatever it might be for other animals, it is for us a vast production, a staged creation—something humanly produced and humanly maintained. Whatever order is in the world is not given in our genes or exclusively supplied by nature. As the biologist J. Z. Young puts it, "the brain of each one of us does literally create his or her own world" (1951: 61); the order of history is, as Eric Vogelin puts it, "the history of order"—the myriad forms in which people have endowed significance, order, and meaning in the world by the agency of their own intellectual processes.

Ernst Cassirer said it, and others have repeated it to the point of deadening its significance: man lives in a new dimension of reality, symbolic reality, and it is through the agency of this capacity that existence is produced. However, though it is often said, it is rarely investigated. More than repeat it, we have to take it seriously, follow it to the end of the line, to assess its capacity to vivify our studies. What Cassirer is contending is that one must examine communication, even scientific communication, even mathematical expression, as the primary phenomena of experience and not as something "softer" and derivative from a "realer" existent nature.

Lest someone think this obscure, allow me to illustrate with an example, an example at once so artless and transparent that the meaning will be clear even if engaging complexities are sacrificed. Let us suppose one had to teach a child of six or seven how to get from home to school. The child has been driven by the school, which is some six or seven blocks away, so he recognizes it, but he has no idea of the relation between his house and school. The space between these points might as well be, as the saying goes, a trackless desert. What does one do in such a situation? There are a number of options. One might let the child discover the route by trial and error, correcting him as he goes, in faithful imitation of a conditioning experiment. One might have the child follow an adult, as I'm told the Apaches do, "imprinting" the route on the child. However, the ordinary method is simply to draw the child a map. By arranging lines, angles, names, squares denoting streets and buildings in a pattern on paper, one transforms vacant space into a featured environment. Although some environments are easier to feature than others—hence trackless deserts—space is understood and manageable when it is represented in symbolic form.

The map stands as a representation of an environment capable of clarifying a problematic situation. It is capable of guiding behavior and simultaneously transforming undifferentiated space into configured—that is, known, apprehended, understood—space.

Note also that an environment, any given space, can be mapped in a number of different modes. For example, we might map a particularly important space by producing a poetic or musical description. As in the song that goes, in part, "first you turn it to the left, then you turn it to the right," a space can be mapped by a stream of poetic speech that expresses a spatial essence and that also ensures, by exploiting the mnemonic devices of song and poetry, that the "map" can be retained in memory. By recalling the poem at appropriate moments, space can be effectively configured.

A third means of mapping space is danced ritual. The movements of the dance can parallel appropriate movements through space. By learning the dance the child acquires a representation of the space that on another occasion can guide behavior.

Space can be mapped, then, in different modes—utilizing lines on a page, sounds in air, movements in a dance. All three are symbolic forms, though the symbols differ; visual, oral, and kinesthetic. Moreover, each of the symbolic forms possesses two distinguishing characteristics: displacement and productivity. Like ordinary language, each mode allows one to speak about or represent some thing when the thing in question is not present. This capacity of displacement, of producing a complicated act when the "real" stimulus is not physically present, is another often noted though not fully explored capacity. Second, each of these symbolic forms is productive, for a person in command of the symbols is capable of producing an infinite number of representations on the basis of a finite number of symbolic elements. As with language, so with other symbolic forms: a finite set of words or a finite set of phonemes can produce, through grammatical combination, an infinite set of sentences.

We often argue that a map represents a simplification of or an abstraction from an environment. Not all the features of an environment are modeled, for the purpose of the representation is to express not the possible complexity of things but their simplicity. Space is made manageable by the reduction of information. By doing this, however, different maps bring the same environment alive in different ways; they produce quite different realities. Therefore, to live within the purview of different maps is to live within different realities. Consequently, maps not only constitute the activity known as mapmaking; they constitute nature itself.

A further implication concerns the nature of thought. In our predominantly individualistic tradition, we are accustomed to think of thought as essentially private, an activity that occurs in the head—graphically represented by Rodin's "The Thinker." I wish to suggest, in contradistinction, that thought is predominantly public and social. It occurs primarily on blackboards, in dances, and in recited poems. The capacity of private thought is a derived and secondary talent, one that appears biographically later in the person and historically later in the species. Thought is public because it depends on a publicly available stock of symbols. It is public in a second and stronger sense. Thinking consists of building maps of environments. Thought involves constructing a model of an environment and then running the model faster than the environment to see if nature can be coerced to perform as the model does. In the earlier example, the map of the neighborhood and the path from home to school represent the environment; the finger one lays on the map and traces the path is a representation of the child, the walker. "Running" the map is faster than walking the route and constitutes the "experiment" or "test."

Thought is the construction and utilization of such maps, models, templates: football plays diagrammed on a black-board, equations on paper, ritual dances charting the nature of ancestors, or streams of prose like this attempting, out in the bright-lit world in which we all live, to present the nature of communication.

This particular miracle we perform daily and hourly—the miracle of producing reality and then living within and under the fact of our own productions—rests upon a particular quality of symbols: their ability to be both representations "of" and "for" reality.[6]

A blueprint of a house in one mode is a representation "for" reality: under its guidance and control a reality, a house, is produced that expresses the relations contained in reduced and simplified form in the blueprint. There is a second use of a blueprint, however. If someone asks for a description of a particular house, one can simply point to a blueprint and say, "That's the house." Here the blueprint stands as a representation or symbol of reality: it expresses or represents in an alternative medium a synoptic formulation of the nature of a particular reality. While these are merely two sides of the same coin, they point to the dual capacity of symbolic forms: as "symbols of" they present reality; as "symbols for" they create the very reality they present.

In my earlier example the map of the neighborhood in one mode is a symbol of, a representation that can be pointed to when someone asks about the relation between home and school. Ultimately, the map becomes a representation for reality when, under its guidance, the child makes his way from home to school and, by the particular blinders as well as the particular observations the map induces, experiences space in the way it is synoptically formulated in the map.

It is no different with a religious ritual. In one mode it represents the nature of human life, its condition and meaning, and in another mode—its "for" mode—it induces the dispositions it pretends merely to portray.

29

All human activity is such an exercise (can one resist the word "ritual"?) in squaring the circle. We first produce the world by symbolic work and then take up residence in the world we have produced. Alas, there is magic in our self deceptions.[7]

We not only produce reality but we must likewise maintain what we have produced, for there are always new generations coming along for whom our productions are incipiently problematic and for whom reality must be regenerated and made authoritative. Reality must be repaired for it consistently breaks down: people get lost physically and spiritually, experiments fail, evidence counter to the representation is produced, mental derangement sets in—all threats to our models of and for reality that lead to intense repair work. Finally, we must, often with fear and regret, toss away our authoritative representations of reality and begin to build the world anew. We go to bed, to choose an example not quite at random, convinced behaviorists who view language, under the influence of Skinner, as a matter of operant conditioning and wake up, for mysterious reasons, convinced rationalists, rebuilding our mode of language, under the influence of Chomsky, along the lines of deep structures, transformations, and surface appearances. These are two different intellectual worlds in which to live, and we may find that the anomalies of one lead us to transform it into another.[8]

To study communication is to examine the actual social process wherein significant symbolic forms are created, apprehended, and used. When described this way some scholars would dismiss it as insufficiently empirical. My own view is the opposite, for I see it as an attempt to sweep away our existing notions concerning communication that serve only to devitalize our data. Our attempts to construct, maintain, repair, and transform reali.y are publicly observable activities that occur in historical time. We create, express, and convey our knowledge of and attitudes toward reality through the construction of a variety of symbol systems: art, science, journalism, religion, common sense, mythology. How do we do this? What are the differences between these forms? What are the historical and comparative variations in them? How do changes in communication technology influence what we can concretely create and apprehend? How do groups in society struggle over the definition of what is real? These are some of the questions, rather too simply put, that communication studies must answer.

Finally, let me emphasize an ironic aspect to the study of communication, a way in which our subject matter doubles back on itself and presents us with a host of ethical problems. One of the activities in which we characteristically engage, as in this essay, is communication about communication itself. However, communication is not some pure phenomenon we can discover; there is no such thing as communication to be revealed in nature through some objective method free from the corruption of culture. We understand communication insofar as we are able to build models or representations of this process. But our models of communication, like all models, have this dual aspect—an "of" aspect and a "for" aspect. In one mode communication models tell us what the process is; in their second mode they produce the behavior they have described. Communication can be modeled in several empirically adequate ways, but these several models have different ethical implications for they produce different forms of social relations.

Let us face this dilemma directly. There is nothing in our genes that tells us how to create and execute those activities we summarize under the term "communication." If we are to engage in this activity—writing an essay, making a film, entertaining an audience, imparting information and advice—we must discover models in our culture that tell us how this particular miracle is achieved. Such models are found in common sense, law, religious traditions, increasingly in scientific theories themselves. Traditionally, models of communication were found in religious thought. For example, in describing the roots of the transmission view of communication in nineteenth century American religious thought I meant to imply the following: religious thought not only described communication; it also presented a model for the appropriate uses of language, the permissible forms of human contact, the ends communication should serve, the motives it should manifest. It taught what it meant to display.

31

Today models of communication are found less in religion than in science, but their implications are the same. For example, American social science generally has represented communication, within an overarching transmission view, in terms of either a power or an anxiety model. These correspond roughly to what is found in information theory, learning theory, and influence theory (power) and dissonance, balance theory, and functionalism or uses and gratifications analysis (anxiety). I cannot adequately explicate these views here, but they reduce the extraordinary phenomenological diversity of communication into an arena in which people alternatively pursue power or flee anxiety. And one need only monitor the behavior of modern institutions to see the degree to which these models create, through policy and program, the abstract motives and relations they portray.

Models of communication are, then, not merely representations of communication but representations *for* communication: templates that guide, unavailing or not, concrete processes of human interaction, mass and interpersonal. Therefore, to study communication involves examining the construction, apprehension, and use of models of communication themselves—their construction in common sense, art, and science, their historically specific creation and use: in encounters between parent and child, advertisers and consumer, welfare worker and supplicant, teacher and student. Behind and within these encounters lie models of human contact and interaction.

Our models of communication, consequently, create what we disingenuously pretend they merely describe. As a result our science is, to use a term of Alvin Gouldner's, a reflexive one. We not only describe behavior; we create a particular corner of culture—culture that determines, in part, the kind of communicative world we inhabit.

Raymond Williams, whose analysis I shall follow in conclusion, speaks to the point:

> Communication begins in the struggle to learn and to describe. To start this process in our minds and to pass on its results to others, we depend on certain communication models, certain rules or conventions through which we can

32

make contact. We can change these models when they become inadequate or we can modify and extend them. Our efforts to do so, and to use the existing models successfully, take up a large part of our living energy. . . . Moreover, many of our communication models become, in themselves, social institutions. Certain attitudes to others, certain forms of address, certain tones and styles become embodied in institutions which are then very powerful in social effect. . . . These arguable assumptions are often embodied in solid, practical institutions which then teach the models from which they start (1966: 19-20).

This relation between science and society described by Williams has not been altogether missed by the public and accounts for some of the widespread interest in communication. I am not speaking merely of the contemporary habit of reducing all human problems to problems or failures in communication. Let us recognize the habit for what it is: an attempt to coat reality with cliches, to provide a semantic crucifix to ward off modern vampires. But our appropriate cynicism should not deflect us from discovering the kernel of truth in such phrases.

If we follow Dewey, it will occur to us that problems of communication are linked to problems of community, to problems surrounding the kinds of communities we create and in which we live.[9] For the ordinary person communication consists merely of a set of daily activities: having conversations, conveying instructions, being entertained, sustaining debate and discussion, acquiring information. The felt quality of our lives is bound up with these activities and how they are carried out within communities.

Our minds and lives are shaped by our total experience—or, better, by representations of experience and, as Williams has argued, a name for this experience is communication. If one tries to examine society as a form of communication, one sees it as a process whereby reality is created, shared, modified, and preserved. When this process becomes opaque, when we lack models of and for reality that make the world apprehensible, when we are unable to describe and share it; when because of a failure in our models of communication we are unable to connect with others, we encounter problems of communication in their most potent form.

The widespread social interest in communication derives from a derangement in our models of communication and community. This derangement derives, in turn, from an obsessive commitment to a transmission view of communication and the derivative representation of communication in complementary models of power and anxiety. As a result, when we think about society, we are almost always coerced by our traditions into seeing it as a network of power, administration, decision, and control—as a political order. Alternatively, we have seen society essentially as relations of property, production, and trade—an economic order. But social life is more than power and trade (and it is more than therapy as well). As Williams has argued, it also includes the sharing of aesthetic experience, religious ideas, personal values and sentiments, and intellectual notions—a ritual order.

Our existing models of communication are less an analysis than a contribution to the chaos of modern culture, and in important ways we are paying the penalty for the long abuse of fundamental communicative processes in the service of politics, trade, and therapy. Three examples. Because we have looked at each new advance in communications technology as an opportunity for politics and economics, we have devoted it, almost exclusively, to matters of government and trade. We have rarely seen these advances as opportunities to expand people's powers to learn and exchange ideas and experience. Because we have looked at education principally in terms of its potential for economics and politics, we have turned it into a form of citizenship, professionalism and consumerism, and increasingly therapy. Because we have seen our cities as the domain of politics and economics, they have become the residence of technology and bureaucracy. Our streets are designed to accommodate the automobile, our sidewalks to facilitate trade, our land and houses to satisfy the economy and the real estate speculator.

The object, then, of recasting our studies of communication in terms of a ritual model is not only to more firmly grasp the essence of this "wonderful" process but to give us a way in which to rebuild a model of and for communication of some restorative value in reshaping our common culture.

NOTES

1 For further elaboration on these matters, see chapter 4.

2 For an interesting exposition of this view, see Lewis Mumford (1967).

3 The only treatment of news that parallels the description offered here is William Stephenson's *The Play Theory of Mass Communication* (1967). While Stephenson's treatment leaves much to be desired, particularly because it gets involved in some largely irrelevant methodological questions, it is nonetheless a genuine attempt to offer an alternative to our views of communication.

4 These contrasting views of communication also link, I believe, with contrasting views of the nature of language, thought, and symbolism. The transmission view of communication leads to an emphasis on language as an instrument of practical action and discursive reasoning, of thought as essentially conceptual and individual or reflective, and of symbolism as being preeminently analytic. A ritual view of communication, on the other hand, sees language as an instrument of dramatic action, of thought as essentially situational and social, and symbolism as fundamentally fiduciary.

5 This is not to suggest that language constitutes the real world as Ernst Cassirer often seems to argue. I wish to suggest that the world is apprehensible for humans only through language or some other symbolic form.

6 This formulation, as with many other aspects of this essay, is heavily dependent on the work of Clifford Geertz (see Geertz, 1973).

7 We, of course, not only produce a world; we produce as many as we can, and we live in easy or painful transit between them. This is the problem Alfred Schutz (1967) analyzed as the phenomenon of "multiple realities." I cannot treat this problem here, but I must add that some such perspective on the multiple nature of produced reality is necessary in order to make any sense of the rather dismal area of communicative "effects."

8 The example and language are not fortuitous. Thomas Kuhn's *The Structure of Scientific Revolutions* (1962) can be seen as a description of how a scientific world is produced (paradigm creation), maintained (paradigm articulation, training, through

exemplars, of a new generation of scientists), repaired (by dismissing anomalous phenomena, discounting counter-evidence, forcing nature more strenuously into conceptual boxes), and transformed (in revolutions and their institutionalization in textbooks and scientific societies).

9 See Dewey (1927). To maintain continuity in the argument, let me stress, by wrenching a line of Thomas Kuhn's out of context, the relation between model building and community: "The choice . . . between competing paradigms proves to be a choice between incompatible modes of community life" (1962: 92).

CHAPTER 2

Mass Communication
and Cultural Studies

In the ragged and extended parenthesis embracing World War II and the Korean War, a major debate resurfaced among American intellectuals concerning the nature and politics of popular culture. The subject at issue was never well defined, and, as is usual in these matters, the antagonists kept answering questions no one was asking. "Popular" in this context referred to certain objects and practices consumed or engaged by all strata of the population. "Culture" referred to expressive artifacts—words, images, and objects that bore meanings. In fact, the debate centered pretty exclusively on popular entertainment—songs, films, stories. The growth of a popular culture—its history, meaning, and significance—was debated by an unlikely collection of disillusioned radicals who had turned from politics in the interregnum between the Nazi-Soviet pact and the Vietnam War, outraged conservatives who saw the popular arts as the great threat to tradition, and smug liberal intellectuals who, at last, following the second Great War, had achieved positions of power and influence. The leaders of the debate, at least as measured by their capacity to irritate, were Dwight MacDonald (1962), C. Wright Mills (1959), and Edward Shils (1959). MacDonald, in contrast to his political Trotskyism, led the conservative antipopulist and antibourgeois assault on popular culture in the name of the folk and the elite. Mills attacked the popular arts from the left, in the name of authentic democratic community and against the manipulation of political economics, and academic elites who controlled the system of industrial production in culture. Shils defended the center of liberal belief: taste was being neither debased nor exploited; artists were freer and better compensated and audiences better entertained; artistic creativity and intellectual productivity were as high as they had been in human history.

Gradually the debate evaporated and the protagonists went on to other, more tractable but less elevating subjects. There was, as with most intellectual debate, no resolution of the issues. When the whole matter was stated in the undressed form the protagonists finally adopted, it was clear they were all correct: surely tradition was being evaporated, surely things in many ways were better than ever before and certainly no worse for the mass of men and women, and surely ordinary people were under a constant barrage of shallow and manipulative culture controlled by a "power elite." But if that was the prudent conclusion, it illustrates that in intellectual matters prudence is not always the most desirable course; rather than resolving a debate, we lost, temporarily at least, a subject matter.

In the 1960s the study of popular culture was absorbed or disappeared into functional sociology and behaviorist psychology—into the "effects" tradition. There were glittering exceptions, of course—Roland Barthes, Raymond Williams, and John Cawelti come to mind—but what remained of the study of popular culture, in forums such as the *Journal of Popular Culture*, drifted off into triviality or bemusement; it was disconnected from any passionate concern or pressing intellectual puzzle. When the subject of popular culture reemerged in the 1970s, it had been stripped of its general moral, aesthetic, and social concerns and absorbed into one overriding problematic: the question of power and domination.

Much has been gained in this journey, but much has been lost also. The original debate raised and then promptly obscured a still puzzling intellectual question: What is the significance of conceiving the world on the terms laid down by popular art, and what is the relationship between this form of consciousness and other forms—scientific, aesthetic, religious, ethnic, mythological—which popular art variously displaces or penetrates or with which it merely cohabits?

The fashion of recent years has been to dismiss the debate on popular culture or treat it as an aberrational prelude to the more serious critical and theoretical work that followed. I resist that fashion because I have become more convinced that the protagonists in the mass culture debate were on the hunt of the real goods. If anything the pertinence of the arguments they set forth has grown over the years (of happiness and despair we still have no measure) for they collectively grasped, however much they differed, how modern societies were put together and the major trajectories of their development. Few people have come close to C. Wright Mills' nuanced understanding of American life in *The Power Elite* (1959). The theory of mass society, at the heart of that book and admirably extended and enriched by William Kornhauser (1959), has not been superseded by writers working the terrain of critical theory or postmodernism or even "effects" research. Indeed, as our understanding of culture has grown, our understanding of social structure has dimmed. Although the theory of popular culture has been powerfully and instructively elaborated by recent European work, that theory remains unadapted to the more fluid, ambiguous, anarchic conditions of North American life, conditions that are, to put too fine a point on it, "Tocquevillian." The continuing value of the older popular culture debate and the Mills-Kornhauser version of mass society is that they powerfully caught the structural conditions of life on this continent.

The weakness of that theory and debate, however, lies in the relatively crude conception of culture they assume. In recent years major advances have been made, under a variety of labels and in an even wider variety of places, in the analysis of culture. In this chapter I would like to review the significance of some of those advances by way of a commentary on and paraphrasing of Clifford Geertz's *The Interpretation of Cultures*. The continuing advantage of Geertz's work is that, while open to important European scholarship, it remains connected, in subtle ways, to Talcott Parsons, under whom Geertz studied, and the milieu of the University of Chicago, where he worked for an early and extended period. Therefore, while absorbing influences from phenomenology, semiotics, British philosophy, and continental literary criticism, Geertz remains in touch with the hard surfaces of American life, even when he is doing ethnography in Bali or Indonesia. Geertz remains open to transatlantic winds of doctrine but still is connected to the instructive lessons that derive from the concrete condition under which he works.

The Interpretation of Cultures is a collection of essays written over fifteen years. In these essays, Geertz, an anthropologist, is on the track of a workable concept of culture. To read the essays chronologically, though they are not so laid out in the book, is to witness the development of an increasingly precise and powerful theory of culture and one that progressively becomes a theory of communication as well. For a student of communication the book is double-edged: it attempts to erect a theory of culture that will aid in understanding the interpretation of specific cultures. It does this by elaborating a theory of symbols and symbolic processes in their relation to social order. Let me attempt to catch this elaboration, first by looking at a dilemma of communication studies, then at a contradiction of social science, and, finally, by a loosely paraphrased and somewhat simplified unpacking of Geertz's essays.

I

In the early 1970s I heard the late Raymond Williams, then a distinguished fellow of Jesus College, Cambridge, remark at a London meeting that "the study of communications was deeply and disastrously deformed by being confidently named the study of 'mass-communication.'" Stuart Hall, then director of the Centre for the Study of Contemporary Culture at the University of Birmingham, responded that at his center they had considered a number of labels, including "communications," to describe their work. In his opinion the wisest decision they had made was to tie the Birmingham Centre to contemporary culture rather than to communications or mass communications. Awash as we are in programs of "communications" and "mass communications" what, pray tell, were Williams and Hall trying to teach us?

Williams argued that it was now time (over a decade ago) to bury the term "mass communications" as a label for departments, research programs, and conferences. The term was disastrous, he thought, for three reasons. First, it limits studies to a few specialized areas such as broadcasting and film and what is miscalled "popular literature" when there is "the whole common area of discourse in speech and writing that always needs to be considered." Second, the term "mass" has become lodged in our language in its weakest sense—the mass audience—and stands in the way of analysis of "specific modern communication situations and of most specific modern communications conventions and forms." Third, because the audience was conceived as a mass, the only question worth asking was how, and then whether, film, television, or books influenced or corrupted people. Consequently, it was always much easier to get funding for these kinds of impact studies than any other kind of research.

It is easy to glide by Williams's distinctive emphasis. He was suggesting that studies of mass communications create unacceptable limitations on study and a certain blindness as well. The blindness is that the term generally overlooks the fact that communication is first of all a set of practices, conventions, and forms, and in studying "mass situations" these phenomena are assumed to exist but never are investigated. Second, the term limits and isolates study by excluding attention to the forms, conventions, and practices of speech and writing as well as to the mass media and therefore necessarily distorts understanding. This distinctive emphasis, which derives in part from European Marxism, should not blind us to the fact that it is shared by American pragmatism as well.

Stuart Hall's objection to the word "communication" is somewhat more opaque, though I think he had a similar intention. Hall believes that the word "communication" narrows study and isolates it substantively and methodologically. Substantively, it narrows the scope of study to products explicitly produced by and delivered over the mass media. The study of communications is therefore generally isolated from the study of literature and art, on the one hand, and from the expressive and ritual forms of everyday life—religion, conversation, sport—on the other. The word "culture," which in its anthropological sense directs us toward the study of an entire way of life, is replaced by the word "communication," which directs us to the study of one isolated segment of existence. Methodologically, the word "communication" isolates us from an entire body of critical, interpretive, and comparative methodology that has been at the heart of anthropology and the study of literature as well as modern Marxism.

We can, of course, easily dismiss this as a misunderstanding and claim that our emphasis on communications and mass communications has not divorced us from the study of speech, writing, and other contemporary products. Too much is being read into the organization of departments and journals. Or, we might argue that limitations have been placed on the range and scope of research, but only to achieve a subject matter amenable to treatment with scientific methods and scientific theories. But these dismissals jump too easily to the lips, and it would be well to suspend judgment until a more generous understanding can be gained of what is distinctive in the Williams-Hall arguments.

One way of catching these distinctive emphases is to suggest that intellectual work on culture and communications derives from different intellectual puzzles and is grounded in two different metaphors of communications. The generalization is too large, of course, and plenty of vividly particular exceptions can be found, but I express preponderant tendencies of thought related to different social conditions. As I suggested earlier, American studies are grounded in a transmission or transportation view of communication. We see communication basically as a process of transmitting messages at a distance for the purpose of control. The archetypal case of communication, then, is persuasion; attitude change; behavior modification; socialization through the transmission of information, influence, or conditioning or, alternatively, as a case of individual choice over what to read or view. I call this a transmission or transportation view because its central defining terms have much in common with the use of "communication" in the nineteenth century as another term for "transportation." It also is related strongly to the nineteenth-century desire to use communication and transportation to extend influence, control, and power over wider distances and greater populations.

By contrast, a ritual view conceives communication as a process through which a shared culture is created, modified, and transformed. The archetypal case of communication is ritual and mythology for those who come at the problem from anthropology; art and literature for those who come at the problem from literary criticism and history. A ritual view of communication is directed not toward the extension of messages in space but the maintenance of society in time (even if some find this maintenance characterized by domination and therefore illegitimate); not the act of imparting information or influence but the creation, representation, and celebration of shared even if illusory beliefs. If a transmission view of communication centers on the extension of messages across geography for purposes of control, a ritual view centers on the sacred ceremony that draws persons together in fellowship and commonality.

Now the differences between these views can be seen as mere transpositions of one another. However, they have quite distinct consequences, substantively and methodologically. They obviously derive from differing problematics; that is, the basic questions of one tradition do not connect with the basic questions of the other.

What is the relationship between culture and society—or, more generally, between expressive forms, particularly art, and social order? For American scholars in general this problem is not even seen as a problem. It is simply a matter of individual choice or one form of determination or another. There is art, of course, and there is society; but to chart the relationship between them is, for a student in communication, to rehearse the obvious and unnecessary. However, in much European work one of the principal (though not exclusive) tasks of scholarship is to work through the relationship of expressive form to social order.

The British sociologist Tom Burns put this nicely somewhere when he observed that the task of art is to make sense out of life. The task of social science is to make sense out of the senses we make out of life. By such reasoning the social scientist stands toward his material—cultural forms such as religion, ideology, journalism, everyday speech—as the literary critic stands toward the novel, play, or poem. He has to figure out what it means, what interpretations it presents of life, and how it relates to the senses of life historically found among a people.

Note what Burns simply takes for granted. There is, on the one hand, life, existence, experience, and behavior and, on the other hand, attempts to find the meaning and significance in this experience and behavior. Culture according to this reading is the meaning and significance particular people discover in their experience through art, religion, and so forth. To study culture is to seek order within these forms, to bring out in starker relief their claims and meanings, and to state systematically the relations between the multiple forms directed to the same end: to render experience comprehensible and charged with affect. But what is called the study of culture also can be called the study of communications, for what we are studying in this context are the ways in which experience is worked into understanding and then disseminated and celebrated (the distinctions, as in dialogue, are not sharp).

Communication studies in the United States have exhibited until recently quite a different intention. They have found most problematic in communication the conditions under which persuasion or social control occurs. Now to reduce the rich variety of American studies to this problematic is, I will admit, a simplification, yet it does capture a significant part of the truth. American studies of communication, mass and interpersonal, have aimed at stating the precise psychological and sociological conditions under which attitudes are changed, formed, or reinforced and behavior stabilized or redirected. Alternatively, the task is to discover those natural and abstract functions that hold the social order together. Specific forms of culture—art, ritual, journalism—enter the analysis only indirectly, if at all; they enter only insofar as they contribute to such socio-logical conditions or constitute such psychological forces. They enter, albeit indirectly, in discussions of psychological states, rational or irrational motives and persuasive tactics, differing styles of family organization, sharp distinctions rendered between reality and fantasy-oriented communication, or the role of the mass media in maintaining social integration. But expressive forms are exhausted as intellectual objects suitable for attention by students of communication once relevance to matters of states and rates have been demonstrated. The relation of these forms to social order, the historical transformation of these forms, their entrance into a subjective world of meaning and significance, the inter-relations among them, and their role in creating a general culture—a way of life and a pattern of significance—never is entertained seriously.

This difference of substance and intent is related also to a difference in strategy in dealing with a persistent meth-odological dilemma of the social sciences and, especially, of different meanings of that critical word *empirical*. In these pivotal matters we may usefully turn to Clifford Geertz and *The Interpretation of Cultures*.

II

At the center of this book is a problem that equality and social class have created for North American intellectuals. We are officially committed to a belief in human reason as the instrument of political action. Without that commitment there is little left of a common political life beyond individual taste, choice, and rights. However, as Reinhard Bendix formulated the matter in "Sociology and the Distrust of Reason" (1971), the modern social sciences are equally com-mitted to the view that human action is either the product of individual preference or, more important for this argument, is governed by intrinsic and unconscious or extrinsic and environmental laws and functions. The latter leave little room for the operation of reason, consciousness, or even individually determined choice. Behavior is modeled on laws of conditioning and reinforcement, or prelogical functions, or preconscious urges and scars such as an inferiority complex or will to power. Now the question that immediately arises is this: Where exactly do these laws and functions come from? We have no other choice than to respond: they are either authored by the scientist for his purposes as a member of a controlling class, or they are part of nature and as such control and determine the behavior of the scientist as well as his subjects. But if the activity of the scientist *qua* scientist is determined by conditioning and reinforcement, by the functional necessities of personality and social systems, by the eruption of the demonic and unconscious, what is left of reason? Scientific thought perhaps has no relation to truth because it cannot be explained by truth; it too is a prejudice and a passion, however sophisticated. If the laws of human behavior control the behavior of the scientist, his work is nonsense; if not, just what kind of sense can be made of it?

This dilemma is at the heart of Geertz's essays and he pursues it most directly in the analysis of ideology. Ideology is a scientific term inherited from the philosophers and converted into a weapon. Intellectuals do not generally think of themselves as in the grip of an ideology and don't much like being called ideologists. As a result, we commonly make a distinction between political science or theory, which theoretically and empirically captures the truth, and ideology, which is a tissue of error, distortion, and self-interest, as in "fascist ideology." Consequently, we proclaim the "end of ideology" because we now have a scientific theory of politics. But how does one make the distinction between these forms? The political theory of scientists might be just one more ideology: distortion and fantasy in the service of self-interest, passion, and prejudice.

There is no easy answer to the question. Geertz calls the dilemma "Mannheim's Paradox" for in *Ideology and Utopia* Karl Mannheim (1965) wrestled heroically with it, though his was a battle without resolution. "Where, if anywhere, ideology leaves off and science begins has been the Sphinx's Riddle of much of modern sociological thought and the

46

rustless weapon of its enemies" (Geertz, 1973: 194). But the dilemma is general: where does conditioning leave off and science begin? Where does class interest leave off and science begin? Where does the unconscious leave off and science begin? The significance of the dilemma for this essay is twofold: first, the study of communication begins when, with the growth of the field of the "sociology of knowledge," the dilemma is faced directly. Second, the principal strategies employed by communication researchers can be seen as devices for escaping Mannheim's Paradox.

Most social scientists do not think much of what they are doing when adopting particular research strategies, and certainly they do not think of themselves as dealing with Mannheim's Paradox. But one important way of looking at the major traditions of social science work is to recognize that there are varying strategies for dealing with "sociology and the distrust of reason." In the study of communication there have been three strategies for attacking the problem, though naturally they parallel the strategies adopted in the other social sciences. The first is to conceive of communication as a behavioral science whose objective is the elucidation of laws. The second is to conceive of communication as a formal science whose objective is the elucidation of structures. The third is to conceive of communication as a cultural science whose objective is the elucidation of meaning. Let me roughly look at these strategies in terms of Geertz's analysis of the perennial problem of ideology.

Two principal explanations of ideology have emerged from the behavioral sciences. Geertz calls them an interest theory and a strain theory, though for us it would be perhaps more felicitous to label them a causal and a functional explanation. A causal explanation attempts to root ideology in the solid ground of social structure. It explains ideological positions by deriving them from the interests of various groups, particularly social classes. It attempts to predict the adoption of ideological positions on the basis of class membership, thereby deriving ideology from antecedent causation. Eventually such an argument starts to creak because it is difficult to predict ideology on the basis of class or, indeed, on any other set of variables. Although ideology is more predictable than many other social phenomena, the net result of causal explanations is relatively low correlations between class position and ideological position. When this form of "essentialism"—one class, one ideology—breaks down, a shift of explanatory apparatus is made. In functional explanations ideology is seen less as caused by structural forces than as satisfying certain needs or functions of the personality or society. Geertz calls this latter view a strain theory because it starts from the assumption of the chronic malintegration of the personality and society. It describes life as inevitably riddled by contradictions, antinomies, and inconsistencies. These contradictions give rise to strains, for which ideology provides an answer. If in causal explanations ideology is derived from antecedent factors, in functional explanations ideology is explained as a mechanism for restoring equilibrium to a system put out of joint by the contrariness of modern life. In one model ideology is a weapon for goring someone else's ox; in a functional model it is a device for releasing tension. In the causal model the petit bourgeois shopkeeper's anti-Semitism is explained by class position; in the functional model the same anti-Semitism is explained as catharsis—the displacement of tension onto symbolic enemies.

These same patterns of explanation are found throughout the behavioral sciences. They attempt to explain phenomena by assimilating them to either a functional or a causal law. Both have their weaknesses: causal laws are usually weak at prediction; functional laws are usually obscure in elucidating comprehensible and powerful functions. Moreover, although both explanations are presented as based on empirical data, the data are connected to operative concepts—such as catharsis or interest—by rather questionable and arbitrary operational definitions.

However, the principal concern is not to question the power of the explanations but to see how they deal with Mannheim's Paradox. The behavioral sciences attempt to deal with the paradox in two ways. First, it can be claimed that the behavioral laws elucidated are only statistically true; therefore, although they apply, like the laws of mechanics, to everyone in general, they apply to no one in particular.

Because such laws explain only a portion of the variance in the data, it can be asserted that the behavior of the scientist is not governed necessarily by it. A second way to escape the dilemma is simply to claim that the laws do not apply to the scientist *qua* scientist because in the act of comprehending the law he escapes its force. The scientist's knowledge gives him a special purchase to critique the assertions of others, particularly to unmask the illusory and self-serving nature of their ideological assertions.

Now neither of these strategies is particularly effective, but perhaps the greatest disservice they perform for ideology— or, for that matter, for any other symbolic form to which they are applied—is that they dispose of the phenomenon in the very act of naming it. They assume that the flattened scientific forms of speech and prose, that peculiar quality of presumed disinterest and objectivity, are the only mode in which truth can be formulated. What they object to in ideology is hyperbole.

The study of communication in the United States has been dominated by attempts to create a behavioral science and to elucidate laws or functions of behavior. And that study has encountered the same dilemmas that appear throughout the social sciences.

Virtually no formal theories of communication have been active in American scholarship. In allied fields, however, there have been formal theories of some scope and power, and they have had at the least an imaginative effect on the study of communications. Modern linguistics, systems theory, and cybernetics are differing attempts to build formal theories of social phenomena. Moreover, under the influence of Noam Chomsky's success in linguistics, movements such as cognitive psychology, cognitive anthropology, and ethno-science have attempted to displace behavioral modes of explanation with formal theories. Varieties of structuralism, derived in significant part from Lévi-Strauss, have been deployed as formal theories applied to mass communication and have been imaginatively, if not operationally, influential (Leymore, 1975).

Formal theories deal with Mannheim's Paradox by turning away from the study of behavior. Therefore, formal theorists avoid postulating or demonstrating lawlike principles governing the behavior of subjects or scientists. This can be seen most clearly in the distinction between competence and performance at the center of one form of linguistic theory, or between language and speech at the center of another. Modern linguists are not attempting to explain linguistic behavior or performance—the actual deployment of actual sentences by actual subjects—but rather linguistic competence—the abstract ability of a native speaker to, in principle, utter the grammatical sentences of a language. Formal theorists begin, then, from an irrefragable, empirical universal—the ability of humans to produce novel utterances (sentences neither heard nor spoken before) or, as with Lévi-Strauss, the presence in all cultures of systems of symbolic opposition (up/down, stop/go, red/green)—and then build theoretical machines, mechanisms, or structures capable of producing these phenomena. The trick is to build the deep structure of mind or culture out of the fugitive materials of everyday acts. While poststructuralism has taken leave of this enterprise, it remains deeply scarred by it.

We can put a different gloss on the same argument. When popular forms such as ideology enter the study of mass communication, they are usually treated as either a force or a function. Unless a formal analysis of the deep structure of the ideology is undertaken (and none has been particularly successful), one is left with searching out the effects of the ideology or its uses and gratifications. The shift from the former to the latter, the normal trajectory of research, is also a shift from persons conceived as relatively trivial machines to persons as complex systems. This shift from causal and toward functional explanations is not merely the product of the narrow history of communications research but reflects, more important, the general history of the social sciences, particularly when those sciences attempt to deal with artifacts and expressions that are explicitly symbolic. There is a sense, of course, in which all human activity in both origins and endings is symbolic. But there is still a useful analytic distinction, to borrow from Geertz, who borrows from Kenneth Burke (1957), between building a house and drawing up a blueprint for building a house, between making love and writing a poem about making love. However much of the symbolic and the artifactual are fused in everyday life, it is nonetheless useful to separate them for analytic purposes. Unfortunately, whenever the symbolic component is inescapably present, a certain theoretical clumsiness overtakes the social sciences. Faced with making some explicit statements about cultural forms, social scientists retreat to obscurantism and reduce their subject matter to social structures or psychological needs. They seem incapable of handling culture in itself—as an ordered though contradictory and heterogeneous system of symbols—and treat merely the social and psychological origins of the symbols.

The several subfields of the social sciences in which symbols and meanings are of critical importance exhibit a similar history. In the study of ideology, religion, and mythology, as well as popular culture, the same attempt is made to reduce symbolic forms to antecedent and causal variables. When this strategy fails, as it inevitably does, a switch in strategy is announced that reduces cultural forms to system-maintaining phenomena—that is, to a functional explanation. Behind the switch in research strategy is a concurrent switch in imagery: from a power model of phenomena to an anxiety model, from an interest theory of action to a strain theory, and from a passive and arational notion of behavior to an active and utilitarian one.

Mass communication research began as an attempt to explain communication effects by deriving them from some causally antecedent aspect of the communication process. Inspired by both behavioristic psychology and information theory, this explanatory apparatus gave rise to a power model of communication wherein the emphasis was placed on the action of the environment, however conceived, upon a relatively passive receiver. This model was made both possible and necessary by a scientific program that insisted on reducing cultural phenomena to antecedent causes. Some of these causes were explicitly conceptualized as psychological variables—source credibility, appeal of the message—whereas others were rooted in the structural situation of the receiver—class, status, religion, income

(Hovland, Janis, and Kelley, 1953; Lazarsfeld, Berelson, and Gaudet, 1948).

An advantage of this model of antecedent causality was that it rooted cultural phenomena in the solid ground of social structure or the conditioning history of individuals. However, it had the disadvantage of yielding ambiguous predictions of behavior. At best, modest correlations of antecedent and resultant variables were achieved, and even modest success was often purchased by carefully screening test populations (Katz and Lazarsfeld, 1955) to heighten the likelihood of significant result.

The history of mass communication research parallels that of other areas of the social sciences that deal with cultural forms. Whether it be deviance (Matza, 1964), art (Geertz, 1973), or religion (Berger, 1967), the attempt is first made to predict the presence of a creed, ideology, deviant pattern, or behavior change on the basis of antecedent exposure and stimulation or on the basis of a social-structural variable—race, class, income, and so on. The results are usually meager, and the conclusion comes down to "some do, some don't." On the basis of conditioning or class or any other of these families of antecedent variables, one concludes that some hold to the creed, some do not; some vote one way, some another; some join fascist movements, some remain apathetic. Unfortunately, one is unable to predict the doers from the underlying model, for only a minuscule amount of variation in the data—significant correlations, but usually less than .5—can be explained by even complex sets of variables. An antiessentialism is forced on us by the data rather than by the philosophy, as David Morley's (1980, 1986) contemporary studies of audiences have shown. The entire imagery of culture as a power—the opiate of the people, the hypodermic needle, the product of the environment—denies the functioning of autonomous minds and reduces subjects to trivial machines. The rich history of cultural symbolism, the complex, meaningful transactions of, for example, religion end up no more than shadowy derivatives of stimuli and structures.

The functional model arises in response to the empirical difficulties encountered in models of antecedent causality.

Moreover, it engenders a shift in imagery and attention: from a view of communication as a power to one of communication as a form of anxiety release and from an interest in the source to an interest in the audience. But most important, it involves a shift in the explanatory apparatus. For in functional analysis the primary emphasis is not on determining the antecedents or origins of behavior but on determining the import or consequences of behavior for the maintenance of systems of thought, activity, or social groups. One explains social phenomena not merely etiologically but teleologically: the way they act as mechanisms to maintain or restore equilibrium within a system.

Functional analysis turns, then, from causes to consequences, which are viewed as a contribution to maintaining (or disrupting) the individual personality or more complex systems of social life. Whether the subject is ideology, religion, or mythology, the effect is the same. Religion, no longer characterized as a product of historical conditioning, is now shown to maintain social solidarity: the "We're all in this together" theory. Ideology, now no longer merely caused by class interest, is shown to provide catharsis by fixating and dispelling anxiety on scapegoats—the "Even paranoids have enemies" theory. Mass communication, rather than causing certain attitudes or behaviors, provides, by diverting audiences from their troubles, feedback into the maintenance of normalized social roles: the "Everything we do is useful" theory.

Functionalism starts, then, from the potential malintegration of systems—social, personality, cognitive. It explains phenomena by attaching them not to causal antecedents but to future states, which they erode or more often maintain. At the level of society functional mechanisms deal with strain—surveying hostile environments; at the level of personality with anxiety, or, in the psychological equivalent to sociological functionalism, with disequilibrium. One is left with the equivocal notion that mass communication may upset or confirm social consensus, survey the environment or deceive an audience, promote solidarity or enhance animosity, relieve or exacerbate social tensions, correlate a response to crisis or fragment a community. Anecdotal evidence can be introduced to support all of these contentions, but there is no way of specifying when and under what circumstances mass communication does any or all of these things.

Although a uses and gratifications analysis on occasion comes close to motives that lie behind the consumption of mass communications, in attempting to discriminate the consequences of the behavior the analysis becomes ambiguous. A pattern of behavior shaped by a certain set of motivations turns out by a plausible coincidence to serve remotely related ends. A person sits down to watch a television program because he wants to be entertained and by some mysterious process ends up dispelling his tensions, restoring his morale, or establishing solidarity with a larger community. These consequences are related to the motivations for the action in an extremely vague, unspecific, and unconvincing way. This problem, again, haunts all functional analysis. As Geertz (1973) has summarized the dilemma,

> a group of primitives sets out, in all honesty, to pray for rain and ends up by strengthening its social solidarity; a ward politician sets out to get by or remain near the trough and ends by mediating between unassimilated immigrant groups and an impersonal governmental bureaucracy; an ideologist sets out to air his grievances and finds himself contributing, through the diversionary powers of his illusions, to the continued viability of the very system that grieves him (p. 206).

Latent functions or false consciousness are devices by which the gap is closed between the intentions and consequences of conduct. This trick was inherited from Malinowski (1962) and his arguments concerning the nature of the primitive mind. In Malinowski's scheme, human action that on its face was patently irrational, superstitious, and magical was linked by a hidden indirection to meanings inherently rational and commonsensical: the primitive mentality disclosed a utilitarian mind. This form of thought left us with but two alternatives in treating behavior; it was either intrinsically primitive and hence irrational and superstitious, or it was susceptible to transformation into utilitarian forms of thought by indication of its intrinsic sensibleness: the unconscious side of thought contributed to the stability of the personality or the ordering of society.

Either strategy has the effect of dissolving the content of the experience—the particular ritual, prayer, movie, or news story—into something pre- or protological without ever inspecting the experience itself as some ordered system of meaningful symbols. The difficulty is, of course, the virtual absence in mass communication research of anything more than a rudimentary conception of symbolic processes. There is much talk about escape, finding symbolic outlets, or solidarity being created, but how these miracles are accomplished is never made clear. In such analyses one never finds serious attention being paid to the content of experience. For example, studies of entertainment claim that fantasy is not completely "irrational" because it eases tension, promotes solidarity and promotes learning—claims that seem ridiculous to anyone who has seen a community divided over the content of movies or been personally disturbed by a recurrent film image. What one rarely finds is any analysis of the voice in which films speak. There is an emphasis on everything except what movies are concretely all about.

The link between the causes of mass communication behavior and its effects seems adventitious because the connecting element is a latent function and no attention is paid to the autonomous process of symbolic formation. Functional analysis, like causal analysis, goes directly from the source to the effect without ever seriously examining mass communication as a system of interacting symbols and interlocked meanings that somehow must be linked to the motivations and emotions for which they provide a symbolic outlet. Content analyses are done, but they are referred for elucidation not to other themes or to any sort of a semantic theory but either backward to the needs they mirror or forward to the social system they maintain.

Despite that, I wish neither to gainsay—or to belabor the traditions of work on mass communication. They are indispensable starting points for everyone. I merely wish to suggest that they do not exhaust the tasks of trained intelligence. There is a third way of looking at the goals of intellectual work in communications. Cultural studies does not, however, escape Mannheim's Paradox; it embraces it in ways I hope to show. In doing so it runs the risk of falling into a vicious relativism, though Geertz himself does not see that as a problem. Cultural studies also has far more modest objectives than other traditions. It does not seek to explain human behavior in terms of the laws that govern it or to dissolve it into the structures that underlie it; rather, it seeks to understand it. Cultural studies does not attempt to predict human behavior; rather, it attempts to diagnose human meanings. It is, more positively, an attempt to bypass the rather abstracted empiricism of behavioral studies and the ethereal apparatus of formal theories and to descend deeper into the empirical world. The goals of communications conceived as a cultural science are therefore more modest but also more human, at least in the sense of attempting to be truer to human nature and experience as it ordinarily is encountered. For many students of cultural studies the starting point, as with Geertz, is Max Weber:

> Believing with Max Weber, that man is an animal suspended in webs of significance he himself has spun, I take culture to be those webs, and the analysis of it to be therefore not an experimental science in search of law but an interpretive one in search of meaning. It is explication I am after, construing social expressions on their surface enigmatical (Geertz, 1973: 5).

That is altogether too arch, so let me explicate the meaning Geertz is after with an artless and transparent example of the type of scene communication researchers should be able to examine. Let us imagine a conversation on the meaning of death. One party to the conversation, a contemporary physician, argues that death occurs with the cessation of brain waves. The test he declares is observable empirically; and so much the better, it makes the organs of the deceased available for quick transplant into waiting patients. A second party to the conversation, a typical middle American, declares that death occurs on the cessation of the heartbeat.

This too is empirically available and, so much the better, occurs after the cessation of brain waves. Life is not only prolonged, but because the heart has long been a symbol of human emotions, the test recognizes the affective side of death, the relation of death to the ongoing life of a community. A third party to the conversation, an Irish peasant, finding these first two definitions rather abhorrent, argues that death occurs three days after the cessation of the heartbeat. This too is empirical; days can be counted as well as anything else. In the interim the person, as at the Irish wake, is treated as if he is alive. The "as if" gives away too much: he is alive for three days after the cessation of heartbeats. Death among such peasants occurs with social death, the final separation of the person from a human community. Prior to that he is, for all intents and purposes, alive for he is responded to as a particularly functionless living being. A fourth party to the conversation argues that death occurs seven days prior to the cessation of the heartbeat. He is, let us say, a member of the tribe Colin Turnbull described so vividly in *The Mountain People* (1972). Among these starving people life ceases when food can no longer be gathered or scrambled for. The person is treated as if he were dead during a phase in which we would declare he was alive. Again, ignore the "as if": the definition is as cognitively precise and affectively satisfying as anything put forth by a neurosurgeon. The definition just is: the particular meaning that a group of people assigns to death.

What are we to do with this scene? We certainly cannot choose among these definitions on the basis of the scientific truth of one and the whimsy of the others. Death is not given unequivocally in experience by inflexible biological and social markers, and this has been true since long before the existence of artificial life-support systems. We can, however, show how differing definitions of death point toward differing values and social purposes: fixations on prolonging life by "artificial means," on preserving the continuity of community existence, to reduce the sharpness of the break between life and death. But as to choosing among them on any presumed scientific grounds, we must, at least at this point, remain agnostics.

What more can be done with this scene? Do we want to ask what caused these individuals to hold to these strange definitions? We might naturally inquire after that, but one cannot imagine producing a "lawlike" statement concerning it other than a tautology such as "all people have definitions of death, however varied, because death is something that must be dealt with." The only causal statement that one might imagine is a historical one: a genetic account of how these views grew over time among various people and were changed, displaced, and transformed. But such an analysis is not likely to produce any lawlike statements because it seems intuitively obvious that every people demands a separate history: there are as many reasons for holding differing definitions of death as there are definitions of death.

Could we inquire into the functions these various definitions serve? One supposes so, but that does not seem promising. There is certainly no a priori reason to assume that such definitions serve any function at all. One can imagine elaborate speculations on the role of death in strengthening social solidarity. But this sort of thing runs into the anomaly of all functional analyses: a tribesman starts to figure out if death has occurred and ends up strengthening the solidarity of society. There is no necessary relationship between these two activities. "The concept of a latent function," Geertz argues, "is usually invoked to paper over this anomalous state of affairs, but it rather names the phenomenon (whose reality is not in question) than explains it; and the net result is that functional analyses . . . remain hopelessly equivocal" (p. 206).

Might one in such a situation go looking for the deep structure of mind underlying these diverse surface definitions? Again, one might do so, but it is hard to see how such an exercise would help us understand this particular scene. We might, à la Lévi-Strauss, go looking for the commonality of semantic structure underlying these definitions of death and therefore out of the variety of definitions produce an elegant vision of a universal meaning of death. But this sort of thing ends up verging on a charade, and as Geertz (1973: 359) concludes in his essay on Lévi-Strauss, there are enough particular individuals and particular scenes such as I have described to "make any doctrine of man which sees him as the bearer of changeless truths of reason—an 'original logic' proceeding from 'the structure of the mind'—seem merely quaint, an academic curiosity."

I chose an example as simple and simpleminded as death because it is about as universal, transhistorical, and trans-cultural a phenomenon as one is likely to get. It is also, in its concrete manifestations, as fiercely resistant to reduction to laws, functions, powers and interests as one can imagine. Even in the postmodern age we are going to die in some vividly particular way and in light of some vividly particular set of meanings. Our inability to deal with the ersatz situation I have created and the innumerable ones we are daily called to comment on is not the result of a failure to understand the laws of behavior or the functions of social practices, though insofar as these things can be discovered, it would not hurt us to understand them. Nor does our speechlessness in the face of empirical events result from failure to understand the universal structure of the mind or the nature of cogni-tion—though, again, we could know more of that too. The inability to deal with events such as the death scene derives from our failure, to put it disingenuously, to understand them: to be able to grasp the imaginative universe in which the acts of our actors are signs. What we face in our studies of communication is the consistent challenge to untangle "a multiplicity of complex conceptual structures, many of them superimposed upon or knotted into one another, which are at once strange, irregular, and inexplicit and which he (the student) must contrive somehow first to grasp and then to render" (Geertz, 1973: 10). To repeat, we are challenged to grasp the meanings people build into their words and behavior and to make these meanings, these claims about life and experience, explicit and articulate so that we might fairly judge them.

Of course, social scientists do place meanings on their subject's experience: they tell us what thought or action means, what other people are up to. But the meanings such scientists produce have no necessary relation to the subjective intentions or sensed apprehensions of the people they study. As one observer acidly put it, "social scientists go around telling people what it is they [people] think." Geertz is suggesting that the first task of social science is to understand the meaningful structure of symbols in terms of which people bury their dead. This has usually been called, as method, verstehen. However, it is no long-distance mind reading but an attempt to decipher the interpretations people cast on their experience, interpretations available out in the public world.

A cultural science of communication, then, views human behavior—or, more accurately, human action—as a text. Our task is to construct a "reading" of the text. The text itself is a sequence of symbols—speech, writing, gesture—that contain interpretations. Our task, like that of a literary critic, is to interpret the interpretations. As Geertz elegantly summarized the position in an essay on the "Balinese Cockfight":

> The culture of a people is an ensemble of texts, themselves ensembles which the anthropologist strains to read over the shoulders of those to whom they properly belong. . . . In the cockfight, then, the Balinese forms and discovers his temperament and his society's temper at the same time. Or more exactly, he forms and discovers a particular face of them. Not only are there a great many other cultural texts providing commentaries on status hierarchy and self regard in Bali; but there are a great many other critical sectors of Balinese life besides the stratificatory . . . that receives such attention. . . . What it says about life is not unqualified nor even unchallenged by what other equally eloquent cultural statements say about it. But there is nothing more surprising in this than in the fact that Racine and Moliere were contemporaries, or that the same people who arrange chrysanthemums cast swords (1973: 452-53).

To speak of human action through the metaphor of a text is no longer unusual, though it is still troubling. The metaphor emphasizes that the task of the cultural scientist is closer to that of a literary critic or a scriptural scholar, though it is not the same, than it is to that of a behavioral scientist. "Texts" are not always printed on pages or chiseled in stone—though sometimes they are. Usually we deal with texts of public utterance or shaped behavior. But we are faced, as is the literary critic, with figuring out what the text says, of constructing a reading of it. Doing communication research (or cultural studies or, in Geertz's term, ethnography) "is like trying to read (in the sense of 'construct a reading of') a manuscript—foreign, faded, full of ellipses, incoherencies, suspicious emendations, and tendentious commentaries but written not in conventionalized graphs of sound but in transient examples of shaped behavior" (p. 10).

To pursue this one step further, suppose we undress the death scene; that is, deverbalize it, strip it of words. What we observe now is not a conversation but a set of actions. We are interested in the actions because they have meaning—they are an orchestration of gestural symbols. We need to decipher—though it is not so mechanical as cracking a code—what is being said through behavior. What we observe are people silently holding a wake, measuring brain waves, rolling relatives into ravines, and, of course, a good deal more. From such fugitive and fragmentary data we have to construct a reading of the situation: to interpret the meaning in these symbols as gestures. The trick is to read these "texts" in relation to concrete social structure without reducing them to that structure. No one will contend that this is particularly easy. There are enough methodological dilemmas here to keep us occupied for a few generations. But to look at communication as, if you will forgive me, communication—as an interpretation, a meaning construed from and placed upon experience, that is addressed to and interpreted by someone—allows us to concentrate on the subject matter of the enterprise and not some extrinsic and arbitrary formula that accounts for it.

Why do we wish to construct a reading? The answer to this question shows both the modesty and importance of communication as a study of culture. The objective of cultural studies is not so much to answer our questions as, Geertz puts it, "to make available to us answers that others guarding other sheep in other valleys have given and thus to include them in the consultable record of what man has said" (p. 30). This is a modest goal: to understand the meanings that others have placed on experience, to build up a veridical record of what has been said at other times, in other places, and in other ways; to enlarge the human conversation by comprehending what others are saying. Though modest, the inability to engage in this conversation is the imperative failure of the modern social sciences. Not understanding their subjects—that unfortunate word—they do not converse with them so much as impose meanings on them. Social scientists have political theories and subjects have political ideologies; the behavior of social scientists is free and rationally informed, whereas their subjects are conditioned and ruled by habit and superstition—not good intellectual soil for a working democracy.

Geertz is suggesting that the great need of the social sciences and one that cultural studies is able uniquely to perform is the creation of a theory of fictions. Fiction is used here in its original sense—fictio—a "making," a construction. The achievement of the human mind and its extension in culture (though it is as much an abject necessity as an achievement) is the creation of a wide variety of cultural forms through which reality can be created. Science, with its claim to be the only cultural achievement that was a veridical map of reality, held us back as much as it advanced our understanding of how this miracle was accomplished. The greatest advance that has been made in recent social theory is the erosion of that field of concepts over which the great intellectual battles of late nineteenth-century life were fought. Of particular significance is the abandonment of the struggle to find the irreducible difference between the "primitive" and modern mind. The distinction between the unbridled superstition of the native and the untrammeled rationalism of the citizen—between the affectively charged life space of the primitive magician and the coolly geometrical world of the modern scientist, to state the case rather too boldly—appears now to have taught us more about the political purposes and personal conceits of social scientists than about the nature of human thought. Once the intellectual membrane separating the primitive from the modern mind was pierced, influence ran in both directions. The mind of the savage slowly yielded its logical structure, and patterns of primitive, though not therefore erroneous, forms of intellection among moderns stood out in bolder relief.

The significance of the discovery of the commonalities in human thought is not that we are both primitive and modern, creatures of both reason and superstition, which seems to be the easily achieved construction placed on this discovery. Rather, its significance lies in the realization that human thought does not consist in the production of irrefragable maps of the objective world (science) and error-filled sketches of a mystic reality. Human thought, in the new model, is seen more as interpretations persons apply to experience, constructions of widely varying systems of meanings the verification of which cannot be exhausted by the methods of science. What persons create is not merely one reality but multiple realities. Reality cannot be exhausted by any one symbolic form, be it scientific, religious, or aesthetic. Consequently, the true human genius and necessity is to build up models of reality by the agency of differing types of symbols—verbal, written, mathematical, gestural, kinesthetic—and by differing symbolic forms—art, science, journalism, ideology, ordinary speech, religion, mythology—to state only part of the catalogue. In trying to understand the meanings people place on experience, then, it is necessary to work through a theory of fictions: a theory explaining how these forms operate, the semantic devices they employ, the meanings they sustain, the particular glow they cast over experience.

Understanding a culture is a complex matter and, as Geertz says, thinking particularly of ritual,

> one can start anywhere in a culture's repertoire of forms and end up anywhere else. One can stay . . . within a single, more or less bounded form and circle steadily within it. One can move between forms in search of broader unities or informing contrasts. One can even compare forms from different cultures to define their character in reciprocal relief. But whatever the level at which one operates, and however intricately, the guiding principle is the same: societies like lives contain their own interpretations. One only has to learn how to gain access to them (Geertz, 1973: 453).

At each point in this circling the task remains the same: to seize upon the interpretations people place on existence and to systematize them so they are more readily available to us. This is a process of making large claims from small matters: studying particular rituals, poems, plays, conversations, songs, dances, theories, and myths and gingerly reaching out to the full relations within a culture or a total way of life. For the student of communications other matters press in: how do changes in forms of communications technology affect the constructions placed on experience? How does such technology change the forms of community in which experience is apprehended and expressed? What, under the force of history, technology, and society, is thought about, thought with, and to whom is it expressed? That is, advances in our understanding of culture cannot be secured unless they are tied to a vivid sense of technology and social structure.

To pull off an effective theory of popular culture requires a conception of persons, not as psychological or sociological but as cultural. Such a model would assume that culture is best understood not by tracing it to psychological and sociological conditions or, indeed, to exclusively political or economic conditions, but as a manifestation of a basic cultural disposition to cast up experience in symbolic form. These forms, however implausible to the investigator, are at once aesthetically right and conceptually veridical. They supply meaningful identities along with an apprehended world.

If human activity is not passive or fully dependent on external stimulation, then a corollary is that activity is not merely an emanation of some substratum of biological needs or socially induced dispositions. Instead, human activity, by the very nature of the human nervous system (Geertz, 1973: 68), is cultural, involving the construction of a symbolic container that shapes and expresses whatever human nature, needs, or dispositions exist. As with much else in this essay, Max Weber (1946: 281), writing of religion, expressed it best. In the process, Weber, as the sociologist Norbert Wiley has said in stealing a phrase from Sartre, managed to "ontologize meaninglessness":

64

Many . . . varieties of belief have, of course, existed. Behind them always lies a stand towards something in the actual world which is experienced as specifically "senseless." Thus, the demand has been implied: that the world order in its totality is, could, and should somehow be a meaningful "cosmos." . . . The avenues, the results and the efficacy of this metaphysical need for a meaningful cosmos have varied widely.

When the idea of culture enters communications research, it emerges as the environment of an organism or a system to be maintained or a power over the subject. Whatever the truth of these views—and there is truth in all of them—culture must first be seen as a set of practices, a mode of human activity, a process whereby reality is created, maintained, and transformed, however much it may subsequently become reified into a force independent of human action (Berger and Luckmann, 1966). This activity allows the human nervous system to function by producing and maintaining a meaningful cosmos at once both aesthetically gratifying and intellectually plausible. It is precisely such a theory of culture—or, if you prefer, a theory of meaning, semantics, or semiotics—that is necessary if culture is to be removed from the status of a power or an environment.

Such a theory is usually avoided by setting human needs and motives outside of history and culture—the eighteenth-century rationalist view that human nature is everywhere the same if its cultural (that is, symbolic) trappings can be stripped away (Geertz, 1973: 35). Yet communication research attains precision or persuasiveness only when it is placed within history and culture; within, that is, the historical experience of particular peoples.

Culture, however, is never singular and univocal. It is, like nature itself, multiple, various, and varietal. It is this for each of us. Therefore, we must begin, following Schutz (1970), from the assumption of multiple realities. Mass communication research generally begins from the assumption of some hard existential reality beyond culture and symbols to which human imaginative productions can be referred for final validation. It is comic to see this argument in analyses of, for example, popular music in which commercial love songs are defined as fantasy and blues or war protest songs as reality (Carey, 1972; Hayakawa, 1957). The difference between these forms is not that one is real and the other fantastic but, rather, that they reflect the tastes of audiences for different modes of casting up experience.

Rather than grading experience into zones of epistemological correctness, we can more usefully presume that given what we are biologically and what culture is practically, people live in qualitatively distinct zones of experience that cultural forms organize in different ways. Few people are satisfied apprehending things exclusively through the flattened perceptual glasses of common sense. Most insist on constantly transforming perception into different modes—religious, aesthetic, scientific—in order to see the particular marvels and mysteries these frames of reference contain. The scientific conceit is the presumption that living in scientific frames of reference is unequivocally superior to aesthetic, commonsensical, or religious ones. The debilitating effect of this conceit is the failure to understand the meaningful realms of discourse in terms of which people conduct their lives.

The immediate significance of popular art has little to do with effects or functions. Popular art is, first, an experience, in Robert Warshow's (1964) terms, an "immediate experience"—that must be apprehended in something like its own terms. However long or intensively one lives in the world of popular art, it is only one of several cultural worlds, by no means consistent or congruent, in which people live. In general, there is little or no relation among these worlds except when people, in answering social science questionnaires, must produce a merger between their entertainment and other regions of life. At most what one finds within popular art is the creation of particular moods—sadness, joy, depression—feelings that descend and lift like fogs, and particular motives—erotic, aggressive—that have vectorial qualities (Geertz, 1973: 97). But whether these moods or motives ever reach beyond the domain in which they exist—for example, theaters and concert halls—into laboratories, street corners, and churches, where other dramas are being enacted and other melodies played, is radically problematic. Usually they do not. The analysis of mass communication will have to examine the several cultural worlds in which people simultaneously exist—the tension, often radical tension, between them, the patterns of mood and motivation distinctive to each, and the interpenetration among them. Simultaneously, it will have to release the assumption that needs and motives encountered in scientific worlds are anything more than one cultural version among many and not some final court against which to judge the veridicalness of other modes of experience.

III

It is unfortunate that to mention cultural studies to most communications researchers resurrects the image of the arguments concerning mass and popular culture that littered the field a few decades ago. That was part of the disaster Raymond Williams referred to in comments mentioned earlier. Yet many who worked in popular culture were on the right track. The question they both raised and obscured was a simple but profound one: What is the significance of living in the world of meanings conveyed by popular art? What is the relationship between the meanings found in popular art and in forms such as science, religion, and ordinary speech? How, in modern times, is experience cast up, interpreted, and congealed into knowledge and understanding?

The remarkable work of Clifford Geertz—remarkable substantively and methodologically, though the latter has not been explored in this essay—and of many others working in phenomenology, hermeneutics, and literary criticism has served to clarify the objectives of a cultural science of communications and has defined the dimensions of an interpretive science of society. The task now for students of communications or mass communication or contemporary culture is to turn these advances in the science of culture toward the characteristic products of contemporary life: news stories, bureaucratic language, love songs, political rhetoric, daytime serials, scientific reports, television drama, talk shows, and the wider world of contemporary leisure, ritual, and information. To square the circle, those were some of the conventions, forms, and practices Raymond Williams felt had slipped by us when we confidently named our field the study of mass communications.

CHAPTER 3

Reconceiving "Mass" and "Media"

The task of hermeneutics, according to Richard Rorty, is to charm hermetically sealed-off thinkers out of their self-enclosed practices and to see the relations among scholars as strands of a conversation, a conversation without presuppositions that unites the speakers, but "where the hope of agreement is never lost so long as the conversation lasts" (Rorty, 1979: 318). On this view scholars are not locked in combat over some universal truth but united in society: "persons whose paths through life have fallen together, united by civility rather than by a common goal, much less a common ground" (p. 318).

This hermeneutic intent is nowhere more needed than in theoretical discussions of the mass media. Of all the areas or subareas within communications, that of the mass media has proved to be the most fiercely resistant to adequate theoretical formulation—indeed, even to systematic discussion. The concepts and methods, which, if inadequate, are at least unembarrassing, when applied to interpersonal communication prove hapless and even a little silly when applied to the mass media. More than a matter of complexity is involved here, though complexity is part of it. Many matters concerning interpersonal communication can be safely encysted from the surrounding world and treated with relatively simple models and straightforward methods. Not so with the mass media, where questions of political power and institutional change are inescapable and usually render hopelessly ineffective the standard cookbook recipes retailed by the graduate schools.

In this chapter I make a modest attempt at argument, or at least make an entry into this perpetually unsatisfying discussion about the mass media. First, let me anticipate a conclusion. In an essay on the history of the telegraph (see chapter 8) I tried to show how that technology—the major invention of the mid-nineteenth century—was the driving force behind the creation of a mass press. I also tried to show how the telegraph produced a new series of social interactions, a new conceptual system, new forms of language, and a new structure of social relations. In brief, the telegraph extended the spatial boundaries of communication and opened the future as a zone of interaction. It also gave rise to a new conception of time as it created a futures market in agricultural commodities and permitted the development of standard time. It also eliminated a number of forms of journalism—for example, the hoax and tall tale—and brought other forms of writing into existence—for example, the lean "telegraphic" style Hemingway learned as a correspondent. Finally, the telegraph brought a national, commercial middle class into existence by breaking up the pattern of city-state capitalism that dominated the first half of the nineteenth century. The point of repeating conclusions arrived at elsewhere is that here I am attempting to elucidate a theoretical structure that will support and give generality to detailed historical-empirical investigation. But the path from the theoretical vacuity surrounding the media to concrete investigations must proceed by way of a number of detours.

I

The ragged ambulating ridge dividing the Enlightenment from the Counter-Enlightenment—Descartes from Vico, if we need names—has surfaced in contemporary media studies as an opposition between critical and administrative research. The ridge that Descartes' action and Vico's reaction carved as an engram in the Western imagination has among its features three peaks.

1 **The noncontingency of starting points**. There is a given place to begin to unravel any problem and a given place where it is unraveled.

2 **Indubitability**. In unraveling problems there are available certain concepts and methods of universal standing and applicability, and insofar as there are not, one can make no claim to knowledge.
3 **Identity**. The world of problems is independent of and accessible to the mind of the knowing observer.

In short, if one begins at the beginning, if one is armed with indubitable concepts and methods, if one stands as an observer gazing upon an independent reality, then there is a path to positive knowledge. Taken together they described and secured the way to positive knowledge and yielded an epistemologically centered philosophy. Most important, they made science paradigmatic for culture as a whole—discrediting or at least reducing other human activities that did not conform to the Cartesian paradigm.

The reaction from the Italian side of the Alps settled all those divides that are with us to this day: Science versus the humanities, objective versus subjective, Rationalism versus Romanticism, analysis versus interpretation. There are three aspects of Vico's reaction worth noting and, I will admit, twisting somewhat to the purpose here. First, the world as such has no essence and therefore no real independence. The "real" is continuously adapted and remade to suit human purposes, including the remaking of humans themselves. It is this world of human activity we can understand with greatest clarity. Second, Cartesian science ought not be viewed as paradigmatic for culture as a whole but as one more form of human expression—a new suburb of the language, in Wittgenstein's phrase. Science, in this view, is one more voice in the conversation of humankind, one more device of self-expression, of communication with other humans. It must be understood, as we would say today, hermeneutically, as part of an extended conversation. Third, there are, then, no timeless invariant methods, concepts, or principles by which things are grasped, only the bounded symbols and knowledge, more or less unique to a given culture, through which the world is rendered intelligible.

I have painted a misleading and exceedingly two-dimensional portrait. The ridge of the Enlightenment does not neatly divide people. Some dextrous scholars try to stand on both sides at once; others are on different sides in different books or at different stages of their careers. Others attempt to save what is valuable in both traditions. Still others (some modern literary critics are examples) assimilate Descartes to Vico and make positive science merely one more literary genre; others assimilate Vico to Descartes and "scientize" all of culture. Finally, some, such as William James, find the whole argument bootless and just walk away from the discussion leaving nothing in its place.

I do not wish to debate any of these issues I have raised but merely to sharpen one of the distinctions, a distinction in Charles Taylor's (1976) terms, between "objectivism" and "expressivism."

Taylor characterizes Descartes' vision as an objectivist one. Descartes saw humans as subjects who possessed their own picture of the world (as opposed to a picture determined by God) and an endogenous motivation. Along with this self-defining identity went an objectification of the world. That is, the world was not seen as a cosmic order but as a domain of neutral, contingent fact to which people were related only as observers. This domain was to be mapped by the tracing of correlations and ultimately manipulated for human purposes. Furthermore, this vision of an objectified neutral world was valued as a confirmation of a new identity before it became important as the basis of the mastery of nature. Later this objectification was extended beyond external nature to include human life and society (Taylor, 1976: 539).

This objectivist view collided not only with deeply held religious beliefs but with secular ones as well. Most people most of the time have felt that reality expressed something, that it was an inscription or a resemblance. Most commonly this expressiveness was seen as spiritualism or animism; reality expressed spirit, the divine and transcendent. It was the doctrine of expressivism that Descartes most thoroughly discredited. In his view reality expressed nothing. It was neutral, contingent, concatenated.

However, expressivism did not go away merely because Descartes attacked it. It reappeared in various forms of romanticism. More important, the notion that reality expressed something reappeared in *Hegel* as the *Geist*: the growth of rational freedom. Later, in Taylor's useful phrase, "Marx anthropologized the *Geist*: He displaced it onto man" (Taylor, 1976: 546). In Marx and much of Marxism reality is not neutral and independent of people. Rather, it expresses them in the sense that it is a product of human activity. In William James's lovely phrase, the "mark of the serpent is overall." Reality expresses at any historical moment the purposes and objectives, intentions and desires of humans. Technology, social relations, and all artifacts are social hieroglyphics. Reality is expressive not because it reveals any nature, human or divine, or any eternal essence of any kind but rather because it is a product of human action in and upon the world.

It is this distinction between objectivist and expressivist views of the world, not between administrative and critical research, that constitutes the fundamental divide among communications scholars. But I accept this distinction only as a prelude to modifying it. I agree, at least to a limited extent, that reality is a product of human activity. But the claim is neither philosophical nor metascientific but a simply historical one. Reality has been made—has been progressively made—by human activity. This is through a process, celebrated by structuralists, whereby nature is turned into culture and by a similar but inverse process whereby culture penetrates the body of nature. The first process is revealed by the simple Lévi-Strauss examples of vegetation transformed into cuisine or animals into totems; the second by the mind ulcerating the stomach, or the more menacing moment when an equation splits the atom. The point is general: The history of the species is simultaneously the history of the transformation of reality. There is now virtually no reach of space, of the microscopic or macroscopic, that has not been refigured by human action. Increasingly, what is left of nature is what we have deliberately left there. But if this is true, then reality is not objective, contingent, and neutral. To imagine such an objectivist science is in fact to imagine a world in which, as Lewis Mumford has argued, humans did not exist. And so did Galileo imagine it (Mumford, 1970:

57-65). But if all that is true, it has a philosophical consequence: there are no given starting points, no Archimedian
points or indubitable concepts, or privileged methods. The
only basing point we have is the historically varying nature
of human purposes.

In presenting the expressionist position I have deliberately
glossed over the serious, even fundamental, disagreements
within this tradition. The fault line—often described by the
terms "materialism" and "idealism"—pivots on the question
of whether reality should be seen as an expression of the
human mind—"the place of the mind in nature," in Ernst
Cassirer's useful phrase—or of human activity, human labor
power. However important the debate on this question, it is
possible to agree to the following on either a materialist or
an idealist reading. The mind—the associative, cooperative
mind—its extension in culture and realization in technique,
is the most important means of production. The most important product of the mind is a produced and sustained reality.

I want now to leave the savannah of continental philosophy for the rather more secure village of American studies.
I shall not refer in what follows to these preliminary matters
but, to steal Stuart Hall's lovely phrase, their "absent presence . . . lay across the route like the sky-trail of a vanished
aircraft" (Hall, 1977: 18).

II

I want to locate the distinction between administrative
and critical research—now transformed into a distinction
between objectivism and expressivism—outside the European tradition and within American studies. Inevitably when
this subject comes up, critical and administrative research
are identified with those two emigrés from the fall of Weimar,
T. W. Adorno and Paul Lazarsfeld. The context of the discussion is thus fixed in advance by the type of research and
sponsorship identified with Lazarsfeld and by the research

and "Hegelianized" version of Marxism identified with Adorno. Indeed the term "critical" did not so much describe a position as a cover under which Marxism might hide during a hostile period in exile. It is useful, however, to resituate the distinction between administrative and critical research within the conversation of American culture and, in particular, in an exchange during the 1920s between Walter Lippmann and John Dewey. I do this not to dramatize the importance of Lippmann or Dewey but rather to underscore the point that one cannot grasp a conversation elsewhere until one can understand a conversation at home. If we accept the contingency of starting points (the time and place where we reside), "we accept our inheritance from and our conversation with our fellow human beings as our only source of guidance" (Rorty, 1979). To attempt to evade this contingency is to hope to become a properly programmed machine, which is what graduate education is so often. In short I turn to Dewey and Lippmann to see if I can grasp their conversation within the tradition we have inherited and shaped. Once having grasped it, we can use it as an entrance to other conversations—foreign, strange, and elliptical.

Walter Lippmann's *Public Opinion* (1922) is, I believe, the founding book in American media studies. It was not the first book written about the mass media in America, but it was the first serious work to be philosophical and analytical in confronting the mass media. The title of his book may be *Public Opinion*, but its subject and central actor is the mass media, particularly the news media. The book founded or at least clarified a continuous tradition of research as well. Finally, the book self-consciously restated the central problematic in the study of the mass media.

In earlier writing on the mass media the central problematic, true to the utilitarian tradition, was freedom. Utilitarianism assumes that, strictly speaking, the ends of human action are random or exogenous. Rational knowledge could not be gained of human values or purposes. The best we can do is rationally judge the fitting together of ends and means. One can attain rational knowledge of the allocation of resources among means and toward given ends, but one can gain no rational knowledge of the selection of ends. Apples are as good as oranges, baseball as good as poetry. All that can be determined is the rational means to satisfy subjective and arational desire. Truth in this tradition is a property of the rational determination of means. In turn, the rationality of means depended upon freedom and the availability of information. More precisely, it was freedom that guaranteed the availability of perfect information and perfect information that guaranteed the rationality of means. In summary, then: if people are free, they will have perfect information; if perfect information, they can be rational in choosing the most effective means to their individual ends, and if so, in a manner never quite explained, the social good will result. So the problem that concerned writers about the press in the Anglo-American tradition was how to secure the conditions of freedom against the forces that would undermine it. These forces were considered to be political and institutional, not psychological. Once freedom was secured against these forces, truth and social progress were guaranteed.

Lippmann changed this problematic. He argued that a free system of communication will not guarantee perfect information, and therefore there are no guarantees of truth even when the conditions of freedom are secure. Moreover, the enemies of freedom were no longer the state and the imperfections of the market but the very nature of news and news gathering, the psychology of the audience, and the scale of modern life. It is important to note the following: Lippmann redefined the problem of the press from one of morals and politics to one of epistemology. The consequence of that move was to radically downplay the role of state and class power—indeed, to contribute, paradoxically in a book about politics, to the depoliticization of the public sphere.

The very title of Lippmann's introductory chapter, the most famous chapter in the book, "The World Outside and the Pictures in Our Heads," reveals his basic assumptions. We can know the world if we can represent accurately what is outside our mind. The possibility and nature of knowledge is determined by the way in which the mind is able to construct representations. The philosophical side of

Lippmann is arguing for a general theory of representation that divides culture into the areas that represent reality well (such as science), those that represent it less well (such as art), and those that do not represent it at all (such as journalism), despite their pretense of doing so (Rorty, 1979: 3). Lippmann's view is that reality is "picturable," and truth can be achieved by matching an independent, objective, picturable reality against a language that corresponds to it. News, however, cannot picture reality or provide correspondence to the truth. News can only give, like the blip on a sonar scope, a signal that something is happening. More often it provides degenerate photographs or a pseudo-reality of stereotypes. News can approximate truth only when reality is reducible to a statistical table: sport scores, stock exchange reports, births, deaths, marriages, accidents, court decisions, elections, economic transactions such as foreign trade and balance of payments. Lippmann's major argument is this: Where there is a good machinery of record, the news system works with precision; where there is not, it disseminates stereotypes. Lippmann's solution to the dilemma was an official, quasi-governmental intelligence bureau that would reduce all the contestable aspects of reality to a table.

One does not have to rehearse the well-known phenomenological and ethnomethodological critiques of official records and tables to see in Lippmann the classic fallacy of the Cartesian tradition, to wit: the belief that metaphors of vision, correspondence, mapping, picturing, and representation that apply to small routine assertions (the rose is red; the Cubs lost 7-5; IBM is selling at 67 1/2) will apply equally to large debatable ones. Numbers may picture the stock market, but they will not tell you what is going on in Central America or, alas, what we should do about Eastern Europe.

There are a number of subsidiary assumptions and doctrines in *Public Opinion*. I will mention only a couple. The basic metaphor of communication is vision. Communication is a way of seeing things aright. Because communication is seen within the requirements of epistemological exactness, it is similarly a method of transmitting that exactness.

Ideally communication is the transmission of a secured and grounded truth independent of power. Because such conditions of truth cannot be achieved outside of Cartesian science, it is necessary to employ cadres of scientists to secure exact representations that can then permit the newspaper to correctly inform public opinion.

Lippmann left an intellectual legacy that is still influential, despite the fact that he refuted many of his own views in subsequent works. He particularly furthered a set of beliefs shared with large stretches of the progressive movement. Lippmann endorsed the notion that it was possible to have a science of society such that scientists might constitute a new priesthood: the possessors of truth as a result of having an agreed-upon method for its determination. The mass media could operate as representatives of the public by correctly informing public opinion. Public opinion is merely the statistical aggregation of the private opinions informed by the news media. The effects of mass communication derive from the epistemological inadequacy of the system of news, as well the prior stereotypes, prejudices, and selective perceptions of the audience. Intellectual-political activity had to be professionalized if truth was to be produced. Finally, and in summary, Lippmann implied that the ground for discussion of the mass media had to be shifted from questions of the public, power, and freedom to questions of knowledge, truth, and stereotypes.

John Dewey reviewed *Public Opinion* in the May 3, 1922, issue of the *New Republic*. He admitted to the virtues of the book, but his sharpest conclusion was that it was the greatest indictment of democracy yet written. Dewey answered Lippmann in lectures given four years later at Antioch College and published in 1927 as *The Public and Its Problems*. It is often a maddeningly obscure book and so rather than trying to summarize it, I will quote from its last three pages a quotation I have mercifully shortened (omitting the many ellipses) without impairing its meaning:

The generation of democratic communities and an articulate democratic public carries us beyond the question of intellectual method into that of practical procedure. But the two questions are not disconnected. The problem of securing diffused and seminal intelligence can be solved only in the degree in which local communal life becomes a reality. Signs and symbols, language, are the means of communication by which a fraternally shared experience is ushered in and sustained. But conversation has a vital import lacking in the fixed and frozen words of written speech. Systematic inquiry into the conditions of dissemination in print is a precondition of the creation of a true public. But it and its results are but tools after all. Their final actuality is accomplished in face-to-face relationships by means of direct give and take. Logic in its fulfillment recurs to the primitive sense of the word: dialogue. Ideas which are not communicated, shared, and reborn in expression are but soliloquy, and soliloquy is but broken and imperfect thought. It, like the acquisition of material wealth, marks a diversion of the wealth created by associated endeavor and exchange to private ends . . . expansion of personal understanding and judgment can be fulfilled only in the relations of personal intercourse in the local community. The connections of the ear with vital and out-going thought and emotion are immensely closer and more varied than those of the eye. Vision is a spectator: hearing is a participator. Publication is partial and the public which results is partially informed and formed until the meanings it purveys pass from mouth to mouth. There is no limit to the intellectual endowment which may proceed from the flow of social intelligence when that circulates by word of mouth from one to another in the communications of the local community. That and that only gives reality to public opinion. We lie, as Emerson said, in the lap of an immense intelligence. But that intelligence is dormant and its communications are broken, inarticulate and faint until it possesses the local community as its medium (Dewey, 1927: 217-19.)

There is much that might be noted about that quotation and much that is implied in it. I will draw out just enough to focus Dewey's conflict with Lippmann and to set the stage for the argument I wish to advance. What is most sharply etched in the quotation is Dewey's espousal of the metaphor of hearing over that of seeing. While his language is mindful of arguments that were to resurface over subsequent decades with Harold Innis and Marshall McLuhan, it is important to note that Dewey is attacking the doctrine of representation in both its political and epistemological forms. He chooses the metaphor of hearing over seeing to argue that language is not a system of representations but a form of activity, and speech captures this action better than the more static images of the printed page. As an instrument of action, language cannot serve a representative function. Truth is, in William James's happy phrase, what "it is better for us to believe," and the test of the truth of propositions is their adequacy to our purposes (Rorty, 1979: 10).

In Dewey's view words take on their meanings from other words and in their relations to practical activity rather than by virtue of their representative character. As a corollary, vocabularies acquire their privilege from the people who use them, not from in Rorty's splendid phrase, "their transparency to the real." Science, rather than a privileged, grounded set of representations, is merely part of the conversation of our culture, though an exceedingly important part. Science is a pattern of discourse adopted for various historical reasons for the achievement of objective truth, where objective truth is no more and no less than the best idea we currently have about how to explain what is going on.

Dewey is, in other words, proposing that conversation, not photography, is the ultimate context within which knowledge is to be understood. Science is one, but only one, strand of that conversation. Science is to be commended not because of the privilege of its representations but because of its method, if we understand method to refer not to technique but to certain valued habits: full disclosure, willingness to provide reasons, openness to experience, an arena for systematic criticism. Dewey did not want a science of society presided over by a priesthood; rather, he wanted a science in society: a means of getting our thinking straight by improving the conversation. In this sense everyone is a scientist. Dewey did not want a new science that would objectify society; he wanted a science that would clarify our purposes, advance our mutual understanding, and permit cooperative action. News is not to be judged, in such a view, as a degenerate form of science trading in stereotypes but as the occasion of public discussion and action—another voice to be heard.

Finally, if reality is what we will to believe in support of our shared purposes, then it is proper to claim that reality is constituted by human action, particularly symbolic action and particularly associative action. Therefore, reality has no essence to be discovered but rather a character to be, within limits, constituted. The instrument of political action, of the generation of a democratic political order, is that form of collective life we call "the public." Therefore, if the public is atomized, eclipsed, made a phantom, democracy is impossible.

Let me summarize Lippmann and Dewey. In Lippmann's view, an effective public opinion exists when the individual minds that make up the public possess correct representations of the world. The newspaper serves its democratic function when it transmits such representations to individual members of the public. An effective public opinion then can be formed as the statistical aggregation of such correct representations. This is at present impossible because of censorship, the limited time and contact available to people, a compressed vocabulary, certain human fears of facing facts, and so on. But the greatest limitation is in the nature of news, which fails to adequately represent, at best signals events, and implants and evokes stereotypes. Therefore, the formation of a correct public opinion requires the formation of independent cadres of social scientists working in quasi-public bureaucracies (the Bureau of Standards was his model) using the latest statistical procedures to produce veridical representations of reality—representations to be in turn transmitted to the waiting individuals who make up the public.

Dewey's response takes a number of turns. Public opinion is not formed when individuals possess correct representations of the environment, even if correct representations were possible. It is formed only in discussion, when it is made active in community life. Although news suffers from many of the deficiencies Lippmann cites, its major deficiency is not its failure to represent. The line between an adequate image and a stereotype is impossible to draw anyway. The purpose of news is not to represent and inform but to signal, tell a story, and activate inquiry. Inquiry, in turn, is not something other than conversation and discussion but a more systematic version of it. What we lack is the vital means through which this conversation can be carried on: institutions of public life through which a public can be formed and can form an opinion. The press, by seeing its role as that of informing the public, abandons its role as an agency for carrying on the conversation of our culture. We lack not only an effective press but certain vital habits: the ability to follow an argument, grasp the point of view of another, expand the boundaries of understanding, debate the alternative purposes that might be pursued.

Behind Dewey's surface-level critique is a deeper one directed at the problem of representation in both its epistemological and political-journalistic senses. Here Dewey is in the most acute conflict with Lippmann. He sees in Lippmann a manifestation of what he most strongly argued against: the spectator theory of knowledge. Lippmann views the public as a second-order spectator: a spectator of the spectator. Scientists observe reality and represent it. This correct representation is then transmitted to a receptive, impressionable audience. Dewey expresses his dissatisfaction with Lippmann's view by contrasting speech with vision. We associate knowledge with vision to emphasize that we are spectators rather than participants in the language game through which knowledge is made or produced. We associate politics with vision and the spectator in order to deny the public any political role other than to ratify a political world already represented—a depoliticized world in which all the critical choices have been made by the experts. He would insist that we are not, however, observers or spectators of a given world but participants in its actual making. How we constitute the world is dependent on our purposes and on our skill at foresight, at imagining the possible states of a desirable politics.

III

There was much that was flawed in Dewey's thought, as I have tried to point out on a number of occasions: a congenital optimism, a romance with the small town, a disastrously simple-minded view of technology. I do think he had the best of this argument, however; and, therefore, we ought to extend, however gently, his pragmatic conception of mass communication.

With Dewey one must begin the analysis of mass communication from within a genuine crisis in culture, a crisis of community life, of public life. This crisis of community life derives from a loss or, better, a failure—to realize the most active principles of associative life in the Western tradition: namely, a democratic social order. Although the roots of this crisis may be described in a variety of compatible ways, for disciplinary purposes, if no other, they can be traced to certain models of communication that dominate everyday life, models through which we create social relationships precluding the possibility of community life. These models, in turn, derive from a commitment to a science of society that paradigmatically describes the essence of communication as a process in which people alternatively pursue influence or flee anxiety, essences that derive from social science models of causality and functionalism, respectively. Indeed, the crisis comes in part from the model of communication, knowledge, and culture one finds in *Public Opinion*. These models undergird not only news but all our cultural productions, the discussions and arguments about these productions, and the media that carry them.

To put this both more colloquially and philosophically, language—the fundamental medium of human life—is increasingly defined as an instrument for manipulating objects, not a device to establish the truth but to get others to believe what we want them to believe. As Albert Camus says, "dialogue and personal relations have been replaced by propaganda or polemic" (Pitkin, 1972: 329). Or, as Hannah Arendt argues, the result of this view of language is that we no longer recognize as a serious possibility the truth revealing

83

function of language, so cut off are we from its power to establish genuine relationships or to create "public space": an institutional arena in which shared public deliberation and free political action are possible (Pitkin, 1972). Or to return to Dewey, although the language is Arendt's: "There is an intimate link between speech and political life. Speech is what makes man a political being and wherever the relevance of speech is at stake matters become political by definition. The polis was a way of life in which speech and only speech made sense and where the central concerns of all citizens was to talk to each other" (Pitkin, 1972: 331). What I take all these arguments to converge on is this: The divorce of truth from discourse and action—the instrumentalization of communication—has not merely increased the incidence of propaganda; it has disrupted the very notion of truth, and therefore the sense by which we take our bearings in the world is destroyed.

If this diagnosis is even approximately correct, it requires that we reformulate our conception of communication not as mere reflection but as action. That is, if communication is, in Wittgenstein's terms, among our central forms of life, then to change the models that describe the terms of communication would open up the possibility of changing this form of life; in fact, it is to change it not merely as a form of talk but as a form of associative life.

Let me reiterate, then, the direction this reformulation must take. We must first discard the view of language as reference, correspondence, and representation and the parallel view that the function of language is primarily to express assertions about the world. Then we must substitute the view that language—communication—is a form of action—or, better, interaction—that not merely represents or describes but actually molds or constitutes the world.

In examining communication as a process by which reality is constituted, maintained, and transformed I am trying to stress that communication as such has no essence, no universalizing qualities; it cannot be represented in nature. Communication simply constitutes a set of historically varying practices and reflections upon them. These practices bring together human conceptions and purposes with technological forms in sedimented social relations. Of the essence of communication we can only say with Heidegger (1968: 277), "We—mankind—are a conversation. . . . The being of man is found in language . . . by which mankind continually produces and contemplates itself, a reflection of our species being." I call this approach cultural studies and its central problem that of meaning in order to contrast it with versions of communication that search for laws and functions and to focus on the hermeneutic side of the task. Meaning in this view is not representation but a constituting activity whereby humans interactively endow an elastic though resistant world with enough coherence and order to support their purposes. The agency by which they do this is certainly representation, but not representations simply of the world. It is the great power of symbols to portray that which they pretend to describe. That is, symbols have an "of" and a "for" side. It is this dual nature that allows us to produce the world by symbolic work and then take up residence in the world so produced. This is a ritual view of communication emphasizing the production of a coherent world that is then presumed, for all practical purposes, to exist. It is to emphasize the construction and maintenance of paradigms rather than experiments; presuppositions rather than propositions; the frame, not the picture.

The objective of doing all this—of looking at the practices that organize communications, the concepts such practices presuppose, and the social relations they bring into existence—is a hermeneutic one: to try to find out what other people are up to, or at least what they think they are up to; to render transparent the concepts and purposes that guide their actions and render the world coherent to them; to extend the human conversation, to incorporate into our world other actors tending other dramas by comprehending what they are saying. Understanding another person or culture, which is the first-order goal and wasting resource of the study of communication, is akin to understanding a scientific theory. You look at the practices people engage in, the conceptual world embedded in and presupposed by those practices, and the social relations and forms of life that they manifest.

Communication is an ensemble of social practices into which ingress conceptions, forms of expression, and social relations. These practices constitute reality (or alternatively deny, transform, or merely celebrate it). Communication naturalizes the artificial forms that human relations take by merging technique and conception in them. Each moment in the practice coactualizes conceptions of the real, forms of expression, and the social relations anticipated and realized in both. One can unhinge the practice at each of the points. The social forms and relations technology makes possible are themselves imagined in and anticipated by the technology. Technique is vectoral and not merely neutral in the historical process. A building, its precise architecture, anticipates and imagines the social relations that it permits and desires. So does a television signal. Social relations of class, status, and power demand both a conceptual structure of persons and a technology to effectuate them. Conceptual structures, in turn, never float free of the expressive forms that realize them or the social relations that make them active agents.

Communication is at once a structure of human action—activity, process, practice—an ensemble of expressive forms, and a structured and structuring set of social relations. To describe communication is not merely to describe a constellation of enshrined ideas; it is also to describe a constellation of practices that enshrine and determine those ideas in a set of technical and social forms. As Clifford Geertz has argued, it should not be necessary, at least since Wittgenstein, to insist that such an assertion involves no commitment to idealism, to a subjectivist conception of social reality, to a belief that people act in circumstances of their own making and choosing, to a naive faith in the power of ideas, or to the romantic notion that the creative imagination can willfully triumph over all the forces sedimented in nature, in society, in the economy, or in the unconscious—biological, collective, lived (Geertz, 1981: 134). Reality is not, as Americans are so quick to make it, a form of private property or a matter of taste. It is not the eternal given either, merely awaiting accurate representation

86

in the individual mind once that mind is emptied of history and tradition, or the veil of false consciousness is lifted, or a better technology of communication perfected. Reality is a product of work and action, collective and associated work and action. It is formed and sustained, repaired and transformed, worshiped and celebrated in the ordinary business of living. To set the matter up in this way is neither to deny, ignore, nor mystify social conflict; in fact, it is an attempt to locate such conflict and make it intelligible.

Reality is, above all, a scarce resource. Like any scarce resource it is there to be struggled over, allocated to various purposes and projects, endowed with given meanings and potentials, spent and conserved, rationalized and distributed. The fundamental form of power is the power to define, allocate, and display this resource. Once the blank canvas of the world is portrayed and featured, it is also preempted and restricted. Therefore, the site where artists paint, writers write, speakers speak, filmmakers film, broadcasters broadcast is simultaneously the site of social conflict over the real. It is not a conflict over ideas as disembodied forces. It is not a conflict over technology. It is not a conflict over social relations. It is a conflict over the simultaneous codetermination of ideas, technique, and social relations. It is above all a conflict not over the effects of communication but of the acts and practices that are themselves the effects.

Conflict over communications is not, however, undifferentiated. It occurs at the level of paradigms and theories, formulas and stereotypes, recipes and programs; that is, conflict occurs over the general determination of the real as well as at the points of exclusion, repression, and denial, where forms of thought, technique, and social relations are cast beyond the glow of the real into the darkness of unintelligibility, subversion, and disgrace. In our time reality is scarce because of access: so few command the machinery for its determination. Some get to speak and some to listen, some to write and some to read, some to film and some to view. It is fine to be told we are the species that actively creates the world and then simultaneously to be told that we are part of the subspecies denied access to the machinery by which this miracle is pulled off. There is no irony intended in saying we have to accept both of those independent clauses. But it reveals as well—and the thought is deliberately allusive—that there is not only class conflict in communication but status conflict as well. Everyone these days seems willing to testify to class domination and to describe it in elegant detail. Alas, we are less willing to describe the internal divisions within dominant classes and the access of dominant and dominated intellectuals to the machinery of reality production: classrooms, journals, books—even newspapers, film, and broadcasting. Status seems less real than class only for those who possess too much of the latter and too little of the former.

John Dewey's notion of public life is naive because in retrospect he seems so innocent of the role of class, status, and power in communication. Lippmann's views seem sophisticated, even if objectionable, because he both understood and accepted the new media and the forms of class power they embodied. Dewey's image of a democratic community was that of a community of equals using procedures of rational thought to advance their shared purposes. His emphasis on the community of inquirers, the public, was designed to highlight the process of the codetermination of reality in the medium of maximum equality, flexibility, and accessibility. We can all talk. He saw more clearly than most the decline and eclipse of public life, the rise of a new breed of professional experts, and the models of communication they were embodying in the new mass media. With the noise of an even angrier and uglier world in our heads we can scarcely follow him, let alone believe him.

We are all democrats, in communication as in everything else, but we are also more than a little in love with power. In *Penguin Island* Anatole France remarked that "in every society wealth is a sacred thing; in a democracy it is the only sacred thing." He is wrong, of course. Let us substitute power for wealth. Modern thought about communication—both that which affirms and that which critiques—reveals the same lust. A critical theory of communication must affirm what is before our eyes and transcend it by imagining, at the very least, a world more desirable.

CHAPTER 4

Overcoming Resistance to Cultural Studies

To repeat: the major issues facing students of mass communication, the macro issues, concern the entire framework within which our studies proceed and, therefore, the nature, purpose, and pertinence of the knowledge we profess. To reorient this framework, I have been making an argument for a particular and distinctive point of view toward the mass media—for something I call, without originality, cultural studies. Much of that argument, made by indirection, has suggested that we would better serve the study of the mass media if we pretty much abandoned our commitments to certain forms of explanation that have dominated the enterprise over the last fifty years or so. We have had our quest for the Holy Grail: the search for a positive science of communications, one that elucidates the laws of human behavior and the universal and univocal functions of the mass media. It is time we give it up, to happily relinquish what John Dewey a couple of generations back called the "neurotic quest for certainty." To abandon the traditional framework would not only invigorate our studies; it would also liberate us from a series of bad and crippling ideas, particularly from a model of social order implicit in this framework, a twisted version of utilitarianism, and from a rhetoric of motives that I have earlier called a power and anxiety model of communications. I am suggesting that we unload, in a common phrase, the "effects tradition." To show how and why, let me first develop the particular form of utilitarianism that undergirds media studies.

Utilitarianism has historically provided the basic model for and explanation of social order in Western democracies, and utility theory, therefore, is the most influential form of social theory. Utilitarianism starts from the assumption that the desires that motivate human action are individual and subjective and are therefore either unknowable to the observer or purely exogenous. These subjective desires, these given and individual preferences, are expressed in human action as an attempt to maximize utility or the pleasure or happiness that the satisfaction of desire brings. Economic theory and capitalist economies are built upon this principle of the maximization of utility. The rest of the social sciences, generally unhappy because utility theory tends to skirt or assume away the problem of social order, desubjectivize utility, drive it outside the head and into the objective world. But the social sciences then relocate utility in our genes, our environment, or our society. Social Darwinism, and its latter-day embodiment, sociobiology, is an example of the first strategy; behaviorism and sociological functionalism are examples of the second and third.

It is these latter positions, particularly behaviorism and functionalism, that provide the underpinning for mass communication research. Indeed, communications research has been little touched by utility theory in either its economic or biological form except—and it is a big exception—that certain assumptions about language and communication (the theory of representation, the self-righting process in the free market of ideas) have undergirded, among economists and communication researchers, the belief that the quest for utility can produce a progressive social order. The "invisible hand" works in both the marketplace of ideas and products. The utilitarian conception of human conduct and society, then, is the implicit subtext of communication research, but it has been twisted out of its originally subjective framework and resituated in the objective world of environment and social structure. It is a form of utilitarianism nonetheless: the objective utilities of natural ecology, the utilities that promote the survival of the human population or the given social order. (Aspects of this formulation are taken from Sahlins, 1976).

It is comforting for many to believe that their small-scale empirical investigations, the limited studies we undertake all the time, are detached from the larger overarching solutions to the problem of social order, to the problem of how persons and societies work when they are working effectively. Unfortunately, they are not. Our studies inevitably articulate into and out of these wider theories. They articulate "out" because they inevitably borrow language, concepts and assumptions from the more encompassing intellectual environment; they articulate "into" for they provide evidence or are used as evidence for and against the soundness of these social theories. Concepts such as attitude, effect, uses, and gratifications are borrowed from utility theory; evidence from "effects" studies is used to support one or another theory of mass society, usually the liberal, utilitarian, or pluralist theory. Indeed, the study of communication effects makes sense and has pertinence only insofar as it actively articulates with these larger positions. We can wish it were otherwise, but there are no neutral positions on the questions that vex society.

There is now, I believe, a large and compelling literature, one written from every point on the compass of knowledge, ethics, and beauty, attacking the behavioral and functional sciences on both epistemological and ethico-political grounds. Idealism and pragmatism have undermined the notions of objectivity and objective truth that ground the explanatory apparatus of such sciences. Marxism, existentialism, and a variety of continental philosophies have elucidated the baleful consequences of such sciences for politics and morals, for conduct and practice. However, it is not necessary to be either so contentious or so philosophical about the entire business.

The argument can be made in the small rather than the large. Contrary to Bernard Berelson's dire prediction of twenty-five years ago, the field of mass communication has not withered away. In fact, it is a successful, growing, highly institutionalized academic enterprise. But despite its academic success, as measured by courses, students, journals, and faculty, it is intellectually stagnant and increasingly uninteresting. It is also plagued by a widening gap between the ambitions of the students and the intellectual and ideological poses of the faculty. Part of the problem (though only part) is that the central tradition of effects research has been a failure on its own terms, and where it is not a failure, it is patently antidemocratic and at odds with the professed beliefs of its practitioners.

As to the first point, the effects tradition has not generated any agreement on the laws of behavior or the functions of communications of sufficient power and pertinence to signal to us that success has been achieved. The entire enterprise has degenerated into mere academicism: the solemn repetition of the indubitable. Our commitments are no longer advancing but impeding inquiry, reproducing results of such studied vagueness and predictability that we threaten to bore one another to death. The surest sign of this state of affairs is the long-term retreat into method at the expense of substance, as if doing it right guarantees getting it right.

However, the "effects tradition" would be a greater failure socially and politically if it were more of a success intellectually, for utility theory produces the classic dilemma for democracy. Utility theory as practiced by economists starts from the assumption, as was stated earlier, that the desires of every individual are distinct from those of all other individuals. If human agents are driven by subjective desire disconnected from the feelings of others, how do they manage to create and sustain the associated cooperative form of social life we call democracy? Why don't people simply gouge one another to the limit, as they often do even in the best of times? No one has produced an adequate answer to that question, and it is usually assumed away with one or another "metaphysical" concept such as the invisible hand of the market. The objective utility theorists give us an answer: our genes make us democrats, or our environment, or the norms of society, though I am here engaging in a bit of burlesque. Besides being a little too optimistic, objective utility theorists achieve an image of democracy at an enormous price: the surrender of any notion of a self-activating, autonomous, self-governing subject. The "new" subject is one controlled or constrained by the laws of biology, nature, or society, laws to which he or she submits because it is not possible to do otherwise. This is the image of humans and the dilemma of democracy with which the entire tradition of mass communication research struggles. It is at the heart of our founding book, Lippmann's *Public Opinion*. It is the reason Paul Lazarsfeld's work was so important. *The People's Choice* turns out not to be the people's choice at all but the choice of an index of socioeconomic status. Such laws of behavior are antidemocratic either because they reveal a subject who is not fit for democracy or they can be used to control the subjects of a mere presumptive democracy. As so often happens in intellectual work, the answers we give get disconnected from the questions we were asking—or, better, they get actively suppressed. As a result, the sharpest criticism of the behavioral and functional sciences ushering forth from philosophical quarters are now dealt with by silence. Under these circumstances, we can continue to wait for our Newton to arise within the traditional framework, but that increasingly feels like waiting for Godot. Or we can try to shift the framework and hold on to what is valuable in the effects tradition, even as we recast it in an alternative conceptual vocabulary.

Let me be clear on one point the speed readers always seem to miss. To abandon the effects tradition does not entail doing away with research methods, including the higher and more arcane forms of counting, that take up so much time in our seminars. Nor does it require turning up the academic temperature to Fahrenheit 451 and indulging in wholesale book burning. No one, except the congenitally out of touch, suggests we have to stop counting or that we can afford to stop reading the "classics" in the effects literature. However, this literature will have to be deconstructed, to use a currently fashionable term, and reinterpreted and the methods and techniques of the craft redeployed. I am trying to be ecumenical about this—not solely for reasons of decency, though that would be sufficient, but for a serious philosophical purpose. There will be no progress in this field that does not seriously articulate with, engage, and build upon the effects tradition we have inherited. A wholesale evacuation or diremption of the theories, methods, insights, and techniques so painfully wrought in the last half-century would be a sure invitation to failure. That is true if only because intelligence continually overflows the constrictions provided by paradigms and methods. But more to the point, the effects tradition attempted to deal with serious problems of American politics and culture, at least on the part of its major practitioners, and it is now part of that culture. Any attempt to avoid it will only consign one to irrelevancy.

However, to reorient the study of mass communication, we will have to change the self-image, self-consciousness, and self-reflection we have of the enterprise: our view of what we are up to, the history we share in common, how we are situated in the societies in which we work, and the claims we make for the knowledge we profess. This is both a little easier and much more painful a surrender than changing a reading list or substituting participant observation or "close reading" for factor analysis and linear regression equations. If we make the shift I have been commending, we would, to borrow some observations from Richard Rorty, talk much less about paradigms and methods and much more about certain concrete achievements. We would talk less about rigor and more about originality. We would draw more on the vocabulary of poetry and politics and less on the vocabulary of metaphysics and determinism. And we would have more of a sense of solidarity with both the society we study and our fellow students than we now have. (This argument is borrowed from Rorty, 1979, 1982, as well as some of his unpublished work.) Above all, we would see more clearly the reflexive relationship of scholarship to society and be rid of the curse of intellectual man (and woman): the alternating belief that we are either a neutral class of discoverers of the laws of society or a new priesthood endowed with credentials that entitle us to run the social machinery. We would, finally, see truth and knowledge not as some objective map of the social order, nature speaking through us, but, in the lovely phrase of William James, as that which is good by way of belief, that which will get us to where we want to go.

Cultural studies make up a vehicle that can alter our self-image and carry forward the intellectual attitudes I have just mentioned. At the very least, this position entails recentering and thinking through the concept of culture relative to the mass media and disposing of the concepts of effect and function. Now I realize that only the excessively adventurous, congenitally unhappy, or perpetually foolhardy are going to leave the cozy if not very interesting village of effects research for the uncharted but surprising savannah of cultural studies without a better map of the territory than I or anyone else has been able to provide. Filling that gap is a major task of the future. The best I can do at the moment is to encourage people to circle within an alternative conceptual vocabulary and an alternative body of literature that will help to mark out this unclaimed territory.

To make things familiar, if not exactly precise, this means connecting media studies to the debate over mass culture and popular culture that was a modest but important moment in the general argument over the effects of the mass media in the 1950s. The debate itself will have to be reconstructed, of course. The basic lines of such reconstruction were set out in the early work of Raymond Williams and Richard Hoggart in England when they attempted to apply the anthropological or primitive society conception of culture to the life and peoples of industrial society: to the language, work, community life, and media of those living through what Williams called "the long revolution" (Hoggart, 1961; Williams, 1958).

The connection of cultural studies to the work of Max Weber is more important yet. Weber attempted to provide both a phenomenology of industrial societies—that is, a description of the subjective life or consciousness of industrial peoples, including the ends or purposes of their characteristic actions—and an analysis of the patterns of dominance and authority typical of such societies. Weber described this enterprise as "cultural science" during the interminable argument over *Naturwissenschaft* and *Kulturwissenschaft*. I much prefer cultural studies to cultural science because I abhor the honorific sense that has accumulated around the word "science." As Thomas Kuhn recently remarked, the term "science" emerged at the end of the eighteenth-century to name a set of still-forming disciplines that were simply to be contrasted with medicine, law, engineering, philosophy, theology, and other areas of study (Kuhn, 1983). To this taxonomic sense was quickly added the honorific one: the distinction between science and nonscience was the same as the Platonic distinction between knowledge and opinion. This latter distinction, along with the correlative distinctions between the objective and the subjective, the primary and the secondary, is precisely the distinction cultural studies seeks, as a first order of business, to dissolve. More than that, I rather like the modest, even self-deprecating connotation of the word "studies": it keeps us from confusing the fish story with the fish. It might even engender a genuinely humble attitude toward our subject and a sense of solidarity with our fellow citizens who are outside the formal study of the mass media while, like us, inside the phenomenon to be studied.

Cultural studies, on an American terrain, has been given its most powerful expression by John Dewey and by the tradition of symbolic interactionism that developed out of American pragmatism generally. It was Dewey's student Robert Park who provided the most powerful analysis of mass culture (though he did not call it that) that was adapted to the circumstances of the country. Without attempting to do so, Dewey, Park, and others in the Chicago School transplanted Weberian sociology in American soil, though happily within the pragmatist attempt to dissolve the distinction between the natural and cultural sciences. Not so happily, though understandably, they also lost the sharper edges of Weberian sociology, particularly its emphasis on authority, conflict and domination, and that will have to be restored to the tradition.

Names solve nothing, I realize, but they begin to suggest at the very least a series of concepts and notions within which media studies might fruitfully circle. To state only part of the catalogue, I might mention experience, subjectivity, interaction, conflict, authority, domination, class, status, and power. As I have earlier argued (Carey, 1983), it was precisely those connections and issues that formed scholars who struck a minor but enduring theme of media studies during the ferment in the 1940s and 1950s: David Riesman, C. Wright Mills, Harold Innis, and Kenneth Burke, a tradition that is simultaneously historic and interpretive, and critical.

Cultural studies, in an American context, is an attempt to reclaim and reconstruct this tradition.

I realize that in an age of internationalism, I have set this argument out ethnocentrically. I do so to make a philosophical point, not a nationalist one. At least since the advent of the printing press, the arguments that constitute social analysis have been ethnocentrically formulated. To try to escape these formulations, to try to import wholesale from somewhere else an analysis that does not develop roots on native grounds, is simply a pose, another way of being an "observer." This is not to say that other voices from other valleys cannot make a major contribution. Weber has been mentioned; Marx cannot for long be avoided; and I have paid homage to Williams and Hoggart. On the contemporary scene one thinks of four European voices that have something of the right spirit in them: Habermas, Foucault, Giddens, and Bourdieu. But such voices must be embedded in and deeply connected with the lines of discourse and the canons of evidence and argument that are decipherable only within the social, political, and intellectual traditions of given national social formations.

The issues surrounding cultural studies have been very much complicated as well as enormously enriched by the increasing prominence in the United States of the work of the Center for the Study of Contemporary Culture at the University of Birmingham, particularly its activity identified with Stuart Hall. Hall's work is theoretically, historically, and often empirically elegant and deeply deserves the influence it has acquired. The Center's research, while distinctively English in orientation and therefore in its limitations, draws heavily on certain traditions of Continental theory and politics, particularly Marxism and structuralism, though, interestingly enough, not on critical theory of the Frankfurt School variety. British cultural studies could be described just as easily and perhaps more accurately as ideological studies for they assimilate, in a variety of complex ways, culture to ideology. More accurately, they make ideology synecdochical of culture as a whole. Ideological studies are, in Stuart Hall's lovely phrase, "the return of the repressed in media studies." Ideology, by this reading, was always the unacknowledged subtext of effects research. Differences of opinion described by psychological scales masked structural fault lines along which ran vital political divisions. The "consensus" achieved by the mass media was achieved only by reading out of the social formation the "deviants": political difference reduced to normlessness. The positive sciences did not provide an analysis of ideology (or of culture); rather, they were part of the actual social process by which ideological forms masked and sustained the social order (Hall, 1982).

Hall's work, and that of many others, has had a rejuvenating effect on a variety of Marxist and neo-Marxist analyses of capitalist societies by North American scholars. Unfortunately, the ferment this rejuvenation has provided in the field is often described by the stale and unproductive contrast between administrative and critical research, a legacy left over from the years the Frankfurt School was in exile. But the difference between cultural studies and the positive sciences is not in any simple sense a mere difference between supporting or criticizing the status quo, although I suppose it is comforting for some to think so.

There are gross and important similarities between British and American cultural studies that derive from certain common origins and influences. Both trace a founding moment to the early 1950s and both have been influenced, to a greater or lesser degree, by the debate over mass culture and the work of Williams, Hoggart, and E. P. Thompson. Both have drawn extensively on symbolic interactionism, although in somewhat different ways. In the British case symbolic interactionism has been limited to providing an approach to the analysis of subcultures and the "problem of deviance." In the American case it has provided a much more generalized model of social action. Similarly, both traditions have been influenced by Max Weber. The principal concept of Weber that has worked its way into British studies is that of legitimation. The rest of Weber's analysis of class, status, and authority, important as it has been to American scholars, has largely been shorn away. Finally, British cultural studies have circled within a variety of meanings of ideology. Those meanings have been provided by the wider debate within

Marxism, particularly by the encounter between Marxism and French structuralism. In fact, beginning with the work of Williams, Hoggart, and Thompson, British cultural studies have made a long detour through French structuralism and, like everything else these days, have been deeply divided over the encounter. Structuralism, in turn, has made little headway in the United States, where it must contend with the far more powerful formalisms provided by information theory and transformational linguistics.

Those wide-ranging and often contradictory influences have been held in remarkable equipoise by Stuart Hall. He has shown an exceptional capacity to be open and generous in absorbing currents of thought while firmly fixed on centering cultural studies on ideological analysis within a neo-Marxist framework. However, despite the power and elegance of his analysis, I think it is likely to strengthen rather than reduce resistance to cultural studies in the United States. That resistance, however understandable, is short-sighted.

The two dominant types of resistance to cultural studies take a positivist and a phenomenological form, though the labels, like all labels, are not quite adequate. As forms of resistance they overlap and share something important in common even though they proceed from different origins and therefore end up in different dilemmas.

The positivist resistance to cultural studies, beyond the ever-present desire to maintain a distinction between hard science and soft scholarship, between knowledge and opinion, is grounded in a deep political instinct. The positive sciences, of which physics is the model and psychology the pretender, grew up in a distinct historical relation not only to capitalism but to parliamentary democracy. Those sciences are the crowning achievement of Western civilization. They are far less ambiguous, in many ways, than either capitalism or democracy. Indeed, the positive sciences epistemologically grounded democracy, provided some guarantee that truth could transcend opinion, and, most of all, provided a model of uncoerced communication in terms of which to judge and modify political practice. In short, the positive sciences are historically linked to certain valuable practices that no one particularly wants to surrender. Therefore, cultural studies, in its attack on the self-understanding of the positive sciences, seems to buy into a moral and political vocabulary which, if not antidemocratic, is at least insufficiently sensitive to the ways in which valued political practices intertwine with certain intellectual habits. More than that, few can completely forget that the positive sciences shored up parliamentary democracy at two particularly perilous moments in its history, the Depression and World War II. Positive science was anchored in a notion of truth independent of politics arrived at by open communication and in the doctrine of natural rights. Hence it provided one means of withstanding the totalitarian temptation.

It is important to be sympathetic to this form of resistance to cultural studies, but in the end the sympathy is misplaced and counterproductive. Because the positive sciences shored up democracy at two bad moments, one need not conclude they can or will do so permanently. In fact, I have already suggested that in the post-World War II phase the positive sciences increasingly assumed an antidemocratic character that was implicit in the commitments of the behavioral and functional sciences. Notions of laws of behavior and functions of society pretty much obliterate the entire legacy of democracy; they substitute ideological and coercive practice for the process of consensus formation via uncoerced conversation. If behind our subjective notions of what we are up to there lie in wait our genes, our conditioning history, or the functions of society exacting their due, then our subjective life, our intentions and purposes, are just so many illusions, mere epiphenomena. The only people who grasp the distinction between reality and appearance, who grasp the laws of conduct and society, are the ruling groups and those who do their bidding: scientific, technical elites who elucidate the laws of behavior and the functions of society so that people might be more effectively, albeit unconsciously, governed. The suggestion that such positive science had to be substituted for uncoerced communication was first put forward in our tradition by Walter Lippmann in *Public Opinion*. John Dewey, instantly responding to the book, described it as the greatest indictment of democracy yet written. By the time of the Vietnam War, Dewey had proved to be prophetic, for the behavioral sciences were central to that intellectual, moral, and political disaster.

Democracy may be damaged by the positive sciences, but it does not need to be buttressed by them or defended and justified in terms of them. The valued practices and habits of the intellectual and political Enlightenment can be better defended by what Richard Rorty has called a "criterionless muddling through," by comparing societies exhibiting qualities of tolerance, free inquiry, and a quest for undistorted communication with societies that do not. We do not need to buttress this comparison by designating certain methods and theories as guarantors of the Truth. Cultural studies are, of course, a thinly disguised moral and political vocabulary. But that is true of all intellectual vocabularies, including the vocabulary of the positive sciences. If students in this field have not learned it from Kenneth Burke, perhaps they are no longer capable of learning, but conceptual vocabularies always contain a rhetoric of attitudes and a rhetoric of motives. There is no way to do intellectual work without adopting a language that simultaneously defines, describes, evaluates, and acts toward the phenomena in question. Therefore, resistance to centering the question of ideology or of adopting cultural studies as a point of view toward the mass media is that it seems to lead one to commit oneself in advance to a moral evaluation of modern society—American in particular, the Western democracies in general—that is wholly negative and condemnatory. It seems, therefore, to commit one to a revolutionary line of political action or, at the least, a major project of social reconstruction. The fear is real. It is also a little silly, if only because there are no revolutionaries anywhere these days, though there are a few counterrevolutionaries about.

If the behavioral and functional sciences contain a moral and political vocabulary, then the problem is not to undertake the hapless task of sundering the sciences from morals and politics. Rather, it is to recognize the inevitable interconnection of these forms of activity and to make them ever more explicit and defensible. The behavioral and cultural sciences should contain an analysis of ideology beyond the crude and reductive one they now have. But they should also make explicit their own ideological implications and persuasions and defend them on their own ground, not by pretending that "science says." (A paradox of our times is that right-wing scholarship, as represented by neoconservatism, does not have much of an analysis of ideology; it just has an ideology. The Left has a dozen different analyses of ideology; it just does not have an ideology—in the sense of a plan for political action.)

Cultural studies look at ideology and theory as varying forms of expression within the same culture. They differ semantically, stylistically, and in terms of their conditions of expression and reception. They do not differ because one contains truth and one error, one knowledge and one opinion, one fact and one fancy, in some a priori way. The task is to see the characteristic kinds of difficulties our ideologies and our theories (and our culture) get us into, then to try to devise ways of getting out of those difficulties.

I have already suggested some of the difficulties that utility theory, the social sciences, liberal ideology get us into. How do we reconcile the individual desires unleashed by capitalism with the demands of associated life, with the justice, equality, and mutual concern necessary for democracy? That dilemma is bad enough, but as soon as we resolve it by the route open through the objective sciences (don't worry, justice is in our genes or in our institutions), we end up in a worse dilemma, one the Left has critiqued with precision. We have, then, a ruling class of social scientists—disinterested, of course—managing the social order on the basis of uncontaminated truth. We are entitled to be skeptical about such a priesthood. Once social scientists adopt the role of seers, we should entertain the notion that their position is based not on their knowledge but on their ability to monopolize positions of power and influence in the social structure. Again, it was Max Weber who looked at intellectual credentials as a device of class closure, who was most trenchant on this point. The supply of valued things in a society, including valued occupations, is strictly limited. Work in industrial societies is hierarchically organized so that valued occupations can be identified and showered with income, amenities, and prestige. Preferred jobs are positional goods, as opposed to material goods, in the well-known distinction of the late British economist Fred Hirsch (1976), and they are valued because they are in short supply. They are valued also because power attaches to them, the power to monopolize valued cultural resources: to monopolize objective knowledge, uncontaminated by ideology, knowledge only the social scientist can grasp. This is hardly a healthy climate for democracy. No one quite knows how to get out of this fix, but we have little chance until we recognize the fix we are in.

In any event, the "getting out" will not be accomplished by getting rid of or devaluing ideology and culture in the name of science; it will be accomplished by plunging science more deeply into culture and ideology. All forms of practice and expression, including science, are cultural forms. They can be understood only in that light.

An instructive lesson here (though I am hardly in the business of extolling or applauding positivists and neo-conservatives) was provided by Daniel Bell and Irving Kristol when they founded *The Public Interest*. They established the journal in 1965 when the orthodox (as opposed to the radical) Left was in control of American politics. Bell and Kristol felt that American society had been badly damaged by the social programs as well as by the cultural and foreign policy initiatives of those in charge. They designed *The Public Interest* as a place for the like-minded to work out a broad social program to change the direction of American life. They did not waste their time defending or explaining the theories and methods of the positive sciences, I can assure you. They did not chase metaphysical bats around intellectual belfries. They simply gathered up a group of social scientists, left the church, and disappeared down the street. They did not even leave a forwarding address or a note in the pew saying "regards." They went off and built a different church on a different intellectual site, on a site that was not as easily shaken by an antipositivist critique. They systematically went about the task of using intelligence, irrespective of method and theory, to reground the social order, undertaking what Stuart Hall would call a hegemonic project but which we might more evenhandedly call a project of social reconstruction. They did not need an outmoded philosophy of science to ground their own image of democracy and intellectual work. Despite having written essays on the "end of ideology," they unabashedly admitted the interconnection between ideology and science and made a case—a remarkably successful case, as it turned out—for their own way of viewing the world and proceeding within it. The task for those who believe that current versions of cultural studies corrupt or compromise democratic practice is not to retreat into value-free objectivist science but to unearth, make explicit, and critique the moral and political commitments in their own contingent work. Intellectual work always depends upon the entire framework of articulated social order—and the ideologies that articulate it—and does not usher forth from some archimedian point in the universe: from some observer "out there" where, as Gertrude Stein said of Oakland, California, there is no there there. If one objects to current versions of cultural studies, then the only answer is to analyze the articulations among theory, practice, and ideology present within the effects tradition—to give up, in short, the pose of the observer and to undertake, explicitly, the task of using intelligence to change, modify, or reconstruct the social order. In short, the answer is to move toward a cultural studies viewpoint, not away from it.

The phenomenological resistance to cultural studies is more difficult to characterize, for it otherwise shares so much in common with cultural studies. Phenomenologists are quite willing to give up the entire positivist framework of the science of human communication or, at a minimum, to settle for a division of labor between the sciences and humanities. They are willing to follow a path—or, better, work a parallel path—to cultural studies up to the point of using the mass media as a context within which to write a phenomenology of modern experience and consciousness. Phenomenologists wish to describe the subjective life, the modern "structure of feeling," in Raymond Williams's arch but useful phrase, in relation to the media of communication, *one* of the paramount forms of experience in relation to which consciousness is formed. In practice this means going only as far as the early work of Williams and Hoggart and particularly not into the intellectual, moral, and political quicksand one encounters when one starts romancing French structuralism. Phenomenologists, in the restricted sense in which I am using the term, are willing to commit themselves to a reconstruction of consciousness through methods as simple as *verstehen* or as complex as hermeneutics. While recognizing that modern consciousness is riddled with antinomies and contradictions formed in relation to and exacerbated by the mass media, and while standing in firm opposition to many forms of life in modern capitalist societies, phenomenologists resist moving power, conflict, domination, or any given set of sociostructural elements to the center of analysis.

Again, I am not at all unsympathetic to this resistance, but I think it is misplaced. It is clear that ideological and cultural analysis can be simply another entry of the Platonic. The distinction between knowledge and opinion is replaced by a distinction between knowledge and ideology. The only gain here is the more explicit political reference of the word "ideology." But what is one buying into by centering the ideological and political? When ideology becomes a term to describe an entire way of life or just another name for what is going on, then the rich phenomenological diversity of modern societies becomes reduced to a flattened analysis of conflict between classes and factions. Economics may have been the original dismal science; cultural/ideological studies now threaten to displace it.

It is worth reminding ourselves why economics became known as the dismal science. Utilitarianism, again, the underpinning of classical economics, pretty much reduced social life to the flywheel of acquisitiveness and accumulation. Economic man became the whole man, the only man. However, the repetitive dullness of acquisition was not the only dismal prospect economics held out. Society became a "world without end, amen!" where the acquisitive itch could never be adequately scratched because of the Malthusian specter. Every gain was balanced by a rise in population, and the children we love became merely the tyrants who turn the wheel of gain.

Cultural studies could also turn into a dismal science if the phenomenological diversity of society is reduced to the single quest for power and domination. By evacuating diversity in the prerevolutionary era, we are left with only one motive with which to run the postrevolutionary society. But the pursuit of power will prove as exhausting and inexhaustible as the pursuit of wealth. The pursuit of power, and theories that rationalize it, nonetheless catches something of the predicament we are in. Power, and the prestige that goes with it, is as archetypal of a bureaucratic age as wealth was of the era of penny capitalism. There is no reason, however, except a positivist one, for a phenomenology of communications to avoid the phenomena of power and domination lest all human relations and all symbols be reduced to the terms of power and politics alone. I support the phenomenological enterprise because I believe any healthy society will possess that part of its spirit that admits to the inevitable and desirable pluralizing of the varieties of experience. Just because one admits power to the household of consciousness and conduct, one need not let it occupy every room, though I admit that, as with many an unwanted guest, one will have to struggle to prevent it from taking over the entire domicile.

Phenomenologists of all stripes are committed to the *varieties* of human experience as providing the deepest pleasure, the wasting resource, and the most complex explanatory problems in modern society. To strip away this diversity, even if it is described as relatively autonomous diversity, to reveal a deep and univocal structure of ideology and politics is to steamroll subjective consciousness just as effectively as did the behaviorists and functionalists. One does not, on this reading, wish to trade the well-known evils of the Skinner box for the less well known but just as real evils of the Althusserian box. Therefore, any movement toward encompassing elements of social structure—class, power, authority—that explain away the diversity of consciousness is to head one down a road just as self-enclosing as the behaviorist terrain phenomenologists have been trying in one way or another to evacuate for most of this century. Why abandon something of rich diversity to build something of self-enclosing monotony? It is precisely the phenomenological diversity of modern society that produces the most compelling and intractable intellectual and political problems. One does not have to be sanguine or approving of this diversity, nor celebrate it as some form of benign pluralism. One has only to recognize that the exceptional tensions in consciousness this diversity generates develop in a particular relationship to the media of communication.

Both of these forms of resistance to cultural studies are of real significance and genuine importance. Neither can be easily or summarily dismissed. I disagree with them, however. I have already said that I do not believe that social democracy needs to be propped up with the objectivist grounding of the positive sciences; that the latter are a weakness of the former; and that we can get along quite nicely by looking at intellectual work, including science, as a muddling through of the dilemmas that history, tradition, and contemporary life have placed before us. Neither do I think it is necessary to abandon the notion of ideology or to close our eyes to the forms of power, authority and domination characteristic of the modern world in order to do justice to its phenomenological diversity. Conflicts and contradictions are as typical and integral to our society as any other. And as irremovable.

I am speaking of more than the master conflicts and contradictions of race, class, and gender. There are more garden-variety contradictions particularly germane to our experience in education. For example, we observe in the swings of student interest among "majors" a wholesale competition for positions in the occupational structure, a contradiction I earlier described with Fred Hirsch's phrase as the struggle over "positional goods." We also observe—indeed, often participate in, despite our liberal ideology—the attempts by parents to purchase through the tuition paid to prestigious universities a place for their children in the occupational structure. This is an old story that federal aid and loan programs have more or less democratized (largely less, of course). That these occupational niches are thought to be entitlements, rewards for educational virtue, or for achievement, presents one kind of contradiction in our presumptively egalitarian society. That such competition for jobs, in which we participate in determining the outcome, at a time when automation widens the gulf between mechanical and immiserating work and the presumed glamour of the professions, presents another kind of contradiction. Both of them live in our classes and curricula and we have no answers to them. However, once we remove those contradictions we will have others, equally difficult and punishing. Similarly, once we remove the master contradictions of race, class, and gender we will immediately generate a new master class, though to anticipate its form we need the imagination of science fiction.

Conflict and contradiction are as inevitable to us as language and the ability to say no. Therefore, ideology and power are central to social life. They are less than the whole cloth, however. After all, ideology plays a larger role in modern life because coercion plays a much smaller role. Ideological state apparatuses have significantly displaced repressive state apparatuses, if that is what we wish to call them, and that is not necessarily a bad thing. No one has yet worked out an adequate analysis of power, conflict, contradiction, and authority. The problem was absolutely central to the rich, diverse, and melancholy work of Max Weber. In fact, part of the phenomenological resistance to cultural studies stems from the simple fact that notions of power and authority that were firmly attached in Weber to matters of action and subjectivity are now more often derived from Durkheim, the social integrationist, for whom power and authority were invisible and unnoted. As a result the analysis is constantly slipping into a functionalism despite the most heroic attempts to prevent it from doing so. It is not absolutely given that the forms of inequality and domination typical of modern society are so odious that they can be maintained only by the silent and invisible agency of cultural reproduction, behind the backs, as it were, of its "subjects." It would be nice if the social order worked by the silent reproduction of cultures and structures. It would spare us from all the misery that conflict and antagonism bring.

Unfortunately, it does not work this way. We live this reproduction in all its turmoil and ambiguity. Durkheim, the theorist of social integration, deliberately downplayed, in contrast to the Marxist tradition, elements of power and conflict. Inspired by the complexity of anthropological studies of social reproduction, he invented notions of "collective representations" and "collective conscience" to explain how societies were held intact in the midst of conflict and strain. When he applied this analysis to modern societies, though my chronology is off here, he tried to show how capitalist societies depended for their very existence and stability on an inherited precapitalist society—the so-called precontractual elements of contract. *Gesellschaft* society, the society regulated by utility and contract, could not work without the integrative mechanisms of *Gemeinschaft* society: nonutilitarian values, beliefs, traditions, and so on. To the old slogan that money is to the West what kinship is to the rest he added that kinship performs a continuing integrative function in advanced societies. In a sense Durkheim inverts the relations of base and superstructure: the capitalist economy thrives on the root system of traditional society. This aspect of Durkheim has been of signal importance and usefulness. But just because culture provides the supportive background to contract it is not necessary to argue that culture is unconscious, irrational, coercive, or automatic. To make this argument is to become either an objective utility theorist or a mechanical Marxist. This leap to culture as unconscious or part of the deep structure makes it difficult to distinguish Marxism from functionalism, except—and it is an important exception—that they make quite different evaluations of the social order that is being silently and automatically integrated.

In short, it is possible, I believe, to press forward with a form of cultural studies that does not perforce reduce culture to ideology, social conflict to class conflict, consent to compliance, action to reproduction, or communication to coercion. More than that, despite the dangers and reservations herein acknowledged, cultural studies in whatever form it survives offers the real advantage of abandoning an outmoded philosophy of science (maybe even getting rid of the philosophy of science altogether) and centering the mass media as a *site* (not a subject or a discipline) on which to engage the general question of social theory: How is it, through all sorts of change and diversity, through all sorts of conflicts and contradictions, that the miracle of social life is pulled off, that societies manage to produce and reproduce themselves? The production and reproduction of society is never guaranteed, automatic or mechanical, and the problematics of the phenomenon are often best revealed in moments of conflict and contradiction and in the rare but powerful episodes of coercive violence, social disorder, and chaos. But whatever the details of the production and reproduction of social life, it is through communication, through the intergraded relations of symbols and social structure, that societies, or at least those with which we are most familiar, are created, maintained, and transformed.

PART II

Technology and Culture

CHAPTER 5

The Mythos of the Electronic Revolution

WITH JOHN J. QUIRK

I

In Thornton Wilder's novel *The Eighth Day*, a typical Illinois town provides the setting for a turn-of-the-century celebration that reflects the anticipations of those Americans who identified change and hope with the coming of the year 1900. Toward the end of the nineteenth century, Americans who had witnessed the destructive effects of industrialization were subject to a naive yearning for a rebirth of native optimism and a resuscitation of the bright promises of science and technology. Wilder's title is taken from the theme of a speech by a community leader who voices the concerns and expectations of those times in words of evolutionary religion. Wilder's speaker envisions the new century as an "eighth day," after Genesis, and men of this century as a new breed, free from the past and heir to the future.

As we near the end of the twentieth century, we are witnessing another prophecy of an "eighth day," punctuated by sophisticated projections of the Year 2000, Mankind 2000, and announcements of an "electronic revolution." In the past, industrial exhibitions and addresses by prominent figures at world's fairs have been employed to enhance the prestige of technological innovations and to enlist the support of public opinion on behalf of science. Today the Commission on the Year 2000, The World Future Society, and Rand Corporation, have become the agencies of prophecy; the public is invited

113

to participate in such elaborate devices as the "World Future Game" of R. B. Buckminster Fuller. Nevertheless, the language of contemporary futurology contains an orientation of secular religiosity that surfaces whenever the name of technology is invoked.

This futurist mentality has much in common with the outlook of the Industrial Revolution, which was heralded by Enlightenment philosophers and nineteenth-century moralists as the vehicle of general progress, moral as well as material. Contemporary images of the future also echo the promise of an eighth day and thus predict a radical discontinuity from history and the present human condition. The dawn of this new era is alternatively termed the "post-industrial society," "post-civilization," "the technetronic society" and "the global village." The new breed of man inhabiting the future is characterized as the "post-modern man," "the protean personality" and "the post-literate-electronic man."

An increasingly prevalent and popular brand of the futurist ethos is one that identifies electricity and electrical power, electronics and cybernetics, computers and information with a new birth of community, decentralization, ecological balance, and social harmony. This set of notions has been most readily associated with Marshall McLuhan, but his position is one in a school of thought that has been articulated and reiterated over many decades and has many spokespersons in our time. The notion of an electronic revolution is supported by a diverse consensus that includes designer R. Buckminster Fuller, musicologist John Cage, futurologist Alvin Toffler, policy scientist Zbigniew Brzezinski, elements of the New Left, theologians inspired by Teilhard de Chardin and computerologists such as Edward Feigenbaum. Outside intellectual circles the notion of an electronic revolution has been repeated and embraced by coteries of advertisers and engineers, corporate and foundation executives, and government personnel.

What brings together this anomalous collection under the banner of the electronic revolution is that they are in a real sense the children of the "eighth day," of the millennial impulse resurfacing in response to social crises and technical change. They have cast themselves in the role of secular theologians composing theodicies for electricity and its technological progeny.

Despite the diversity of their backgrounds and positions on other questions, there is within their rhetorical descriptions of the electronic revolution a common set of ideas. They all convey an impression that electrical technology is the great benefactor of mankind. Simultaneously, they hail electrical techniques as the motive force of desired social change, the key to the re-creation of a humane community, the means for returning to a cherished naturalistic bliss. Their shared belief is that electricity will overcome historical forces and political obstacles that prevented previous utopias.

Zbigniew Brzezinski pins his view of the future to the belief that "ours is no longer the conventional revolutionary era; we are entering a novel metamorphic phase in human history" that is "imposing upon Americans a special obligation to ease the pains of the resulting confrontation" between our society and the rest of the world. In his new version of manifest destiny, Brzezinski suggests that technetronic America will supersede any other social system because all other revolutions have only "scratched the surface . . . alterations in the distribution of power and wealth," whereas the technetronic revolution will "affect the essence of individual and social existence."

With typically American optimism, Brzezinski enunciates the compatibility of democracy, decentralism and technology. "Yet," he continues, "it would be highly misleading to construct a one-sided picture, a new Orwellian piece. Many of the changes transforming American society augur well for the future." Among those trends Brzezinski identifies "greater devolution of authority" and "massive diffusion of scientific and technical knowledge as a principal focus of American involvement in world affairs" given that "technetronics are eliminating the twin insulants of time and space." The resulting situation is one in which a band of social scientists, above party and faction, is enabled to "reduce social conflicts to quantifiable and measurable dimensions, reinforce the trend towards a more pragmatic problem solving approach to social issues."

In McLuhan's scenario it is the artist rather than the scientist who is heir to the future. Nonetheless McLuhan dresses electricity in a cloak of mystery as the new invisible hand of providence: "The electronic age, if given its own unheeded lee-way, will drift quite naturally into modes of cosmic humanism." Far more metaphysical than Brzezinski, McLuhan sees in electricity the capacity to "abolish space and time alike" as it confers "the mythic dimension on ordinary industrial and social life today." Finally, McLuhan's penchant for religious metaphors leads to a characterization of electricity as Divine Force: "The computer, in short, promises by technology a Pentecostal condition of universal understanding and unity." Whether the rhetoric of the electronic revolution appears in sacred or secular form, it attributes intrinsically benign and progressive properties to electricity and its applications. It also displays a faith that electricity will exorcise social disorder and environmental disruption, eliminate political conflict and personal alienation, and restore ecological balance and a communion of humans with nature.

The new high-tech glamor firms in electronics, computers, communications, robotics, and genetic engineering that seem to be in infinite supply promise everywhere to provide a cornucopia of jobs, markets, and products, to rejuvenate ailing economies, to refund declining universities, to reemploy the unemployed and redundant, to offer vast and satisfying opportunities to those new to the labor force, to produce environmental harmony as high tech displaces the smokestacks of low tech, and even to eliminate, through user friendliness, the last alienation and estrangement between people and their machines. Such a faith, however, contrasts sharply with developments in electricity and electronics in recent decades. The manifest consequences of electricity are clearly in opposition to a decentralized, organic, harmonious order. The use of electronic technology has been biased toward the recentralization of power in computer centers and energy grids, the Pentagon and NASA, General Electric and Commonwealth Edison. Further, the "electronic society" has been characterized by thermal and atmospheric pollution from the generation of electricity and the erosion of regional cultures by television and radio networks the programming of which focuses upon a single national accent in tone and topical coverage at the expense of local idiom and interest.

Electronic high-tech industry apparently requires a benign human environment, less restrictive social legislation, and less militant labor unions. But these are less requirements than demands, and the frenzied competition they set off among the states, lead to an insistence on pastoral places for the upper middle class to work free from the intrusion of the poor and disadvantaged, the absence of even minimal government regulation, and the elimination of trade unions.

Educated elites in turn pick up the theme that our competitive failing results from a widespread scientific illiteracy and propose, as with the Sloan Foundation, a new definition of the liberal arts emphasizing mathematics, computer science, and technological expertise. Anxious middle-class parents, eager to purchase a place for their children in the occupational structure, pack them off to computer camps or direct them even earlier toward Harvard via infant training at the personal home computer. The advertising of computer companies resurrects the oldest image of the literate man and weds him to the new computation devices: the priesthood of all believers, everyman a priest with his own Bible, becomes in the new rendition the priesthood of all computers, everyman a prophet with his own machine to keep him in control.

This leads to a dilemma: either modern "electricians" possess insight into the future that we are barred from possessing or the revolution announced in their rhetoric is mere wishful thinking or, worse, a new legitimation of the status quo. The latter thought is particularly disturbing, for we may be witnessing the projection into the twenty-first century of certain policies of American politics and industry that in the past have had particularly destructive effects. We also may be mystified concerning the possibility through the grand eloquence of electrical nomenclature. Electricity is not exactly new, however, and in the history of technology and its social use we may find the terms to appraise the possibilities and potentialities of the electronic revolution.

There is no way to interpret sensibly the claims of electrical utopians except against the background of traditional American attitudes toward technology. For the chastening effect we should therefore remind ourselves of the typical American response to the onset of industrialization and the development of mechanical technology.

America was dreamed by Europeans before it was discovered by Columbus. Atlantis, Utopia, the Passage to India—this land was the redemption of European history before it was the scene of American society. The controlling metaphor that invoked this promised land was Nature, the healing power of an unsullied virgin wilderness. Americans subsequently came to define their "nation's nature" in terms of a pastoral idiom inherited from the European utopians. Mechanical technology was welcomed here, but it was to undergo a characterological change when received into the Garden of America. Machinery was to be implanted into and humanized by an idealized rural landscape. The grime, desolation, poverty, injustice, and class struggle typical of the European city were not to be reproduced here. America's redemption from European history, its uniqueness, was to be through unblemished nature, which would allow us to have the factory without the factory system, machines without a mechanized society.

A vital and relevant tradition in American studies, inspired by Perry Miller and Henry Nash Smith and continued by Leo Marx and Alan Trachtenburg, has traced the recurrent theme of the "machine in the garden." This was a unique American idea of a new dimension in social existence through which people might return to an Edenic estate through a harmonious blending of nature and manufactures. Each new invention or device was heralded as a means to move toward the goal of a new environment made possible by the geographical and historical options afforded the young nation. This vision was of a middle landscape, an America suspended between art and nature, between the rural landscape and the industrial city, where technological power and democratic localism could constitute an ideal way of life. As dreamed by intellectuals, preached by ministers, painted by artists, romanticized by politicians, dramatized by novelists, this society was to be located symbolically and literally midway between the overdeveloped nations of Europe and the primitive communities of the western frontier. America's virgin land and abundant resources would produce an indigenous solution to industrialization on this continent, a solution that would rejuvenate all Europeans who ventured into the New World and would allow us to leap over the disadvantages of the European system of industrialization. America was, in short, exempt from history: from mechanics and industrialization we would derive wealth, power, and productivity; from nature, peace, harmony, and self-sufficiency.

Influential Enlightenment philosophers anticipated this rhetoric in forecasting the American future. Condorcet, for example, was convinced that America was freed from the dead hand of the past and "would double the progress of the race" and "make it doubly swift." He believed that America was safely insulated from the Old World turmoil, possessed of sufficient space for preservation of rustic virtues, and could translate material progress into moral improvement and social bliss. It was this attitude that converted Jefferson and his agrarian followers to acceptance of the Hamiltonian program of manufactures and infant industry. Jefferson suspended his skepticism about factory economics and came to differentiate between "the great cities in the old countries . . . [where] want of food and clothing . . . [had] begotten a depravity of morals, a dependence and corruption" and America, where "manufactures are as much at their ease, as independent and moral as our agricultural inhabitants, and they will continue so long as there are vacant lands for them to resort to."

A special importance was attached periodically to specific technologies that performed key services. Jefferson himself once remarked that newspapers were more necessary than government itself, and he equated the technology of print and the protection of the rights of a free press with literacy and liberty. Patriotic historians even dated the birth of national consciousness from the publication of the first newspaper in Boston in 1704. Finally, the Bill of Rights guaranteed constitutional protection to technology with its clause on freedom of the press.

Later, steam engines occupied a particular place in the pantheon of technologies through their capacity to link the continent by railroad and waterway and to create new commercial bonds. Eventually there were essays on and oratorical praises of "The Moral Influence of Steam" and "The Indirect Influence of Railroads." A typical passage of the era, this from an address by Charles Fraser to the Mercantile Library Association of Charleston, South Carolina, invests machinery with metaphysical properties: "An agent was at hand to bring everything into harmonious cooperation . . . triumphing over space and time . . . to subdue prejudice and to unite every part of our land in rapid and friendly communication; and that great motive agent was steam."

Lifting the hyperboles of technological sublimity to a philosophical plane, Emerson paired steam and electromagnetism with transcendentalism: "Machinery and transcendentalism agree well. . . Stage-Coach and Railroad are bursting the old legislation like green withes. . . . Our civilization and these ideas are reducing the earth to a brain. See how by telegraph and steam the earth is anthropoligized." In Emerson's aphorism we have a graphic example of the intellectual's awe of technology and the confusion of technological fact with spiritual symbolism.

The rhetoric of the technological sublime, as Leo Marx has felicitously labeled these tributes to the technology of steam and mechanics, constituted the false consciousness of the decades before the Civil War. Neither the printing press nor the steam engine forestalled that fateful conflict, however, or ensured that the victory won by Lincoln and Grant would not be lost during Reconstruction. During the Civil War and in the decades thereafter, the American dream of the mechanical sublime was decisively reversed. It became increasingly evident that America was not exempt from history or isolated from the European experience of industrialization. The war itself called into question the dream of a continental democracy. In its aftermath American cities were turned into industrial slums, class and racial warfare were everyday features of life, economic stability was continually interrupted by depression, and the countryside was scarred and ravaged by the railroads, coal and iron mining, and the devastation of forests. But reality was unable to reverse rhetoric, and in the last third of the nineteenth century, as the dreams of a mechanical utopia gave way to the realities of industrialization, there arose a new school of thought dedicated to the notion that there was a qualitative difference between mechanics and electronics, between machines and electricity, between mechanization and electrification. In electricity was suddenly seen the power to redeem all the dreams betrayed by the machine.

There were many exemplars of the turn from the mechanical to electrical sublime, but a useful starting figure is the principal American economist of the nineteenth century, Henry Charles Carey. His father, Mathew Carey, an Irish rebel refugee and founding member of the Society for the Promotion of National Industry in Pennsylvania, had published the influential series of writings with which Henry Clay underpinned his "American Plan" for protection of native industries and vast internal improvements in canals and highways. Henry Charles Carey himself rejected Manchester economics and argued for a unique viewpoint in American industrial policy. He suggested that the introduction of the factory and the injection of industry on the native scene would have quite different results in this country than had been the case in Europe. Technology on this continent would produce wealth and industrial efficiency but without the wage slavery and environmental disasters of British and European centers.

In 1848, Carey wrote *Past, Present and Future*, a book that formulated a programmatic statement of these ideals in a distinct alternative, "regional associationism." He held that his new system would be realized when regional patterns of "association" between industry and agriculture were founded and merged into a cooperative economy. He thought that his plan would permanently secure decentralized, small-scale units in politics as well as economics. In addition, Carey believed that a union of agriculture, industry, and universal education in mechanical skills would prevent divisions between country and city and conflicts between social classes.

When Henry Charles Carey was born, Washington was president; in the year he died, Henry Ford began work on motorcars in Michigan. During his life, the idea of regional associationism went unrealized as centralization of industry, money and influence, and the exploitation of immigrant labor became the overwhelming realities of American life. Carey did not, however, give up the American Plan but projected it in the language of electricity. In his last book, *The Unity of Law*, Carey substituted the language of electricity for the language of mechanics, identifying the physical laws of electricity and magnetism, then being discovered, with the laws of society and projecting electricity as the new bond between nature and society. One dense but important quotation will illustrate this shift:

> Electricity presents a far more striking resemblance to the brain power which is its correspondent in the societary life. So striking indeed is it that when we need to express the idea of rapid action of the societary thought and will, we find ourselves compelled to look to the physical world for the terms to be employed, availing ourselves of those of electricity and magnetism. . . .
>
> The actual relation of each and every member of a community as giver and receiver, teacher and learner, producer and consumer is positive and negative by turns and relatively to every difference of function and force in his associates, the whole mass constituting a great electric battery to which each individual contributes his pair of plates. Perfect circulation being established as a consequence of perfect development of all individualities, the economic force flows smoothly through every member of the body politic, general happiness and prosperity, improved mental and moral action following in its train . . . wealth and power . . . everywhere in the ratio in which each and every pair of plates is placed in proper relation with each other; the vitalized circuit being thus established throughout the entire mass and made to bear, with the concentrated energy of the whole upon every object of general interest. . . . The more this power is exercised in the direction of promoting rapid circulation among the plates of which the great battery is composed, the greater

is the tendency to the development of an inspiration and an energy closely resembling the service of the lightning of heaven subdued to human use.

In this passage Carey signals the advent of a new rhetoric, another form of the industrial Edenic, which we can term, following Leo Marx, the rhetoric of the electrical sublime. The passage itself indicates how Carey utilized the dialectical categories positive and negative not as antithetical terms but as signifying a unity among opposites. Thus disharmony and conflict are mere appearances that point to underlying harmonies. Similarly, as a form of popular culture the rhetoric of the electrical sublime attempted to merge all those contradictory desires of the American imagination. Electricity promised, so it seemed, the same freedom, decentralization, ecological harmony, and democratic community that had hitherto been guaranteed but left undelivered by mechanization. But electricity also promised the same power, productivity, and economic expansion previously guaranteed and delivered by mechanical industrialization. Other events that occurred during the decade in which Carey penned the preceding passages presaged which of these contradictory desires were to determine American social policy. During the 1870s Edison and Bell developed the electronic technology that was to be the basis of the new civilization; Gould, Vanderbilt, and others carried on the "telegraph war" and other patent fights for the right to control the new technology; and the basis for industrial giants, such as General Electric, that were finally to exploit the new technology was perfected. Edison, Bell, and other wizards were exploited as symbols of the new civilization, used to curry public favor and demonstrate the beneficence of the new technology, while new empires in communications and transportation were created behind the mask of an electrical mystique.

Not everyone was mystified about the real meaning of the new technology. Intellectuals, however, both in Europe and America, could devise nothing more effective than a purely literary strategy for dealing with the situation. Jacob Burkhardt and Anatole France in Europe and Henry Adams and Samuel Clemens in this country devised the strategy of inverting the technological sublime and portraying the new technology as a specter of disaster. In his novel *Connecticut Yankee in King Arthur's Court*, Samuel Clemens published what was probably America's first dystopia or antiutopian science fiction. The American idea comes full circle in the novel as Hank Morgan is projected backward in space and time only to be encircled when he realizes that the electric fence erected by his own order for self-protection actually entraps him. This is an important event in American letters precisely because it contrasts so sharply with the Whitmanesque optimism of Clemens's earlier Mark Twain work.

Similarly, Henry Adams was obsessed with the laws of thermodynamics and the specter of entropic disaster. *The Education of Henry Adams* is filled with pages of disillusionment of the kind that led Adams to locate the exact shift from the "old universe" of Boston genteel culture to the new phase of history determined by sheer power in the events of the year 1844: "the opening of the Boston and Albany Railroad; the appearance of the first Cunard steamers in the bay; and the telegraphic message which carried from Baltimore to Washington the news that Henry Clay and James K. Polk were nominated for the Presidency."

Despite the morbid views of literary intellectuals, the rhetoric of the electrical sublime was appropriated by reformers and regenerated by visionary utopians. The reformers and idealists blamed the corporation for defeating the possibilities of the electrical revolution. Edward Bellamy's speculations in *Looking Backward* and *Equality* and William Dean Howells's fictional *A Traveller from Altruria* were reversions to sublime aspiration and returns to optimistic attitudes toward electricity. Bellamy, a socialist propagandist, and Howells, a genteel reformer and member of the Boston Bellamy Club, envisioned the social use of radio and television and rapid transport. For them electric power for communication and transportation were to facilitate the diffusion of culture, dispersion of population, and decentralization of control: in Howells' phrase, "getting the good of the city and the country out of the one and into the other."

124

Historically, the precedent for coupling pastoralism with technological power was the first prophecy of an electrical revolution. In 1770, a minor philosopher and dramatist, Louis Sebastien Mercier, wrote a novel of the future, *L'An 2440*, in which electricity was portrayed as both a material and a moral instrument. In Mercier's electrical utopia there were imagined inexhaustible lamps and lights, motion pictures for cultivation and education of the populace in public virtues, and the higher enjoyment of sensory stimulation. A hundred years later the idea of an electrical utopia had great appeal to Europeans as well as to Americans.

In his valuable studies, Lewis Mumford credits the Russian anarchist and geographer, Prince Petr Kropotkin, with the first forward-looking interpretation to the effect that electrical technics could rescue civilization from the banes and burdens of industrialism and restore communal conditions. In his *Fields, Factories and Workshops* (1913), Kropotkin recommended that electric power could serve to create "industrial villages" where handicrafts, manufactures, agriculture, and scientific investigation could be combined in small-scale regional economies. In Kropotkin's scheme, "domestic industry" was to be alternated with the "moral and physical advantages" of agrarian toil, and an egalitarian situation of mutual cooperation was to promote solidarity in the common endeavors of experimentation and production.

At the same time, the German scientist Werner von Siemens wrote to his colleagues that an alliance of inventors and statesmen should be promoted:

> now is the time to build electric power stations throughout the world. . . . Thereby the small workshop and the individual working by himself in his own home will be in a position . . . to compete with the factories that generate their power cheaply by steam-engines and gas-engines . . . [and] will in the course of time produce a complete revolution in our conditions, favour small scale industry, add to the amenities and ease of life—by ventilators, lifts, street tramways, etc.

In England, Ebenezer Howard, author of *Garden Cities of Tomorrow: The Peaceful Path to Real Reform*, produced an Anglicized version of Bellamyism in which he assured his readers that "the smoke fiend is well within bounds in Garden City," where "all machinery is driven by electric energy." These strains of thought converged in an important group, the International Association for the Advancement of Science, Art, and Education, an intellectual league of the early twentieth century. Among its membership were the British social thinker, Graham Wallas, who today is only remembered for coining the phrase "The Great Society," and the forgotten man of the study of ecology, the Scottish biologist and town planner Patrick Geddes.

On the eve of World War I, Graham Wallas, disenchanted with Fabianism and its bureaucratic formulae, wrote *The Great Society*. In a series of passages Wallas anticipated the disillusionment with technological society, the failure of the welfare state on qualitative issues, and "the quest for a new environment whose stimulation of our existing disposition shall tend toward the good life." Ironically, Wallas's consciousness of the problems posed by advanced technology was not to be generally recognized until the era when Lyndon Johnson inadvertently accepted Wallas's phrase as an administration trademark. Wallas observed that

> those who first developed these inventions [steam and electricity] expected that their results would be entirely good. . . .
> . . . And, now, we find ourselves doubting, not only as to the future Happiness of individuals in the Great Society but as to the permanence of the Great Society itself.
> . . . When one looks, for instance, at the beautiful drawings which have lately been prepared by a body of citizens for a new Chicago, one feels that they are suited to giants and not to men.

As a therapeutic strategy, Wallas advocated a revival of dialogue and discussion to counterbalance the overwhelming forces of impersonal organization and mass communication. In values and vocabulary, Wallas emphasized the placement of technology within open spaces and evoked the idyllic image of a decentralized rural environment:

> If I try for myself a visual picture of the social system which I should desire for England and America there comes before

me a recollection of those Norwegian towns and villages where everyone . . . seemed to respect themselves, to be capable of happiness as well as pleasure and excitement . . . in the employment of all their faculties. I can imagine such people learning to exploit the electric power from their waterfalls, and the minerals in their mountains, without dividing themselves into dehumanized employers or officials and equally dehumanized hands.

A now neglected thinker, Patrick Geddes was the first systematic writer to see beyond science fiction, social criticism, and romantic agrarianism in order to construct a visionary utopia consonant with urban conditions. In the first quarter of the twentieth century, Geddes's seminal influence and personal persuasiveness gained followers among regional planners, civic groups, and social movements. The goal set by Geddes and his adherents was nothing less than a "realizable Eutopia" here and now. Geddes was the first to offer a full-scale utopia systematically within a theory of electrical technology that attempted to develop the qualitative difference between mechanical and electrical technology. He predicted a "great transition from a machine and money economy towards one of life, personality and citizenship." He saw the modern phase as "something between" the "old paleotechnic" mechanisms and "neotechnic" innovations. Here, Geddes noted, "there are two very distinct Industrial Ages, characterized by steam and electricity respectively."

Geddes's own background played a central role in his utopianism. A patriotic Scot, a republican, and a regionalist who for years refused an offer of knighthood, Geddes identified with the Celtic revival in culture and supported local rule for Gaelic Ireland and Scotland. He also identified with Zangwill's experiment in Palestine and with Gandhi's attempt to revive domestic industry in India. Geddes viewed the centralization of financial and industrial power in capitals such as London and Berlin and a few satellites as antithetical to cultural traditions and the integrity of the intellect. He frequently denounced "colonization, conquest and empire" because of their exploitation, militarism, and destruction of viable economies and cultures in subjected nations. And he rejected the Fabian strategy of the Social

Democratic Federation and the extremism of the Left because of the temporizing with authoritarianism and bureaucracy and the condescension toward local institutions.

As a young student, Geddes had eschewed Ruskin and Morris for their "tidings of the establishment, for the hundredth time, of a new utopia." But the evidence of cultural decay, combined with the dissipation of human and natural resources, impressed Geddes with a sense of urgency and the imperative need for a solution. During a tour of Britain, Kropotkin delivered lectures and distributed pamphlets on the potential for an age of plenitude. Geddes and others were touched by Kropotkin's alternative because, as Geddes said, it "burst upon us in the midst of a great industrial crisis."

In a series of works, Geddes and his colleague Victor Branford treated burning questions covered in the titles *Cities in Evolution*, *The Coming Polity*, and *The Making of the Future*. Geddes's gospel obtained great currency, especially in America. During lecture tours and a stay at the New School for Social Research, Geddes gathered attention and disciples. In turn, America made a deep impression upon Geddes. He later wrote:

> Here America is of leading interest, with its labor saving inventions, its electricians, its efficiency engineers. . . This incipient social order is emerging as Neotechnic . . . more efficient, less wasteful of nature. Pinchot, with his renewing forests, is thus like Plunkett in Ireland with his renewing farms. . . . We are thus passing beyond mere Neotechnics, in which the opposition of labor and capital goes on in the city, without thought of the country, and, opening fully into a Geotechnic phase . . . beyond the dream of historic Utopias . . . the creation, city by city, region by region, of the Eutopia; each a place of health and well being, even of glorious, and, in its way, unprecedented beauty.

Internationally, Geddes was awarded the informal title of "the apostle of the sanitary picturesque" and "the big brother of reform." In the United States he conferred with such associates as John Dewey, Jane Addams, and Thorstein Veblen. Lewis Mumford became Geddes's major disciple, and Geddes's programs were embodied in the newly formed

Regional Planning Association of America, whose charter members included Gifford Pinchot, Henry Wright, and Stuart Chase. In these circles Geddes sparked a movement around the goals of public electric power and community planning. The Regional Planning Association launched a "giant power" crusade to integrate the new technology with conservationism and democratic localism. In the words of Gifford Pinchot, then governor of Pennsylvania, the keynote for the power crusade was sounded:

> Steam brought about the centralization of industry, a decline in country life, the decay of many small communities, and the weakening of family ties. Giant Power may bring about the decentralization of industry, the restoration of country life, and the upbuilding of small communities and the family . . . . If we control it, instead of permitting it to control us, the coming electrical development will form the basis of civilization happier, freer, and fuller of opportunity than the world has ever known.

But the real beneficiaries of the rhetoric of the electrical sublime were the electric light and power companies that presided over the new technologies. The public relations techniques pioneered by Samuel Insull and other executives were so effective in their invocation of the new civilization they were building under the aegis of "giant power" that even the *New Republic* was reluctant to criticize them until the Depression and the resultant scandals caused their fall from favor.

During the Depression, American "electricians" contended that the promises of electricity had been subverted by "vested interests" but that hydroelectric power and a new type of political organization would redeem the original message of Geddes. During the 1930s, the "giant power" crusade was renewed but now under the auspices of government rather than industry. A spokesman for the League for Industrial Democracy, Stuart Chase, put forward "A Vision in Kilowatts" in *Fortune* magazine in 1933:

> It [electric power] not only marches to ever greater quantitative output but it also transforms the entire economic

structure as it goes. In its full development, electricity can yoke a whole continental economy into something like one unified machine, one organic whole. The parts may be small, flexible, located where you please, but with their central station connections. Electricity can give us universally high standards of living, new and amusing kinds of jobs, leisure, freedom and an end to drudgery, congestion, noise, smoke, and filth. It can overcome the objections and problems of a steam civilization. It can bring back many of the mourned virtues of the handicraft age without the human toil and curse of impending scarcity that marked the age.

The New Deal seized upon the motif of a "New Power Age" for its creation of the Tennessee Valley Authority and the Rural Electrification Administration. President Franklin Delano Roosevelt and his advisers invested TVA and REA with the role of models for a new America, an inspirational symbol around which to rally people to renew their confidence in America and its capacity for rehabilitation. Addressing the World Power Conference in 1936, Roosevelt proclaimed the New Deal ideal of a pragmatist's utopia:

> Now we have electric energy which can be and often is produced in places away from where fabrication of usable goods is carried on. But by habit we continue to carry this flexible energy in great blocks into the same great factories, and continue to carry on production there. Sheer inertia has caused us to neglect formulating a public policy that would promote opportunity for people to take advantage of the flexibility of electric energy; that would send it out wherever and whenever wanted at the lowest possible cost. We are continuing the forms of over-centralization of industry caused by the characteristics of the steam engine, long after we have had technically available a form of energy which should promote decentralization of industry.

Roosevelt concluded that our command over electrical energy could lead to an industrial and social revolution, that "it may already be under way without our perceiving it."

The Tennessee Valley Authority was intended to serve as a showcase for the positive linkage of electricity, decentralization, and citizen participation in reclamation of the landscape. The TVA was not intended merely to generate energy and produce fertilizer. In the words of the president, it was also to grant the Middle South an examplary way of life: "a social experiment that is the first of its kind in the world, a corporation clothed with the power of government, but possessed of the flexibility and initiative of private enterprise," "a return to the spirit and vision of the pioneer," which "touches and gives life to all forms of human concern." "If we are successful here," Roosevelt concluded, "we can march on, step by step, in a like development of other great natural, territorial units . . . and distribution and diversification of industry."

David Lilienthal's dedicatory address to the TVA summarizes and recapitulates the rhetoric of the electrical sublime:

> This valley will be the first to enjoy to the full the fruits of this new age, the Age of Electricity. Those who have its blessings in abundance will come into a new kind of civilization. New standards of living, new and interesting kinds of jobs, totally new industrial processes, an end to drudgery, congestion, waste . . . such things are in store for us. For in this valley in another decade, electricity will hardly be reckoned in cost, so cheaply can your communities then supply it.

The TVA idea acquired numerous foreign admirers. Probably the most ardent was Madame Keun, a French visitor, whose *A Foreigner Looks at TVA* grasped the salient motifs of the American imagination that underlined the New Deal approach. In her book the TVA appeared as a "happy balance between the Jeffersonian dream of the self-sufficient agricultural community and the mechanical advantages of the power age." The TVA experience, she thought, showed that "in a capitalistic democracy . . . that imperishable quest of man for the millennium can be pursued by evolutionary adaptation."

At home and abroad the TVA ideal was considered the original model from which other regions and countries might adapt a prime vehicle of social democracy. In 1944, Henry A. Wallace argued for many TVAs around the world under the rhetorical rubric of "Universal Electrification." Wallace

131

suggested that a postwar expansion of the TVA would constitute a powerful force for peace, link economic interests on a noncontroversial basis, and obviate international tensions from the Danube to the Ganges. For, as Wallace put it, "valleys are much the same everywhere." After World War II Arthur Schlesinger, Jr., saw the TVA as a weapon in the cold war that, if properly employed, "might outbid all the social ruthlessness of the Communists for the support of the people of Asia."

We shall not review the fate of the TVA here; it is an ambiguous legacy at best. Certainly it has not proved to be a vast and catalytic social experiment. Rather than being a progressive force in the economy, it has identified itself with the electrical goods industries that have clustered around it, and the TVA has even been accused of corrosive strip-mining practices and of rate fixing during the Dixon-Yates controversy. Rather than being a harbinger of economic and political democracy for the valley, it has bureaucratized its interests and rhetoric and identified itself with the status quo. Rather than leading to a new social age, it has merely used electricity to elevate the traditionally narrow and socially wasteful standards of efficiency. Indeed, the entire American romance with dam building, fertilizer, and electrical power—in both domestic and foreign policy—increasingly looks like a profound misadventure. Exported as programs of development to other nations, it has involved the United States in political misadventures that equate American democracy with American technology and has resulted in proposals such as the Mekong Delta Authority and the McNamara project to electrify the DMZ. Applied to climatic zones different from those of the United States and Europe, the dam-building mania has produced economic and ecological disasters.

The TVA experience demonstrates the folly of identifying technical projects with the creation of democratic community. As contemporary rhetoric is doing with electronics, TVA rhetoric coupled ideas about electrical sublimity with attitudes concerning contact with nature and saw in the merger the automatic production of democracy. As a result, the TVA mesmerized liberals and prevented a serious evaluation of its failures; only Rexford Tugwell seems to have maintained the degree of detachment necessary to understand that the "TVA became more of an example of democracy in retreat than of democracy on the march."

It was Lewis Mumford who placed the TVA and similar ventures into greater perspective. In *Technics and Civilization* (1963) and other works during the 1920s and early 1930s, he had blamed "the metropolitan milieu" and "the cult of paper money" for the postponement of the new order prophesied by Patrick Geddes, Kropotkin, and the "garden cities" planners. By midcentury, a disillusioned Mumford found new culprits in the pragmatic liberals of the type who established the TVA:

> The liberal's lack of a sense of history carries a special liability: it makes him identify all his values with the present . . . . Like their counterparts, in the Soviet Union and China, our own leaders are now living in a one-dimensional world of the immediate present unable to remember the lessons of the past or to anticipate the probabilities of the future. . . . Similarly, the TVA is as characteristic of our American economy as DuPont or General Motors.

But Mumford did not have a strategy for dealing with the reversal of his original hopes. His articulation of the rhetoric of the electrical sublime had, if anything, contributed to the situation he found so abhorrent. It remained for the now obscure Canadian academic, Harold Innis, to produce the first systematic criticism of the new technological behemoth.

It is one of the more remarkable ironies of this entire narrative that Marshall McLuhan should have come under the influence of his colleague at the University of Toronto, Harold Innis. For Innis uncovered the most vulnerable point in the rhetoric of the electrical sublime and disputed all those claims for electricity that McLuhan celebrated. Innis principally disputed the notion that electricity would replace centralization in economics and politics with decentralization, democracy, and a cultural revival. Innis placed the "tragedy of modern culture" in America and Europe upon the intrinsic tendencies of both printing press and electronic media to reduce space and time to the service of a calculus of commercialism and expansionism.

Innis's insightful analysis was founded upon a long tradition of scholarship and thorough research. At the University of Chicago, Innis was influenced by research in urban sociology and also by the work of Thorstein Veblen. In his own studies of the Canadian staple trade and the broad relationships between Europe and North America, Innis developed the perspective upon which he based his historical and social criticism. He refuted the frontier hypothesis of Turner, "so gratifyingly isolationist, . . . that the source of inspiration and action was not at the center but the periphery of western culture."

Innis assessed the importance of historical and geographical factors and their relation to the means of communication and transportation. He developed from those assessments the theory that the ways in which communication and transportation systems structure (or "bias") relations of time and space were at the base of social institutions. Innis divided communication and social control into two major types. Space-binding media, such as print and electricity, were connected with expansion and control over territory and favored the establishment of commercialism, empire, and eventually technocracy. On the other hand, time-binding media, such as manuscript and human speech, favored relatively close communities, metaphysical speculation, and traditional authority.

Innis argued that the "bias" of modern technology was to undermine both space and time, history and geography:

> Industrialism implies technology and the cutting of time into fragments suited to the needs of the engineer and the accountant. The tragedy of modern culture has arisen as inventions . . . have destroyed a sense of time. . . . Obsession with present-mindedness precludes speculation in terms of duration and time. . . . The general restiveness inherent in an obsession with time has led to various attempts to restore concepts of community.

In addressing the works of Geddes, Innis assayed the long-term effects of electrical power. In an essay entitled

"The Penetrative Powers of the Price System," Innis argued that whatever temporary manifestations of decentralization and democratization might seem associated with electrical power, these were merely superimpositions upon a larger trend toward increased territorial expansion, spatial control, commercialism, and imperialism.

This capacity of the new electrical technology, Innis pointed out, enhanced the capacity of imperial powers to bring satellite areas within the orbit of their control. No amount of rhetoric could varnish or reverse the pattern of technological control, Innis held; only the workmanship of politics and scholarship, the consistent attempt to maintain another counterculture, offered any viability.

Innis felt that the demise of culture in the modern world could be prevented only by a deliberate curtailment of the influence of technics and those institutions in which technics were encased and by a strenuous cultivation of the realms of art, ethics, and politics. Like Patrick Geddes and Graham Wallas, he identified the oral tradition, with its emphasis on dialogue and dialectic, values and philosophical speculation, as the countervailing culture to the technological culture of sensation and mobility.

But the support of such an oral tradition, and its embodiment in cultural enclaves, requires that elements of stability be preserved and extended, that communities of association and styles of life be freed from the blinding obsolescence of technical change. However, the demands of growth, empire, and technology itself, Innis noted, placed primary focus upon the global development of electric power and electronic media as they fostered expansion and administration at a distance.

The increasing facility with which electronic media penetrated national boundaries worried Innis because it increased the capacities of imperialism and cultural invasion. Innis considered "monopolies," whether of electrical technology or, for that matter, rigid orthodoxy, threats to human freedom and cultural survival. He perceived beneath the surface of the cold war and the mission-oriented scholarship of "post-war adventurers in the universities" and "pseudo-priests of science" exactly such a threatening momentum.

Despite what Marshall McLuhan said concerning the effect of television on the senses, the impact of such communications media stems from a simple technological fact: each of the modern media has increased the capacity for controlling space. They do this by reducing signaling time (the gap between the time a message is sent and the time it is received) between persons and places. Print solved the problem of producing standardized communications rapidly and in sufficient units to administer large areas. While allowing for production efficiency, print does not possess an efficient distribution system and is dependent upon ship, rail, and air transportation to gain rapid and widespread circulation. The development of electronic communication beginning with telegraph and perfected by radio and television solved simultaneously the problems of rapid production and distribution.

Modern media of communications have, however, a common effect: they widen the range of reception while narrowing the range of distribution. Large audiences receive but are unable to make direct response or participate otherwise in vigorous discussion. Consequently, modern media create the potential for the simultaneous administration and control of extraordinary spaces and populations. No amount of rhetoric will exorcise this effect. The bias of technology can be controlled only by politics, by curtailing the expansionist tendencies of technological societies and by creating avenues of democratic discussion and participation beyond the control of modern technology.

In his last years Innis was pessimistic about the prospects. The development of radio and television, the enormous influence of American communication interests on the allocation of international frequency patterns, and the expansion of communication industries abroad were leading to a more exquisite form of cultural imperialism. In *Changing Concepts of Time* (1952), Innis commented that "vast monopolies of communication occupying entrenched positions involved a continuous, systematic, ruthless destruction of elements of permanence essential to cultural activity."

What Innis saw most clearly was that the main meaning of electronics was not in the provision of entertainment and information through radio and television. He recognized that the speed and distance of electronic communication enlarged the possible scale of social organization and greatly enhanced the possibilities of centralization and imperialism in matters of culture and politics. Perhaps the final meaning of electronics is in the use of telephony and computers to enlarge enormously the spatial bias of modern humans: in short, to take us to the moon and make possible the colonization and political control of "outer space" by the most electronically advanced cultures—those of the United States and the Soviet Union.

Innis's pessimism concerning the future was deepened by the knowledge that the one group that understood the course of history and the dangers of modern technology—namely, scholars and scientists—had themselves internalized the technical psychosis and had become "hot gospellers of truth" producing in the name of science "new monopolies to exploit faith and credibility."

The analysis and advice of Harold Innis have been largely unavailing. Since the 1960s we have lived with a series of prophetic voices proclaiming a technological revolution to be realized through the marriage of computers and television, communications and information processing. We are deep in furrowed ground, etches in the national imagination of long standing. Current prophets and prognosticators see in yet another generation of electrical machines technological solutions to what are in fact persistent political problems. Alvin Toffler first put us in "future shock," a disease we did not know we had, in order to prepare us for "The Third Wave." "Megatrends" differ from ordinary trends in that they cannot be resisted or redirected and are, alas, benign in their consequences anyway. Figures such as Toffler and John Naisbitt are manifestations in popular culture of a vision of a desirable future loosely shared by a variety of groups: the major engineering societies, leading corporations with global stakes in high tech, universities looking for substitutes for declining federal support, the military seeking to augment its share of the gross national product, and the State Department searching for new technological means to maintain an American hegemony.

137

What, then, is the responsibility of intellectuals concerning the electronic revolution?

We submit that it is not the convocation of a Vision '80, a Mankind 2000 project, or a congress of futurologists. The history of the theory of "neo-technic utopia" reveals that an intellectual involvement in elaboration of plans for the application of technology has been an inadequate approach. These attempts have failed because the bias of electronic power and communication is antithetical to dispersed use and small-scale control.

The promotion of the illusion of an "electronic revolution" borders on complicity by intellectuals in the myth-making of the electrical complex itself. The celebration of the electronic revolution is a process whereby the world of scholarship contributes to the cults of engineering, mobility, and fashion at the expense of roots, tradition, and political organization. As Harold Innis pointed out, the demise of culture could be offset only by deliberately reducing the influence of modern technics and by cultivating the realms of art, ethics, and politics. This requires action to counter and direct rather than disguise the bias of the electronic revolution; it means cultural and qualitative checks rather than more quantitative definitions of the quality of life; it requires decoupling the humanistic from the technological instead of offering a contradictory image of humanized technology.

Obviously, the electronic revolution cannot be managed by purely literary strategies, by creating images of the antisublime, or "black humor" allegory, or by creating new zones of romantic isolation and innocence. Yet this is precisely the profession of Orwellian science fiction and confrontation-protest techniques. These are neo-Luddite activities that bespeak a belief that apocalypse is upon us and that only a symbolic crusade, "wounding the Pentagon," or exorcising bad Karma can save us. Like the electronic revolutionaries, antitechnologians suggest that we are living in a new age unlimited by previous history, politics, and technology. They merely reverse the mythology about the electronics powerhouses. In a faulty response, they seek illusory mirages, reprogrammed sensibility, a chemical pastoral, a politics of style. By bypassing the steady work of scholarship and politics, this engagement in intransigence, resistance, and electric circuses only Americanizes the myth of Sisyphus. Paranoia about mass media and a sense of powerlessness are the simplistic obverse of the mythos of the electronics. The stance of powerlessness debilitates and means more powerlessness.

In *Player Piano*, Kurt Vonnegut predicted the ultimate defeat of any neo-Ludditry in his "American in the Electronic Age." As his would-be counterrevolutionaries proclaim: "Those who live by electronics die by electronics." "We'll rediscover the two greatest wonders of the world, the human mind and hand . . . walk wherever we're going . . . . And read books, instead of watching television." But the new Ludditry fails to offer alternative ways of life. Consequently, the technological imperative expands into new domains despite the protest.

There is another *zeitgeist* of irrelevance that tries to set up special locations and insulations, literal human reservations, where electronics can be mastered and tamed by secular prayer and imagination. In B. F. Skinner's *Walden II* and Huxley's *Island*, a merger of folklore and futurism takes place on the artificial plane of utopianism. In Huxley's words, "electricity minus birth control plus heavy industry equals totalitarianism, war and scarcity," but "electricity plus birth control, minus heavy industry equals democracy, peace and plenty." This is the type of new commonplace that renames manipulation as rehabilitation, technocratism as humanism, and so on.

We advocate that intellectuals deal with realities and speak to the living concerns of the populace rather than escape from politics or return to folklore. At present it is incumbent upon us all to resuscitate what remains of a universe of discourse, political language, and democratic vocabulary. Already our conceptual and perceptual capabilities have been bombarded and our moral dimensions denuded by the mythology of technology and the folklore of a past idyllic.

The first task is to demythologize the rhetoric of the electronic sublime. Electronics is neither the arrival of apocalypse nor the dispensation of grace. Technology is technology; it is a means for communication and transportation over space, and nothing more. As we demythologize, we might also begin to dismantle the fetishes of communication for the sake of communication, and decentralization and participation without reference to content or context. Citizens now suffer in many areas from overloads of communication and overdoses of participation. We should address ourselves directly to the overriding problems: the uprooting of people from meaningful communities and the failure to organize politically around authentic issues. Thus functional participation and geographical decentralization cannot solve problems in government, factories, and schools that are constitutional and not merely mechanical. The political questions are not centralism versus decentralism but democratization; not book versus computer in education but an adequate curriculum; not representative versus participatory institutions but the reconciliation of immense power and wealth with the ideals of liberty and equality. It might be that real control over the electronic media will necessitate more formal centralism. The point is really a pragmatic one in the nonphilosophical sense of the word.

To reduce the twin delusions of technics and myth, we must convey these concerns to the public. Intellectuals should demonstrate the relevance of scholarly integrity and rationality by critical studies that can reach an audience in sympathetic terms. The focus should not be negativistic but in favor of the values of the arts, ethics, and politics where people find fulfillment. As Perry Miller put the matter in his eloquent essay, "The Duty of Mind in a Machine Civilization," "We may say without recourse to romantic isolationism that we are able to resist the paralyzing effects upon the intellect of the looming nihilism of what was formerly the scientific promise of bliss . . . millions of Americans, more than enough to win an election, have only vague notions, barely restive worries, as to the existence of any such enmity. . . . Upon all of us, whoever we may be, rests the responsibility of securing a hearing from the audience."

That hearing must be secured in a language of democracy that is demythologized and in which political words are again joined to political objects and processes. At least this seems to be a responsibility for formation of a "party of the mind."

CHAPTER 6

Space, Time, and Communications

A TRIBUTE TO HAROLD INNIS

During the third quarter of this century, North American communications theory—or at least the most interesting part of it—could have been described by an arc running from Harold Innis to Marshall McLuhan. "It would be more impressive," as Oscar Wilde said while staring up at Niagara Falls, "if it ran the other way." Innis's work, despite its maddeningly obscure, opaque and elliptical character, is the great achievement in communications on this continent. In *The Bias of Communication, Empire and Communication, Changing Concepts of Time* and in the essays on books on the staples that dominated the Canadian economy, Innis demonstrated a natural depth, excess, and complexity, a sense of paradox and reversal that provides permanent riddles rather than easy formulas. His texts continue to yield because they combine, along with studied obscurity, a gift for pungent aphorism, unexpected juxtaposition, and sudden illumination. Opening his books is like reengaging an extended conversation: they are not merely things to read but things to think with.

But beyond these intellectual qualities Innis had an admirable and indispensable moral gift expressed throughout his life but perhaps most ardently in his opposition to the cold war and the absorption of Canada into it and in his defense of the university tradition against those who would use it as merely another expression of state or market power.

The very opaqueness and aphoristic quality of his writing, when combined with its critical moral stance, has left his work open to be assimilated into and contrasted with newer developments in scholarship that have occurred since his death: developments in cultural geography, Marxism and critical theory, cultural anthropology and hermeneutics. But the significance I am after derives from Innis's place in North American communication theory and, in particular, in relation to work in the United States.

I

Research and scholarship on communication began as a cumulative tradition in the United States in the late 1880s when five people came together in Ann Arbor, Michigan. Two were young faculty—John Dewey and George Herbert Mead—and two were students at the time—Robert Park and Charles Cooley. The final element of the pentad was an itinerant American journalist by the name of Franklin Ford, who shared with Dewey—indeed, cultivated in him—the belief that "a proper daily newspaper would be the only possible social science."[1]

Like most intellectuals of the period, this group was under the spell of Herbert Spencer's organic conception of society, though not enthralled by social Darwinism. The relationship between communication and transportation that organicism suggested—the nerves and arteries of society—had been realized in the parallel growth of the telegraph and railroad: a thoroughly encephalated social nervous system with the control mechanism of communication divorced from the physical movement of people and things.

They saw in the developing technology of communications the capacity to transform, in Dewey's terms, the great society created by industry into a great community: a unified nation with one culture; a great public of common understanding and knowledge. This belief in communication as the cohesive force in society was, of course, part of the progressive creed. Communications technology was the key to improving the quality of politics and culture, the means for turning the United States into a continental village, a pulsating Greek democracy of discourse on a 3,000-mile scale. This was more than a bit of harmless romanticism; it was part of an unbroken tradition of thought on communications technology that continues to this day and that Leo Marx (1964) named and I appropriated as the "rhetoric of the technological sublime."

Three other features of the work of the Chicago School, as it was called, are worth noting. First, methodologically they were in a revolt against formalism, in Morton White's (1957) happy phrase: they attempted to return social studies to a branch of history and to emphasize the interdisciplinary nature of social knowledge. Second, they were under the spell of the frontier hypothesis, or at least a certain version of it. The significance they found in the frontier was not that of the heroic individual breaking his way into the wilderness; rather, they emphasized the process whereby strangers created the institutions of community life *de novo* in the small towns of the West. This process of community creation, of institution building was, they argued, the formative process in the growth of American democracy. Again, although there is more than a little romance with the pastoral in all this, it also led to a positive achievement. In the absence of an inherited tradition the active process of communication would have to serve as the source of social order and cohesion. Moreover, the Chicago School scholars conceived communication as something more than the imparting of information. Rather, they characterized communication as the entire process whereby a culture is brought into existence, maintained in time, and sedimented into institutions. Therefore, they saw communication in the envelope of art, architecture, custom and ritual, and, above all, politics. And this gave the third distinctive aspect to their thought: an intense concern with the nature of public life. As Alvin Gouldner (1977) has reemphasized, the idea of the public is a central notion in their thought, and although they agreed with Gabriel Tarde that the public is something brought into existence by the printing press, they went beyond him in trying to work through the conditions under which the public sphere gives rise to rational and

144

critical discourse and action. In the 1920s these concerns crested and yielded a continuous stream of literature on communications, a central feature of which was a concern with the "vanishing public" or the "eclipse of the public" (Dewey, 1927). Despite their youthful optimism, many of the Chicago School came to see that although the mass media brought the public into existence, they later threatened the possibility of public life and with it the possibility of rational discourse and enlightened public opinion.

Harold Innis studied at the University of Chicago when Park and Mead were on the faculty and this tradition was in full flower. Moreover, these same intense concerns with communication were ripe within the city at large: in Jane Addams's Hull House, in Frank Lloyd Wright's architecture offices, in the writings of Louis Sullivan, and, above all, in the textures of the University of Chicago. There was a continuity and connection between Innis and the Chicago School, though Marshall McLuhan's claim that Innis "should be considered as the most eminent member of the Chicago group headed by Robert Park" (1964, p. xvi) is an absurdity. Park had no direct influence on Innis, and Innis was too singular a thinker to be described as a member of any school. Innis's transcript at the University of Chicago reveals he took a very narrow range of courses strictly limited to traditional topics within political economy. His only outside work was one course in political science on municipal government offered by the greatest Chicago political scientist of the time, Charles Merriam.[2] My only claim is this: the significance of Innis is that he took the concerns of the Chicago School and, with the unvarnished eye of one peering across the 49th Parallel, corrected and completed these concerns, marvelously widened their range and precision, and created a conception and a historically grounded theory of communications that was purged of the inherited romanticism of the Chicago School and that led to a far more adequate view of the role of communications and communications technology in American life.

By the time Innis started to write about communications, Chicago sociology had pretty much run itself into the sand. During the 1930s it was transformed into symbolic interactionism, a social psychology of the self and others drawn from the work of Mead. However elegant this work might be, it was also safely tucked away from the questions of politics, rationality, power, and social change that Chicago sociologists had earlier engaged.

American studies in communications then came under two influences. The first arose from work on psychological behaviorism initiated by John B. Watson immediately prior to World War I. Watson, both a professor at Columbia and a vice-president of J. Walter Thompson advertising agency, drew upon an accumulating body of work, principally from E. L. Thorndike, in animal psychology, and laid down a model of human action in which mind played no part in the arrangement of behavior. Transmitted into the study of communication, this provided the basis for a program of study in which communication became a branch of learning theory, in which learning was defined as the acquisition of behaviors and in which behaviors were governed in turn by conditioning and reinforcement. By removing mind from behavior, the possibility of rational action was removed also, but this was the precise and willing price to be paid for constructing a model of human social action on the postulates of physical science. Powerfully aided by the practical research demands of World War II, behaviorism gave rise to a power or domination model of communication in which study was narrowed into a focus on the means by which power and control are made effective through language, symbols, and media.

The second influence was more indirect but came initially from the powerful demonstration effect of the Hawthorn experiments. Conducted in a Western Electric plant in the Chicago suburbs, these studies gave rise to the often noted Hawthorn effect: that worker productivity rose over the cycle of the experiments because of the experiments themselves—Hawthorn gives us Heisenberg. What is less often noted is that the experiments were presumably a test of a model derived from Durkheim: that the factory should be viewed as an integrated social system to which the worker had to be adjusted. The findings of the experiments then gave rise to a new social role, a band of ambulatory counselors

whose task it was to resocialize the workers to their griev-
ances. That is, the major lesson of the Hawthorn experiments
was the discovery of the power of communication to serve
as a means of therapy in the service of social control of
the worker.

These movements in thought coalesced under Paul Lazarsfeld and his students, and communication studies in the
immediate postwar years, impelled by the war effort and
coordinate developments in cybernetics, were organized
strictly as a subdiscipline of social psychology. Moreover,
the models that guided this research yielded two alternative
formulations of communication: in one model communication was seen as a mode of domination, in another as
a form of therapy; in one model people were motivated to
pursue power and in the other to flee anxiety. I characterize
such models in this way to emphasize one simple point: these
models were not merely models of communication, representations of the communication process. They were also
models for the enactment of the communication process,
powerful models of an actual social practice. Finally, the
growth of these models within the intellectual community
and the marriage of this social science to imitations of the
physical sciences signaled a shift in the nature of American
social scientists in general and communication students
in particular. I refer here to the transformation of social
scientists from a prophetic to a priestly class. It signaled
the ingestion of social science into the apparatus of rule
and a surrendering of the critical function of independent
intellectuals.

These transformations in the study of communications
connected, in turn, with a deeply recurrent cultural pattern in North America whereby the growth of technology
in general—the printing press, literacy, communications
technology in particular—is seen as part of a larger narrative of progress. The history of communications technology becomes the story of the expansion of the powers of
human knowledge, the steady democratization of culture,
the enlargement of freedom and the erosion of monopolies
of knowledge, and the strengthening of the structures of
democratic politics. From the onset of literacy through

the latest in computational gadgets, it is the story of the progressive liberation of the human spirit. More information is available and is made to move faster: ignorance is ended; civil strife is brought under control; and a beneficent future, moral and political as well as economic, is opened by the irresistible tendencies of technology.

This was the situation, admittedly reduced to a sketch, that pertained when Harold Innis died in the early 1950s. It is against this background that the achievement of Innis should be assessed. Innis produced a body of historical and theoretical speculation that sets out the major dimensions of communications history and the critical propositions and problems of communication theory, and he did so with maximal pertinence to circumstances in North America. This is the critical point. All scholarship must be and inevitably is adapted to the time and place of its creation. That relation is either unconscious, disguised, and indirect or reflexive, explicit, and avowed. Marx was among those who understood that scholarship must be understood in terms of the material conditions of its production as the prerequisite to the critical transcendence of those conditions. In an extended commentary on North American (and the only North American economist he took to be of importance, Henry Charles Carey) Marx described the distinctiveness of the North American social formation even as it resided within the framework of Western capitalism:

> Carey is the only original economist among the North Americans. Belongs to a country where bourgeois society did not develop on the foundation of the feudal system, but developed rather from itself; where this society appears not as the surviving result of a centuries-old movement, but rather as the starting-point of a new movement; where the state, in contrast to all earlier national formations, was from the beginning subordinate to bourgeois society, to its production, and never could make the pretence of being an end-in-itself; where, finally, bourgeois society itself, linking up the productive forces of an old world with the enormous natural terrain of a new one, has developed to hitherto unheard-of dimensions and with unheard-of freedom of movement, has far outstripped all previous work in the conquest of the

forces of nature, and where, finally, even the antitheses of bourgeois society itself appear only as vanishing moments (Marx, 1973: 884).

Innis happily accepted as a starting point the inevitably ethnocentric bias of social science. Despite the enormous range of his scholarship, he was tied to the particularities of North American history and culture and the peculiar if not unprecedented role that communications played on the continent. He recognized that scholarship was not produced in a historical and cultural vacuum but reflected the hopes, aspirations, and heresies of national cultures. American and British scholarship was based, he thought, on a conceit: it pretended to discover Universal Truth, to proclaim Universal Laws, and to describe a Universal Man. Upon inspection it appeared, however, that its Universal Man resembled a type found around Cambridge, Massachusetts, or Cambridge, England; its Universal Laws resembled those felt to be useful by Congress and Parliament; and its Universal Truth bore English and American accents. Imperial powers, so it seems, seek to create not only economic and political clients but intellectual clients as well. And client states adopt, often for reasons of status and power, the perspectives on economics, politics, communication, even on human nature promulgated by the dominant power.

This commitment to the historical and particular led Innis to pursue communications in a genuinely interdisciplinary way. He was simultaneously geographer, historian, economist, and political scientist and he located communications study at the point where these fields intersected. Like the Chicago School, he shared in the revolt against formalism and ransacked experience without regard to discipline. Most critically, he rescued communications from a branch of social psychology and freed it from a reliance on natural science models. He was committed to the notion of pluralistic centers of scholarship as essential to cultural stability. To this end he attempted to restore to economics and communications a historical model of analysis. The central terms that he brought to the study of communications—the limitations of technology, the spatial and temporal bias inherent in technology, the monopolies of knowledge toward which they tend and which they support, the analysis of social change, selective advantage, cultural stability and collapse— were not the terms of a verification model. They were, instead, a made-in-the-kitchen group of concepts with which to examine the actual historical record. Variations in history and geography demanded in scholarship concomitant variation in social theory and cultural meanings. Like Patrick Geddes, the Scottish biologist whom he resembles and from whom he borrowed, Innis believed that the search for intellectual universals could proceed only through the analysis of radical particularities of history and geography. This relationship between imperial powers and client states, whether in the sphere of economics, politics, or communications, was expressed in his work by a series of polarities with which he described political and cultural relations: relations between metropole and hinterland, center and margin, capital and periphery, or, in the more abstract terms he preferred, time and space.

In short, Innis provided in communication studies, at a moment when virtually no one else in the United States was doing so, a model of scholarly investigation that was historical, empirical, interpretive, and critical. His work was historical, as I have said, in the precise sense that he wanted to test the limits of theoretical work, to show the actual variations in time and space that rendered transparent the dangerous claim of universal theory. The historical imagination checked off the bias of the theoretical one. It was empirical in that he attempted to exhume the actual historical record and not those ironclad laws of development with which we have been plagued from Hegel forward. His work was interpretive in that it sought the definitions, the varying definitions, people placed upon experience in relation to technology, law, religion, and politics. Finally, his work was critical in the contemporary sense in that he was not proposing some natural value-free study but a standpoint from which to critique society and theories of it in light of humane and civilized values.

Innis also reformulated the ideas of the Chicago School often in a quite explicit way and attacked, albeit indirectly, the notions of communications that had gained currency in American historical and scientific scholarship. In particular, from his earliest work he argued against the major versions of the frontier hypothesis "so gratifyingly isolationist that the source of inspiration and action was not at the centre but at the periphery of Western culture." Every frontier, in short, has a back tier. The "back tier" interest was determined by the extent to which the frontier products strengthened its economy, supplemented rather than competed with its products, and enhanced its strategic position (Heaton, 1966). The first back tier was Europe, and to that extent North American economic and communications development was part of the trajectory of European history. The development of this continent was decisively determined by the policies and struggles of European capitals. The consequences of those policies and struggles were outlined in his studies of staples: fur, fish, timber, and so on. With the gradual decline of the influence of Europe, the back tier shifted to the North American metropolitan centers—both Canadian and American—but effective control shifted toward New York and Washington relative to both the Canadian and American frontiers. The studies of paper and pulp brought that home and also led to the realization that in mechanized forms of communications new types of empire and back-tier/frontier relations were elaborated.

> The United States, with systems of mechanized communication and organized force, has sponsored a new type of imperialism imposed on common law in which sovereignty is preserved *de jure* and used to expand imperialism *de facto* (Innis, 1950: 215).

In this observation he founded the modern studies that now exist under the banner of media imperialism, but his sense of the complexity of that relationship was considerably more subtle than that of most contemporary scholars. In particular, Innis knew something of the tensions, contradictions, and accommodations that existed between trading and communications partners. This allowed him, from the beginning, to pierce the organic metaphors that so often led the Chicago scholars astray and masked the facts of history, geography, and power in a veil of metaphysics. Even if society were like an organism, there would be some controlling element, some centralized brain in the body, some region and group that would collect the power necessary to direct the nerves of communication and the arteries of transportation. There would be no transformation of the great society into the great community by way of disinterested technology but only in terms of the ways in which knowledge and culture were monopolized by particular groups.

Innis saw in the growth of communication in the late eighteenth and nineteenth centuries a continual process of decentralization and recentralization that moved forward in a dialectical way as small hinterland communities attempted to outrun metropolitan influence, only to be absorbed back into it later. The prevailing pattern of communication prior to the American Revolution was a classically imperial one. Messages moved on an east-west axis between London and the colonies. Communication between the colonies moved slowly and erratically, and in general the colonies communicated with one another via London. Following the revolution this same pattern prevailed for a time. News in early American newspapers was almost exclusively European in origin, and communication was stronger between the port cities and England than between the cities and their own American hinterland. Internal communication was slow and problematic, good only on the Atlantic sea corridor and only then when not adversely affected by weather. American towns and cities were relatively isolated from one another and connected only by common port cities or European capitals.

Following the War of 1812 the country embarked on a vigorous campaign for what were benignly called "internal improvements," the object of which, again benignly expressed, was an attempt to bind the nation together or connect the east with the west. In fact, what developed was the same pattern of communication of the colonial period but now with New York replacing London as the central element in the system. As Arthur Schlesinger, Sr. (1933) emphasized, what grew up over the first half of the eighteenth century was a pattern of city-state imperialism. The major cities of the East vigorously competed with one another to replace London as the geographic center of trade and communications.

By the early 1800s New York was firmly established as the center of American communication and controlled the routes of trade and communication with the interior, a position it has never relinquished. It maintained first contacts with Europe through shipping and therefore information passed among American cities by being routed through New York. But every major city on the East Coast made its bid for control of the interior. New York's hegemony was secured by the Hudson River, the Erie Canal, and the resultant access to Chicago via the Great Lakes allowing New York to service and drain the Mississippi Valley. Philadelphia also attempted to control the West through an elaborate series of canals whose failure brought Pennsylvania to the verge of bankruptcy. Baltimore attempted through the first national highway, from Cumberland, Maryland, to connect into the Ohio River and terminate in St. Louis at the headwaters of the Missouri. Baltimore later tried with the Baltimore and Ohio Railroad, the first national railroad, to build this connection surer and faster; and even Boston, although blocked from the West by New York, attempted to become a railroad center and create access independent of the Erie Canal. As Alan Pred's (1973) studies have documented most thoroughly, the effect of the hegemony of New York was to draw the hinterland cities within its information field and to isolate the other East Coast cities.

New York's hegemony was in turn strengthened by the construction of the Illinois Central Railroad from Chicago to New Orleans. At the time of its building it was popularly called the "great St. Louis cut-off" because it was designed to isolate St. Louis from its natural trading partner, Baltimore. When the first transcontinental railroad was placed along the northern route, this again strengthened the centrality of New York. New York and therefore its merchants, firms, and elites controlled an increasingly centralized system of information that tied the northern tier together and even acted as a source of supply for many Canadian cities. It just as effectively isolated the South. By every measure of communication the South, with the exception of New Orleans, was isolated from the rest of the country. There were poor interconnections between southern cities, and southern cities dealt with one another and the rest of the North only by first channeling communication through New York.[3]

Although this pattern of information movement has been importantly altered since the 1840s, its persistence, at least in outline, is even more striking. To be sure, the trade routes of culture laid down by the canal and railroad have been altered by the telegraph, wire services, magazines, films, telephone, broadcasting, and jet aircraft. But the centrality of New York in the flow of communications and culture, the importance of the New York-Washington corridor, and the metropole-hinterland connections that flow east and west are still there to be observed. In other words, despite the enormous size of the United States, a particular pattern of geographic concentration developed that gave inordinate power to certain urban centers. This development undercut local and regional culture. Although it aided in forming a national culture, it disguised how local— even provincial—this national culture was: a national and even international culture was defined increasingly by how the world was seen from a couple of distinctively local places. The point is that since 1800 we have lived with essentially a dominant eastern corridor of American communication that has created an effective monopoly of knowledge in news and entertainment. Concretely, today this means that a few national figures and themes are pretty much exclusively focused on politics and entertainment, that local issues are of interest only when they can be alchemized into national issues of concern in a few urban centers, and that the drama of news and entertainment must be made increasingly slick and abstract to appeal to national and, increasingly, international audiences.

Innis was also sensitive to the means by which the hinterland was in a continual struggle both to escape and to accept metropolitan dominance. There was an important truth in the Chicago School's notion of the importance of local community-building as a formative democratic experience.

In his essay entitled "Technology and Public Opinion in the United States" (1951), Innis attempted to show how localities and regions resisted the spread of communication, how the relationship was decided by a protracted series of conflicts over the spread of standard time, the mail order house, parcel post and rural free delivery, the department store and regionalized corporation. Moreover, he was concerned to point out how the Western newspaper was an instrument for resisting metropolitan dominance, how the telegraph initially strengthened the local and regional press until that too was undercut by the power of the wire services and chain papers. That is, the spread of a spatially biased system of communication was not even and uniform but resulted in a complicated interplay of resistance and acceptance that we have yet to adequately lay out in detail.

Moreover, the pattern of national spatial organization was reproduced in the organization of city after city and county after county. Seymour Mandelbaum's *Boss Tweed's New York* (1965) is a marvelous though often complacent study of the reorganization of New York City essentially on a metropole-hinterland model. My own studies suggest that same model of development holds true at the regional and county levels.

The United States, then, at all levels of social structure pursued what I call a high communications policy, one aimed solely at spreading messages further in space and reducing the cost of transmission. That is what Innis meant by exploiting the spatial bias of modern communication. Communication was seen, in other words, solely in the envelope of space and power. That communication might be seen as something else, as a container of human interaction that allows for the persistence and growth of culture, is a view that never entered policy. The distinction between power and container technology parallels Innis's distinction between space and time. But what Innis saw more clearly than most was how modern institutions were thoroughly infected by the idea of space. The universities were not exempt. Economics, political science, urban planning, sociology, and the physical sciences charted the problems and challenges of society in space. Even time was converted to space as the social sciences, enamored of prediction, characterized the future as a frontier to be conquered. Even historians caught the bug using time merely as a container to tell the narrative of progress: politics, power, empire, and rule.

In summary, as the United States pursued an almost exclusive policy of improving communication over long distance, as it saw communication as a form of power and transmission, the effective units of culture and social organization underwent a radical transformation. There was a progressive shift from local and regional units to national and international ones, though not without considerable struggle and conflict. Individuals were linked into larger units of social organization without the necessity of appealing to them through local and proximate structures. Communication within these local units became less critical for the operation of society and less relevant to the solution of personal problems. Finally, the growth of long-distance communication cultivated new structures in which thought occurred—national classes and professions; new things thought about—speed, space, movement, mobility; and new things to think with—increasingly abstract, analytic, and manipulative symbols.

II

Innis's first major work was his doctoral dissertation, a history of the Canadian Pacific railroad. While studying the path of the railroad he discovered that it largely overlaid the routes of the old fur trade, and this led him to an interest in the economic staples (fish, furs, timber, pulp) that had been the basis of the Canadian economy. The discovery of the path of the fur trade led him to examine the competition of New France and New England for control of the North American continent. Subsequently, in his greatest work, *The Fur Trade in Canada* (1930), he argued against looking at history in terms of the prevailing paradigms of the time: the formal stages of German history or the American "frontier hypothesis." He contended, in particular opposition to the "Turner School," that the settlement and development of Canada and the United States largely constituted an extension into the New World of the power and politics of Europe, particularly Spain, England, and France. He described North America by three broad bands: the Canadian North, defined by the Laurentian shield and the routes of the fur trade connecting New France and Europe by the coin of commerce; the American South, tied by staples, such as tobacco and cotton, to England; and between the two the mixed economy of the American North. The continent as a whole represented the adaptation of European culture to new geography. The patterns of trade were not a pure response to indigenous factors but rather were controlled even into the nineteenth century by policies of London, Madrid, and Paris. Moreover, the factors central to North American development were not such ethereal matters as frontier individualism but the rather harder facts of the biology of beavers, the role of staples in international trade and community settlement, and the persistence of unused capacity over the trade routes, which acted as constant stimulus to immigration. Innis also paid considerable attention to the differing social and economic motives of the imperial powers, motives that drove the French to the Rockies when the English were still at the Piedmont, and of the fatefulness of the contact between the tribal and oral cultures of the Indians with the literate culture of Europe, a contact that shattered Indian culture as they became dependent upon European goods and integrated into the European price system (Axtell, 1985). *The Fur Trade in Canada* is less a portrait, then, of North American particularism than of Europeanization of North America as an outpost of the first modern empires.

From his studies of the fur trade came the germ of two ideas that were later to control his studies of communication and his analysis of the relations of space and time. The first idea can be put as a question. What facilitated the great migration of European power, people, and culture beyond the perimeter of Europe into a "new world"? The second idea was an implication of the staple theory outlined in that book but developed later: communication, when considered in terms of the medium that facilitated it, might be seen as the basic staple in the growth of empire.

First the question of European migration. The expansion of Europe into North America was based on a cluster of inventions in shipbuilding, navigation, and warfare. These inventions affected individual nations quite differently. However, the central impulse in each country was improvements in communications: high-speed sailing craft, reliable instruments of navigation, and, most important, printing.

As the first uses of writing were in matters of empire, warfare, and the state—assessing and collecting taxes, keeping records, dispatching military couriers, counting slaves, the bookkeeping of livestock captured, casualties, and confiscation—so too the first uses of printing were in the administration of nation and empire. We have come to think of writing and printing as elevated arts identified with holy books and literary art, but their immediate utilities were in the practical realm (Clanchy, 1979).

In the absence of printing, sporadic forays utilizing the new technology would have been attempted. However, printing encouraged the coordinated and systematic expansion of European empires First, it encouraged the *centralization* of national authority through a uniform code of law, a standardized vernacular, a uniform educational system, and a centralized administration capable of integrating separate provinces, regions, and principalities. Second, it permitted the *decentralization* of national administration through the portability and reproducibility of a lightweight yet durable form of communication. National companies of trade, exploration, and settlement could be created— such as the Hudson's Bay Company, the company of One Hundred Associates, the Jamestown Bay Company—that could be directed and, to a degree, monitored and controlled through the marriage of print and relatively rapid navigation. It was print and navigation that allowed European nations to burst the bonds of geography and spread into a "new world."

While print permitted and even encouraged this imperial expansion, print, as the colonial powers soon discovered, had its limitations. The French empire stretched from the maritimes to New Orleans, was thinly settled, and was held together only by military strength. The weakness of communication in the American colonies permitted an effective federalism to develop despite British efforts to counter it. Not until the nineteenth century, with the decrease in time of Atlantic crossing and the growth of an effective mail service, did control of the American colonies become possible from London, but by then history had turned a corner.

If Innis was led to study communication originally by the contact of the tribal and oral cultures of the Indians with literate European cultures and by the role of print in facilitating imperial expansion, he was led to move communication to the center of his studies when he expanded his analysis of Canadian staples into wood pulp and paper. Here he made a significant discovery, albeit not a serendipitous one, for it is foreshadowed clearly in his earlier work. With the rapid expansion of the American newspaper industry following the invention of the "penny press," American demand for Canadian pulp and paper was intensified. The rapid growth of the American economy pressed the United States into an increasingly worldwide search for raw materials. Canada, by the conspiracy of geography and the history of European empire, was cast as a staple economy providing such raw materials to England and the United States. Consequently, many of the decisions central to Canadian development were made in London, New York, and Washington, increasingly in this century in the United States. To support its imports the United States exported capital, commodities, and, increasingly, culture. In his studies of paper Innis discovered the true Canadian double bind. The United States imported the raw material of printing from Canada under the doctrine of freedom of trade, a doctrine of Manchester economics that the United States selectively adapted to its interests. It then exported back into Canada the finished products fashioned from Canadian raw materials: newspapers, books, magazines, and, above all, advertising and defended its exports with the doctrine of freedom of information. Here was the Canadian dilemma: caught between the scissors of American demand for paper and American supplies of newspapers, magazines, and books, its independent existence in North America was threatened.

It was this realization that turned Innis to the study of the relations of time and space, to the relationship between the routes of trade and routes of culture. He initially characterized the history of the modern West as the history of a bias of communication and a monopoly of knowledge founded on print. In one of his most quoted statements Innis characterized modern Western history as beginning with temporal organization and ending with spatial organization. It is the history of the evaporation of an oral and manuscript tradition and the concerns of community, morals, and metaphysics and their replacement by print and electronics supporting a bias toward space.

Innis argued that changes in communication technology affected culture by altering the structure of interests (the things thought about) by changing the character of symbols (the things thought with), and by changing the nature of community (the arena in which thought developed). By a space-binding culture he meant literally that: a culture whose predominant interest was in space—land as real estate, voyage, discovery, movement, expansion, empire, control. In the realm of symbols he meant the growth of symbols and conceptions that supported these interests: the physics of space, the arts of navigation and civil engineering, the price system, the mathematics of tax collectors and bureaucracies, the entire realm of physical science, and the system of affectless, rational symbols that facilitated those interests. In the realm of communities he meant communities of space: communities that were not in place but in space, mobile, connected over vast distances by appropriate symbols, forms, and interests.

To space-binding cultures he opposed time-binding cultures: cultures with interests in time—history, continuity, permanence, contraction; whose symbols were fiduciary —oral, mythopoetic, religious, ritualistic; and whose communities were rooted in place—intimate ties and a shared historical culture. The genius of social policy, he thought, was to serve the demands of both time and space; to use one to prevent the excesses of the other: to use historicism to check the dreams of reason and to use reason to control the passions of memory. But these were reciprocally related tendencies. As cultures became more time-binding they became less space-binding and vice versa. The problem again was found in dominant media of communication. Space-binding media were light and portable and permitted extension in space; time-binding media were heavy and durable or, like the oral tradition, persistent and difficult to destroy. In propositional form, then, structures of consciousness parallel structures of communication.

The printing press created new forms of cultural association best expressed as the introduction of a horizontal dimension into modern states and into international relations as well and as an alteration in the meaning and relations of social classes. Charles Beard selected 1896 as the pivotal year in modern American history because the political conventions of that year introduced horizontal cleavages into society that were overlaid on existing vertical ones.

Deep underlying class feeling found its expression in the conventions of both parties and particularly that of the Democrats, and forced upon the attention of the country in a dramatic manner a conflict between great wealth and the lower middle and working classes which had hitherto been recognized only in obscure circles. The sectional or vertical cleavage in American politics was definitely cut by new lines running horizontally through society (Beard, 1914: 164).

It is not accidental that Beard chose the period in which a national communication system, through the agency of the news service and the national magazine as well as rural free delivery and the mail order house, was emerging to mark this new historical phase. He is implicitly contrasting horizontal forms of association with local and regional communities. These latter communities naturally possessed a class structure, but such structure revealed class variations on a common culture: vertical divisions within communities and not horizontal units across them. Improvements in long-distance communication created a series of national classes or, better, class-factions, first in business but eventually spreading out into every domain of human activity. These national horizontal units of organization created by space-binding forms of communication possessed greater reality in terms of culture and power than the local units from which they sprang. The upshot of the Progressive Movement, of which Beard himself was a part, was not, in the phrase of John Dewey, the transformation of a great society into a great community but what Robert Wiebe has called a segmented society: innumerable horizontal communities tied together across space, attenuated in time, and existing relative to one another not as variants on an explicitly shared culture but, in David Riesman's apt term, as "veto groups." Moreover, there was little relation among these segments except the exercise of power and manipulation.

Beard states, then, the relation between time and space and between long- and short-distance communication Innis later exploited. If communication is physically effective over short distances and weak and attenuated over long ones, we would expect that the units of culture, politics, and the common concern that would emerge would be grounded in place, in region, in local communities. These communities would be vertically stratified, but it would still be sensible to speak of a shared culture and politics among them. Small deviations in space would produce great differences in culture and interests. Larger units of social organization that emerged would be not national but federal: amalgamations of local structures into more comprehensive communities. However, as long-distance communication improves, both local and federal relations evaporate into a stratified national community. Large numbers of people physically and culturally separated become effective national communities of culture and politics. As long-distance communication improves and short-distance deteriorates, we would expect that human relationships would shift to a horizontal dimension: large numbers of people physically separated in space but tied by connection to extra-local centers of culture, politics, and power.

III

Innis was everywhere intent on demonstrating the paradoxical nature of char.ges in the technology of communications. Nowhere was this sense more apparent than in his critique of the American Constitution and the first clause protecting freedom of the press. Although traditional liberal values can be found sprinkled throughout his work, he saved some of his most savage language for assaults on the common interpretation of the Anglo-American notion of freedom as it was institutionalized in views of the press. He argued that the First Amendment did not so much grant freedom of speech and press as give constitutional protection to technology and in this sense restricted rather than expanded freedom:

> Freedom of the press has been given constitutional guarantees as in the United States [and] has provided bulwarks for monopolies which have emphasized control over space. Under these conditions the problem of duration or monopoly over time has been neglected, indeed obliterated. Time has been cut into pieces the length of a day's newspaper (Innis, 1954: 89-95).

The free press clause served largely to consolidate the position of the newspaper's monopoly of knowledge and eventually, through the newspaper's dependence on advertising and news, was instrumental in telescoping time into a one-day world, in spreading the values of commercialism and industrialism and furthering the spatial bias of print. In granting freedom of the press, the Constitution sacrificed, despite the qualifying clause, the right of people to speak to one another and to inform themselves. For such rights the Constitution substituted the more abstract right to be spoken to and to be informed by others, especially specialist, professional classes.

The full impact of printing did not become possible until the adoption of the Bill of Rights in the United States with its guarantee of freedom of the press. A guarantee of freedom of the press in print was intended to further sanctify the printed word and to provide a rigid bulwark for the shelter of vested interests (Innis, 1951: 138).

Innis refused to yield to the modern notion that the level of democratic process correlates with the amount of capital invested in communication, capital that can do our knowing for us, and fervently hoped that his work would break modern monopolies of knowledge in communication and further restore the political power of the foot and the tongue.

There certainly was something romantic in Innis's affection for the oral tradition, but there was much more: a concern with the very possibility of public life. He identified the oral tradition with the Greeks and with Plato's attack on writing in the Phaedrus:

> If men learn this writing it will implant forgetfulness in their souls; they will cease to exercise memory because they rely on what is written, calling things to remembrance no longer from within themselves but by means of external marks; what you have discovered is a recipe not for memory but for reminder. And it is not true wisdom that you offer your disciples, but only its semblance (Hackworth, 1972: 157).

The objections to writing here are twofold: it is inherently shallow in its effects, and essential principles of truth can be arrived at only dialectically. Writing is shallow in its effects because reading books may give a specious sense of knowledge that in reality can be attained only by oral question and answer; and such knowledge in any case goes deep only when it is inscribed in memory, "when it is written in the soul of the learner" (Hackworth, 1972: 159).

We associate democracy with widespread literacy and a world of knowledge as transcending political units. Yet even though literacy can give rise to a form of democracy, it also makes impossible demands. Literacy produces instability and inconsistency because the written tradition is participated in so unevenly.

Improvements in communication . . . make for increased difficulties of understanding. The cable compelled contraction of language and facilitated a rapid widening between the English and American languages. In the vast realm of fiction in the Anglo-Saxon world, the influence of the cinema and the radio has been evident in the best seller and the creation of special classes of readers with little prospect of communication between them. . . . The large-scale mechanization of knowledge is characterized by imperfect competition and the active creations of monopolies of language which prevent understanding (Innis, 1951: 25-29).

That is, modern technology actually makes communication much more difficult. Rational agreement and democratic coherence become problematic when so little background is shared in common. As Bertha Phillpotts argued in 1931:

Printing so obviously makes knowledge accessible to all that we are inclined to forget it also makes knowledge easy to avoid. A shepherd in an Icelandic homestead . . . could not avoid spending his evenings listening to the kind of literature which interested the farmer. The result was a degree of really national culture, such as no nation of today has been able to achieve.[4]

Literate culture is much more easily avoided than an oral one, and even when it is not avoided, its actual effects may be relatively shallow. Lacking an oral culture, one may easily fall prey to experts in knowledge who do our knowing for us, who inform us but whose knowledge does not easily connect to our actual experience and to the basic transactions of life.

In short, Innis believed that the unstated presupposition of democratic life was the existence of a public sphere, of an oral tradition, of a tradition of public discourse as a necessary counterweight to printing. In the more telegraphic prose of his notebooks Innis observed:

Commercialism tends to make for imperfect competition between levels of reading public and to fix various groups within level. Average man cut off from literature. Problems of making fiction a channel of communication between publics

. . . reading public disintegrated by imperfect competition in publishing industry (Innis: 30).

The First Amendment, then, did not secure the permanence of public life; in fact it acted against it because it finally placed the weight of education on the written tradition. Modern media of communication, largely for commercial purposes, created a system of communication that was essentially private. Private reading and the reading audience replaced the reading public and the public of discussion and argument. The system of communication that actually evolved was grounded, therefore, not merely in a spatial bias but in a privatized one as well. It was privatization more than the Bill of Rights that led to the decline of censorship: "Decline in the practice of reading aloud led to a decline in the importance of censorship. The individual was taken over by the printing industry and his interest developed in material not suited to general conversation" (Innis, 1952: 10). Under such conditions the public becomes a mere statistical artifact, public taste a measure of private opinion that has been both cultivated and objectified but not realized in discourse. With that the public sphere goes into eclipse.

The strength of the oral tradition in Innis's view was that it could not be easily monopolized. Once the habits of discourse were widespread, the public could take on an autonomous existence and not be subject to the easy control of the state or commerce. Therefore, the major intellectual project of Innis's later life, a project of importance to both politics and the university, was the restoration of the oral tradition—by which he meant a set of talents at memory, speech, and argument and a sphere, a place or institutional home, in which such a tradition might flourish. "Mass production and standardization are the enemies of the West. The limitations of the mechanization of the printed and the spoken word must be emphasized and determined efforts to recapture the vitality of the oral tradition must be made" (Innis, 1950: 215). Here he agreed with John Dewey. Speech is the agency of creative thought; printing of dissemination. It was precisely the imbalance between the processes of creativity and dissemination that Innis sought to correct.

Mechanical communication transformed the reading and listening public into a reading and listening audience with disastrous consequences for democracy.

Innis's attachment to the oral tradition finally, then, had a modern purpose: to demonstrate that the belief that the growth of mechanical communication necessarily expanded freedom and knowledge was both simplistic and misleading. For that to happen there would have to be a parallel and dialectical growth of the public sphere, grounded in an oral tradition, where knowledge might be "written in the soul of the learner." Freedom of the press *could* suppress freedom of expression.

Innis argued that *any* form of communication possessed a bias; by its nature it was most adept at reducing signaling time and controlling space or strengthening collective memory and consciousness and controlling time. This bias hardened into a monopoly when groups came to control the form of communication and to identify their interests, priestly or political, with its capacity.

In economic terms monopoly simply means the control of supply by a single source. If knowledge is viewed as a commodity, as something that can be possessed and distributed, then it too can be monopolized: the sources of knowledge, skill, or expertise can be reduced to one. Obviously, for monopolies of knowledge to grow, some division of labor must be present, for as with other commodities, monopolies can grow only when people are dependent upon an external source of supply. When they are capable, through control of knowledge and resources, of producing goods for themselves, monopolies are inhibited. In Innis's view commercialism was a system that ultimately transferred all control from the person and community to the price system: where people are fed every product, including knowledge, by a machine they merely tend.

The strength of the oral tradition, in Innis's view, derived from the fact that it could not be easily monopolized. Speech is a natural capacity, and when knowledge grows out of the resources of speech and dialogue, it is not so much possessed as active in community life. But once advanced forms of communication are created—writing, mathematics, printing, photography—a more complicated division of labor is created and it becomes appropriate to speak of producers and consumers of knowledge. Through the division of labor and advanced communications technology, knowledge is removed from everyday contexts of banquet table and public square, workplace and courtyard, and is located in special institutions and classes. In extreme form we come to speak of a knowledge industry, and meanings are not dignified as knowledge until they are processed through that industry or certified by designated or self-designating occupations, classes, organizations, or even countries.

Innis argued that the effect of modern advances in communication was to enlarge the range of reception while narrowing the points of distribution. Large numbers are spoken to but are precluded from vigorous and vital discussion. Indeed audiences are not even understood. Professional classes appropriate the right to provide official versions of human thought, to pronounce on the meaning present in the heads and lives of anonymous peoples. In *Changing Concepts of Time* he commented that vast "monopolies of communication occupying entrenched positions involved a continuous, systematic, ruthless destruction of elements of permanence essential to cultural activity" (1952: 15). He is claiming something more than the now commonplace observation that over time the media of communication become increasingly centralized and conglomerate. He is not merely claiming that with the growth of the mass media and the professionalization of communication a few journalists, for example, achieve vast readership while other people are reduced to representation in the letters to the editor. He is claiming that the commodity called "information" and the commodity called "entertainment" and the knowledge necessary to produce these things of the world become increasingly centralized in certain elites and institutions. The civic landscape becomes increasingly divided into knowledgeable elites and ignorant masses. The very existence of a commodity such as "information" and an institution called "media" make each other necessary. More people spend more time dependent on the journalist, the publisher, and the program director. Every week they wait for *Time*.

The new media centralize and monopolize civic knowledge and, as importantly, the techniques of knowing. People become "consumers" of communication as they become consumers of everything else, and as consumers they stand dependent on centralized sources of supply.

The development, then, of monopolistic—or, if that is too strong, oligopolistic—structures of knowledge and knowing and the professional classes that control them expropriates the more widespread, decentralized body of human impulses, skills, and knowledge on which civil society depends. Given a network of such monopolies backed by corporate economic and political power, we reach a stage under the impulse of advanced communication at which there is simultaneously advancing knowledge and declining knowing. We keep waiting to be informed, to be educated, but lose the capacity to produce knowledge for ourselves in decentralized communities of understanding. All this apparatus generates is continuous change and obsolescence: time is destroyed, the right to tradition is lost.

IV

Satellites and cable television, video phones and computer information utilities, telex and direct broadcasting, multinational corporations and common markets have posed anew all the questions Innis raised. Unfortunately, response to these developments possesses none of the power and scope of the political and cultural economy Innis developed. The age of electrical machines has been savagely portrayed in dystopian tracts of the same kind that emerged at the onset of industrialization. Others have tried to analyze the new technology in terms of the qualitative differences between mechanics and electricity, between paleotechnic and neotechnic technology. Still others have pinned their analysis to the difference between communications organized on socialist as opposed to capitalist principles. Another solution to our dilemmas is offered by a cadre of technocrats committed to no political theory who energetically demonstrate how the new technology will solve every problem of politics, the economy, health, and even loneliness and isolation. They propose to solve the "problem of communication" by identifying the entire human habitat with it. Finally, modern utopians have resurrected the original language of industrialism and presented a bright new world aborning by the automatic action of electrical machines. One finds among them the pleasant notion that we are now outgrowing the nation-state and that a new form of world order is emerging, a global village, a universal brotherhood or world government on a shrunken planet—spaceship earth.

Most of this is pleasant if not dangerous nonsense. What we are witnessing is another increase in the scale of social organization based upon electronic communication. We are witnessing the imperial struggle of the early age of print all over again but now with communication systems that transmit messages at the extremes of the laws of physics. We are witnessing larger federations of power developing out of the nation-state: the Soviet bloc, the Common Market, North America. Institutional structures are already being evolved in multinational corporations, regional federations, and modern cartels. Multinationals could not exist without jet planes, advanced computers, and electronic communication. Such organizations are even creating, through electronics, a new culture. In the nomadic travels of ITT executives the telephones become an obsession, as Anthony Sampson puts it,

> not only because ITT makes them but because they abolish distance and provide a reassuring link with home base. The more uprooted the way of life, the more dependent the multinational managers become on their company, which forms the carapace within which they travel. I overheard one ITT manager in his Brussels hotel joking on the telephone for twenty minutes with New York. . . . Inside these giant organisms differences of nationality seem often less important than differences of company (Sampson, 1974: 99).

There is also a pattern of decentralization occurring. First, through satellite communication there occurs a thrusting out of cultures into new regions of space. This movement is part of a system of national and regional rivalries, which find expression in satellite broadcasting. When in a few years television images will be transmitted over national boundaries to home receivers, the United States and the Soviet Union as the two largest electronic powers can enlarge the region and particularity of their influence.

Beyond the use of satellites for direct, nation-to-person broadcasting, there is a second dimension to the current decentralization and extension in space of electronic communication. The second arena in which the United States and the Soviet Union are in competition is the arena of space itself. The advent of exploration and utilization of space is in its infancy, and one cannot predict what the ultimate uses of these lifeless colonies will be, though one should not be surprised if we again send people "into transportation." The delays in space exploration did not derive from deficiencies of rocket thrust. The real delay was the development of a system of communication that would allow space travel to be controlled from earth. As printing went with seagoing navigation and the telegraph with the railway, electronic and computer-based communication go with the space ship. In the absence of communication that matches the speed of light and exceeds the speed of the brain, some hardy pioneer might have tried to thrust himself off to the moon, although capital costs alone, as in the age of navigation, make that unlikely. The availability of electronic communication, with its capacity to increase control by reducing signaling time, has turned space into the next area of expansion. The meaning of electronic communication is not in the news that informs us or the entertainment that distracts us but in the new possibility to turn space into a domain of geographical and political competition for the most electronically advanced nations.

Electronics has the potential for the perfection of a utilitarian attitude and the indefinite expansion of the administrative mentality and imperial politics. Electronics, like print in its early phases, is biased toward supporting one type of civilization: a powerhouse society dedicated to wealth, power, and productivity, to technical perfectionism and ethical

171

nihilism. No amount of rhetorical varnish would reverse this pattern; only the work of politics and the day-by-day attempt to maintain another and contradictory pattern of life, thought, and scholarship. As Innis pointed out, the demise of culture could be dispelled only by a deliberate cutting down of the influence of modern technics and cultivation of the realms of art, ethics, and politics. He identified the oral tradition with its emphasis on dialogue, dialectics, ethics, and metaphysics as the countervailing force to modern technics. But support of such traditions or media requires that elements of stability be maintained, that mobility be controlled, that communities of association and styles of life be freed from the blinding obsolescence of technical change. However, the demands of growth, empire, and technology put an emphasis—in education, politics, and social life generally—on those media that fostered administrative efficiency such as print and electronics. Only by supporting the countervailing power of substantive rationality, democracy, and time would the bias of technology be controlled. That is the task that Innis summarized in one of his greatest essays, "A Plea for Time."

Notes

1 The phrase comes from notes taken by Charles Cooley on a Dewey lecture in Ann Arbor as quoted in Matthews (1977).
2 The Registrar of the University of Chicago was kind enough to send me a copy of Innis's transcript with grades appropriately and delicately blanked out.
3 The analysis relies on Pred (1973, 1980), but the outlines of the argument are present in Innis (1930), particularly the concluding chapter.
4 As quoted in Goody (1968). This section borrows from and paraphrases the work of Goody and Watt therein.

CHAPTER 7

The History of the Future

WITH JOHN J. QUIRK

In *The Image of the Future* (1961) F. L. Polak has traced the human preoccupation with the future to its ancient roots in Delphic oracles and astrological priesthoods. However, the modern history of the future originates with the rise of science and onset of the age of exploration. Armed with the techniques of modern science, especially the new measuring devices of precise clocks and telescopes, a secular priesthood seized hold of the idea of a perfect future, a zone of experience beyond ordinary history and geography, a new region of time blessed with a perfect landscape and a perfection of man and society. Nevertheless, there exists a continuity from the ancient astrologers of the temple, tribe, and city to modern scientists, for both are elevated castes who profess special knowledge of the future—indeed, establish a claim of eminent domain over the next stages of human history.

Modern oracles, like their ancient counterparts, constitute a privileged class who monopolize new forms of knowledge and alternatively panic and enrapture large audiences as they portray new versions of the future. Moreover, modern scientific elites often occupy the same double role of oracles to the people and servants of the ruling class as did the astrologers of ancient civilization. And they rely on a similar appeal to authority. Ancient astrologers used their ability to predict the behavior of planets to order social life through the calendar and to regulate agriculture. The knowledge of astronomical order in turn supported their authority as all-purpose seers capable of taming the future. Similarly, modern scientists use their capacity to predict the behavior of narrow, closed systems to claim the right to predict and order all human futures.

And yet while the future as a prophetic form has a long history, the future as a predictable region of experience never appears. For the future is always offstage and never quite makes its entrance into history; the future is a time that never arrives but is always awaited. To understand the dilemma of the future, we might take a cue from the scholar reflecting on the loss of interest in history, who asked, "Does the past have a future?" and ourselves inquire, "What sort of a past has the future had?" The future as an idea indeed has a definite history and has served as a powerful political and cultural weapon, particularly in the last two centuries. During this period the idea of the future has been presented and functioned in American and British life in three quite distinct ways.

First, the future is often regarded as cause for a revitalization of optimism, an exhortation to the public to keep "faith," and is embodied in commemorative expositions of progress, world fairs, oratorical invocations, and the declaration of national and international goals. Second, the future, in the politics of literary prophecy, is attractively portrayed as the fulfillment of a particular ideology or idealism. The past and present are rewritten to evidence a momentous changing of the times in which particular policies and technologies will yield a way out of current dilemmas and a new age of peace, democracy, and ecological harmony will reign. Third, the future has acquired a new expression in the development of modern technologies of information processing and decision making by computer and cybernated devices. Here the future is a participation ritual of technological exorcism whereby the act of collecting data and allowing the public to participate in extrapolating trends and making choices is considered a method of cleansing confusion and relieving us from human fallibilities.

I

Throughout American history an exhortation to the future has been a standard inaugural for observing key anniversaries and renewed declarations of national purpose. At celebrations of science and industry and in the orations of public officials, the invocation of a sublime technological future elevates the prosaic and pedestrian commonplaces of the "American creed" with its promises of progress and prosperity to an appeal for public confidence in established institutions and industrial practices. This exhortation to the sublime future is an attempt to ward off dissent and to embellish cosmetically the blemishes of the body politic with imagery of a greater future for all.

The strategy of the future as exhortation was exemplified by the Centennial Exhibition staged in Philadelphia in 1876. The American Centennial was observed through the preferred nineteenth-century symbol of progress and optimism, the industrial exhibit. The initial purpose of the exhibit was to testify to American unity eleven years after the Civil War. However, the magnetic attraction of the exhibit was the Hall of Machinery with thirteen acres of machines connected by pulleys, shafts, wheels, and belts to a giant Corliss engine in the central transcept. Symbolically, President Grant opened the Centennial by turning the levers that brought the giant engine to life, assisted by Dom Pedro, the Emperor of Brazil. The Corliss engine dominating the Centennial illustrated the giantism of nineteenth-century mechanical technology, which enraptured both public and politicians. The machines were symbols of the grandeur and strength of the American people and a hopeful sign for the second century of American life. Even literary types such as William Dean Howells were overcome by the Corliss engine: "in these things of iron and steel . . . the national genius freely speaks; by and by the inspired marbles, the breathing canvases, the great literature; for the present America is voluble in the strong metals and their infinite uses" (Brown, 1966: 130).

While the giant hardware of the "Age of Steam" dominated the exhibit, the new electrical machines also held sway in the Centennial halls where the electric lamp and Alexander Graham Bell's telephone were on display.

In inaugurating the fair, President Grant noted that of necessity our progress had been in the practical tasks of subduing nature and building industry, yet we would soon rival the older nations in theology, science, fine arts, literature, and law. For while this was a celebration of 1876, it had an eye clearly fixed on 1976, the next centennial, progress toward which was guaranteed by native advances in mechanics and industry. However, America of the 1870s displayed numerous symptoms not altogether in harmony with the prevailing mood of the Centennial. The entire two decades following 1873 were highlighted by a worldwide depression. Earlier "improvements" in communication and transportation had led to an unprecedented degree of international integration in the economy. Failures in the economy fanned out over this international network so that the "communications revolution" of the 1830s generated, as one observer put it, three unprecedented historical phenomena: "an international agrarian market, an international agrarian depression and, as a climax, international agrarian discontent" (Benson, 1951: 62). Bitter discord reverberated through American society, lurking even in the shadow of the Centennial Exhibition. Labor unrest in the Pennsylvania coal fields led to strikes and union organization and to the hanging of ten members of the Molly Maguires in 1877. During 1876, President Grant had to dispatch troops to the South to control violence in the aftermath of the disputed election of Rutherford Hayes. The Centennial itself was disrupted on the Fourth of July by Susan Anthony's presentation of the Women's Declaration of Independence. Frederick Douglass, the contemporary black leader, was an official guest at the Centennial opening, although he had difficulty getting past police to the receiving stand; however, his token presence did not retard the spread of Jim Crow legislation through the South, undoing whatever gains had accrued to blacks in the aftermath of the Civil War. Finally, nine days before the climactic Fourth of July celebration, news arrived of Custer's defeat at Little Big Horn (Brown, 1966: passim). Such realities of American life—the problems of racial and ethnic relations, of political democracy, of the industrial proletariat, and of chronic depression did not pervade the official rhetoric of the Centennial with its eyes fixed firmly on Tomorrow.

For another Centennial celebration we dutifully created a commission on National Goals, a Bi-Centennial Committee, agencies, and commissions to foretell the year 2000. Moreover, the same problems that haunted 1876 marred the bi-centennial landscape. And, finally, while the favored symbols of technological progress have changed—satellites, spaceships, computers, and information utilities, having replaced steam engines and dynamos—the same style of exhortation to a better future through technology dominates contemporary life. This exhortation to discount the present for the future has therefore been a particular, though not peculiar, aspect of American popular culture. It is, in a trenchant phrase by Horace Kallen (1950: 78), "the doctrine and discipline of pioneering made art."

The reasons behind this orientation are easy enough to state, though difficult to document briefly, for the very creation of the United States was an attempt to outrun history and to escape European experience, not merely to find a new place but to found a "New World." The idea of a "new land," a virgin continent, had been part of the European utopian tradition. The discovery of America during the age of exploration removed utopia from literature and installed it in life.

This notion of our dispensation from European experience, free to realize the future without the baggage and liabilities of the past, has always been central to American belief. It first appears in a religious context, in the belief that a uniform, nonsectarian Christianity would be possible in "New England" because of the absence of European institutions and traditions. In the nineteenth century, dramatic advances in technology and industrialization were seen as an analogy to the spread of American religion, so that the spiritual improvement wrought by Christianity was linked to those "internal improvements," particularly improvements in transportation and communication. By midcentury canals, railways, and the telegraph became the most important forms of missionary activity.

The course and domain of spiritual empire increasingly became identified with that practical enterprise, manifest destiny, the course of the American empire. America's dispensation from history gave it a missionary role in the world: to win the world to an absolute truth—at first religious, then technical; to create a radical future "of a piece with the titantic entrance into the 'new world' of steam and electricity" (Miller, 1965: 52).

Whenever the future failed, as it often did during the nineteenth and twentieth centuries, appeal was made to yet another new future patching up the miscarriage of previous predictions. Most important, preachers and politicians appealed to Americans to retain faith in the future as such; they appealed to the future as a solvent and asked the public to believe that the latest technology or social project would fully justify past sacrifices and the endurance of present turmoil.

Fifty years after the Philadelphia Centennial, the foremost American historians of the period, Charles and Mary Beard, who were not unconscious of the difficulties of postwar America, were fascinated nonetheless by the vastness of the industrial inventory presented at the Sesquicentennial Exposition in contrast to what was shown in 1876. Moreover, they saw America's social destiny in "the radical departures effected in technology by electrical devices, the internal combustion engine, the wireless transmission of radio", changes, they felt, "more momentous even than those wrought by invention in the age of Watt and Fulton." They argued that the new technology removed the gloom and depression of the age of steam and provided a new motive force to rearrange American social patterns. Electricity would emanicipate humankind and integrate the city with the country as radio brought cosmopolitanism "as if on the wings of the wind." They concluded in lyrical prose that the "influence of the new motors and machines was as subtle as the electricity that turned the wheel, lighted the film and carried the song" (Beard and Beard, 1940: 746).

Several years later, in the midst of the Great Depression, Franklin Delano Roosevelt ritually exhorted the American people, reminding them,

> We say that we are a people of the future . . . the command
> of the democratic faith has ever been onward and upward;
> never have free men been satisfied with the mere maintenance
> of the status quo. . . . We have always held to the hope, the
> conviction, that there was a better life, a better world, beyond
> the horizon (Nevins, 1971: 400-401).

Similarly, at the 1933 Century of Progress Exposition in
Chicago, where Thomas Edison was being memorialized and
the electrical exhibit featured the themes of conquest of time
and space, Roosevelt tried to banish doubts and fears by
reference to "the inauguration of a Century of even greater
progress—not only along material lines; but a world uplifting
that will culminate in the greater happiness of mankind."

The function of such rhetoric was once characterized
by the late C. Wright Mills (1963: 302): "The more the
antagonisms of the present must be suffered, the more
the future is drawn upon as a source of pseudo-unity
and synthetic morale." The future in exhortation becomes a
solvent; the very act of moving forward in time constitutes a
movement away from past problems and present difficulties.
The future becomes a time zone in which the human condition is somehow transcended, politics evaporated, and a
blessed stage of peace and democratic harmony achieved.
The historian Allan Nevins (1971: 398) clearly expressed this
native ideology:

> Unity in American life and political thought certainly does
> not stem from general agreement on any body of doctrines. . . .
> The meaning of democracy in Oregon is very different from
> its meaning in Alabama. We are often told that we are held
> together as a people not so much by our common loyalty to
> the past . . . as by our common faith and hopes for the future.
> It is not the look backward . . . but the look forward that gives
> us cohesion. While we share some memories, the much more
> important fact is that we share many expectations. . . . The
> great unifying sentiment of America is hope for the future. . . .
> For national unity it is important to maintain in the American
> people this sense of confidence in our common future.

These views have potent political uses. The ideology of
the future can serve as a form of "false consciousness,"

a deflection away from the substantial problems of the present, problems grounded in conflicts over wealth and status and the appropriate control of technology, toward a future in which these problems, by the very nature of the future, cannot exist. As rationalizers for the British empire in the last century urged not only recognition of but belief in the Industrial Revolution, so Nevins, like other apologists, asks that our "minority groups" must have their sense of deprivation relieved by partaking of "faith in sharing, on equal terms, in a happier future." Similarly, one of Richard Nixon's first acts as president was to create a National Goals Research Staff. The staff was charged with orienting Americans toward the bicentennial and the year 2000, so that we might "seize on the future as the key dimension of our decisions" (*Futures*, 1969: 459).

Culturally and politically, then, the idea of the future functions in much the same way as the notion of the "invisible Hand of Providence" operating in the dreams of "heavenly cities" in the eighteenth and nineteenth centuries; it provides a basis for faith in the essential rectitude of motives and policy in the midst of the disarray of the present. The rhetoric of the future in the twentieth century has offered, in Aldous Huxley's words (1972: 139), a "motivating and compensatory Future" that consoles for the miseries suffered in the present. To Huxley's critical mind, the literature of the future provided to modern generations what the Methodist sermon on hard times now and heavenly rewards later had for the first English working class at the onset of the Industrial Revolution: the rhetoric of a sublime future as an alternative to political revolution and a stimulus to acquiescence. In the new literature of the future, the salvation is not other-worldly but terrestrial revolution and its correlates in moral, social, and material betterment. As Huxley (1972: 140) concluded, "the thought of . . . happiness in the twenty-first century consoles the disillusioned beneficiaries of progress."

From the enormous corpus of prophetic writing about the future, we have selected a few British and American authors who illustrate the essential features of this literature. Although the authors' motives and backgrounds differ, certain distinct common themes distinguish futurist literature. Invariably the newest technologies of communication and transportation are seen as means for the lasting solution to existing problems and a radical departure from previous historical patterns. Also, the landscape of the future is suggestively drawn as one in which a sublime state of environmental balance, social harmony, and peace is achieved.

In *Futures* magazine, I. F. Clarke (1969) identified the first major technological forecast written in the English language as the work of an anonymous author published in 1763 under the title *The Reign of George VI, 1900-25*. This premier utopia, which may be said to have initiated the age of extrapolation, depicted the future as a mere perfection of the ethos of the reign of George III. It projected the consolidation and expansion of the empire over the continents of Europe and North America with a Pax Brittannica of secure hegemony by means of vastly improved communication and transportation supporting commerce, foreign service, and military force. Published in the same year as the end of the French and Indian War and thirteen years before the uprising of the thirteen colonies, it professed to see a time when England's perennial rivals gladly accepted orders from London. Coeval with Watt's steam experiments, it suggested that the English countryside would be embellished by the waterways and routes of new industry, that cities might remain quaint, and that the society of aristocratic amenities would be perpetuated. During the predominance of the British Empire, a literature of the imperial future sought to impress the reading public with such sublime reasons for continued expenditure and sacrifice on behalf of Anglo-Saxon destiny. It also became in time a ground for arguing against revolutionary ideology as Chartism, Marxism, and republicanism challenged the system.

An apotheosis of nineteenth-century optimism followed in the train of the Great Exhibit of 1851 as the prevalent ethos of Victorian complacency imagined a global community of interests to be the inevitable by-product of communication and transport in the cause of trade and empire. There were some dissenters who pierced the Crystal Palace mystique and correctly read into industrialization its pernicious tendencies to dwarf man and nature under advancing machinery. The dominant note remained one of beneficent *social corollaries* to be derived from the conquests by technology of the earth and the barriers of time and space. Ironically, these included gifts for which we are still waiting, such as freedom from drudgery, a wedding of beauty and utility, and an end to warfare and cosmopolitan consciousness.

A prime document of this period is illustrative of the point that today's future is yesterday's future as well. In *The Silent Revolution: Or the Future Effects of Steam and Electricity upon the Condition of Mankind*, a projection from the perspective of 1852, Michael Angelo Garvey portrayed the world as the Great Exhibit writ large where all the problems of industrialism were finally resolved. The smoke-filled slum and the Malthusian specter were to be eliminated as transportation redistributed population to new colonies and allowed a new and elevated working class access to "pure air and joyous landscape." Sharing the mistaken notion of most futurists that social conflict results from insufficient communication and isolation, Garvey personified the technology of travel and telegraphy. The railway was "if not the great leveler" then "the great master of ceremonies," who is "daily introducing the various classes" and "making them better acquainted in common." In a further "future period," Garvey projected a system of total communications anticipating the notions of Marshall McLuhan: "a perfect network of electric filaments" to "consolidate and harmonize the social union of mankind by furnishing a sensitive apparatus analogous to the nervous system of the living frame" (Garvey, 1852: 103-104, 134, 170).

This perfect future was of a piece with other Victorian prophecies despite the proximate realities of Irish famine and labor unrest, the Crimean War, and other manifestations of discord and dispute. But the ulterior motive for the imperial era future literature was patently clear in *The Silent Revolution*. Garvey pleaded for his readers to maintain their loyalty to the regime, the proper caretaker of the future, and to avoid noisy agitation for reform or revolt. The "silent revolution" was a substitute for a social revolution, a rhetorical method to keep not only the majority but minorities silent about questions of imperial policy.

The literature of the future of the empire continued to mirror and mold prevailing opinion of the British elite well into the twentieth century. Its attitudes regularly overshadowed critical warnings about the fate awaiting overextension abroad and retention of obsolete institutions at home. Although the citations from twentieth-century versions of the literature of the imperial futurists already seem arcane to us because of the depletion of English power, it is well to realize the degree to which American futurism in the present context—for instance, in Zbigniew Brzezinski's (1970) "Technetronic Society"—derives its inspiration from the British *Pax Americana* augmented by electronic instruments of communication for the conduct of foreign policy and warfare and the pacification of the home populace.

In *The World in 2030 A.D.*, a view from the year 1930, the Earl of Birkenhead tried to blend imperialism and futurism to ward off erosion of public confidence caused by the depression and the rise of dictators. To offer a relief from the over 230 years of turmoil, Birkenhead predicted a characteristic turning point identical to that delineated by current writers about the future: "Today we are witnessing the death of a society and tradition which have existed since the first French Revolution and the Industrial Revolution" (Birkenhead, 1930: 116). This change, however, was not to be political or social but technological. Electrification of the English countryside and decentralized, smokeless factories were to comprise a handsome landscape of laboratories resembling an "interminable park" and dispensing the plentitude of an "industrial Arcadia."

Public disaffection from remote government might be treated by obtaining formal participation through electronic communications, so that "it will be feasible once more to revive *that form* of democracy which flourished in the city states of Ancient Greece" (Birkenhead, 1930: 8-9). Broadcasting of special debates could be followed by instant opinion polling through devices inserted in telephone exchanges. But this meant no real transfer of power to the people because in Birkenhead's analysis, government should probably be handed to a class of expert specialists whose electronic consultation might be a mere formality, a guise of democracy for the electronic Leviathan.

Furthermore, Birkenhead envisioned the future world as continuing management of world affairs and the evolution of international organization around the nucleus of the British Commonwealth with India, South Africa, and even Dublin again inside its orbit. The future world would be made safe for the RAF patrol over the pipelines in Iraq and for upper-class amenities of silent Rolls Royces and riding to hounds. In sum, "the world in 2030" was to be nothing more than the wishful dream of an 1830 Tory mentality given technocratic expression.

So pronounced was the tendency of the British intelligentsia to conceive of the future solely in terms of the empire that it affected even Liberals, Fabians, and scientific modernizers such as J. B. S. Haldane. H. G. Wells, the most inventive of the futurists during the first part of the twentieth century, was initially a member of a circle who viewed the Empire as "the pacific precursor of a practical World State" (Wells, 1929: 126) and the royal military equipped with the latest technology of communication and transport as the forerunners of a "world police" able to be dispatched quickly to any trouble spot to quell insurrectionary activity.

In contradistinction to the imperialist futurists, there arose an alternative view of the future genuinely dedicated to the decentralization of power and industry, a rehabilitation of the natural landscape, and a revival of regional cultures. Its major figures were the Russian anarchist and naturalist, Peter Kropotkin, and the Scottish regionalist, Patrick Geddes. Kropotkin's vision of an "industrial village" of the future foresaw the dispersion of production and population to communal and workshop levels (Kropotkin, 1913). The transmission of electricity would replace the huge steam engine, dehumanized factories, and alienation of labor. This attractive idea was further elaborated by Geddes as a theory of the reversal of the adversities of the Industrial Revolution and the arrival in the near future of a "eutopian" mode of life.

During and after World War I, Geddes and his colleague sociologist Victor Branford edited a series of books and pamphlets collectively published as *Interpretations and Forecasts, The Making of the Future*, and *Papers for Present* (Geddes, 1917). Geddes's foremost American disciple, Lewis Mumford, has credited this biologist and town planner with the introduction of "the future, as so to speak, a legally bounded terrain in social thought" (Barnes, 1966, p. 384). Geddes earned the title "big brother of reform" through his activist field experiments from Chicago and Edinburgh to India and Palestine. His intellectual influence extended to contemporaries such as Jane Addams and John Dewey and reemerged in updated versions in the work of figures such as Paul Goodman and Marshall McLuhan.

Geddes's own portrayal of the future drew a dialectical contrast between old and new forms of technology. Electricity was to be the key to a "great transition" from forms of concentration to decentralization, from pollutants to ecology, from urban congestion and false cosmopolitanism to regional and folk revival: "We may divide the age of machinery into the paleotechnic age of smoke and steam engine, and the neotechnic age of electricity and radium, the conquest of noise and the utilization of waste" (Geddes, 1917: preface). The aim of the future for Geddes was a neotechnic "Eutopia" under a "partnership of man and nature" in a world redesigned to resemble a garden.

There is a remarkable similarity between Geddes's conception of the future and notions entertained by contemporary futurology. Geddes expected the passing away of politics, parties, and ideologies. In place of political activism, he and Branford advocated a third alternative *beyond* right and left to be carried out by "peace armies" of "university militants" going to the peoples of the world in projects of environmental reconstruction, conservation, educational reform, and civic design. Imperialism would be superseded by autonomous regional federations. This neglect of political facts and factors in Geddes's ideas has been evaluated by Mumford as the critical oversight in his view of the future world.

Geddes's future was premised on several other errors. The new technology as applied brought about increased centralization and concentration and domination over the landscape by powerhouses. And it extended the range of control by imperialistic power centers over indigenous cultures and regions.

The ideas of Geddes and Kropotkin had their influence in the United States among leading conservationists, regional planners, and social critics. The transfer to the American scene of Geddes's neotechnic formulations was especially due to the works of Lewis Mumford.

In 1934, in his *Technics and Civilization*, Mumford attributed a series of "revolutionary changes" to "qualitative" effects of electricity itself, particularly hydroelectric turbines and incipient automated machinery in the factory. These he supposed to include a "tidying up of the landscape" by "Geotechnics" in the "building of reservoirs and power dams" and a lifting of the "smoke pall" as "with electricity the clear sky and clear water . . . come back again." The sublime landscape of the radiant future would be one of an intermarriage of town and country, agriculture and industry, and even distribution of surplus population and of wealth (Mumford, 1963: 255-256).

From radio and "person-to-person" electronic communication Mumford hoped for a universal democracy by technology: "there are now the elements of almost as close a political unity as that which was once possible in the tiniest cities of Attica" (Mumford, 1963: 241).

Still, Mumford's Americanization of Geddes's gospel was subjected to the same irony of history as had overtaken previous projections of the future. The hydroelectric project and reservoir eventually further uprooted and eroded the environment. The air, water, and land were neither cleared nor cleansed, as we who now inhabit this future landscape well know. The megalopolis continued to grow. Total automation is still more predicted than realized, while the C.I.O.'s organizing drive began in earnest just as Mumford wrote of the end of the working class. Politically, it was an age of dictators and centralized rule.

Mumford himself was compelled to admit that there had been a "miscarriage of the machine," given that civilization was still stalled in a "pseudomorphic" stage: "The new machines followed the pattern laid down by previous economic and technical standards." In subsequent reevaluation Mumford has seen that belief in electricity as a revolutionary force was in fact mistaken; even "in those plans that have been carried through, the realization has retrospectively disfigured the anticipation" (Mumford, 1959: 534).

Nevertheless, Mumford's themes have reappeared in future literature. I: was thirty-six years ago that he composed a section on "shock absorbers," the essence of which reappeared in Alvin Toffler's *Future Shock* (1971). Toffler has revived themes of the sublime technological revolution of forty years vintage as a means of peering toward the year 2000. Toffler's recent work is embellished by the same recurring symbolism of the futurist genre. There are a number of "final and qualitative" departures in store for the new millennium. According to Toffler, the new society has "broken irretrievably with the past," transcending geography and history.

What we encounter in Toffler is a portrait of the future as a new realm of dispensation from the consequences of the Industrial Revolution. The era of automation is pictured as a change "more important than the industrial revolution." The new industries of electronics and space technology are characterized by "relative silence and clean surroundings" as contrasted with the imagery of "smoky steel mills or clinking machines." The end of the assembly line dispenses with classic class conflict by placing a "new organization man" in the leading role as historical protagonist. Anticipatory democracy will be instituted in "town halls of the future," where critics of technics will be outdistanced by a futurist movement. Dissident minorities and recalcitrant middle Americans will be coopted into programmed participation into future-planning games. Groups will be dissuaded from opposition to the space program and have their dissent funneled into support for improved technology. Cadres of specialists will be attached to various social groups so that expertise will be married to the solicitation of consent.

Another illustrative comparison can be taken from the literature of the 1930s and 1970s. Contemporary rhetoric of a sublime national future merely places the computer and transistor where the powerhouse generators once held sway as predominant technology. A striking similarity may be seen in the parallel between the initial celebration of the Tennessee Valley Authority as a New Deal showcase and the recent projection of the electronic counterculture in *The Greening of America* (Reich, 1970).

Contrary to prevalent interpretations, the New Deal had its futurist impulses in efforts to enact projects for the construction of new communities, the decentralization of power, the reclamation of the landscape, and the electrification of the American countryside. This aspect of New Deal thought reflected the ideas of the old progressive conservationists, such as Gifford Pinchott, who have been influenced by Geddes and the regional planning movement.

The TVA was the subject of a vast oratorical and journalistic outpouring centering on its image as a model of the future. For instance, it was held to be a "Revolution by Electricity" by Paul Hutchinson (1937), editor of *The Christian Century*, who lifted his idiom from Lewis Mumford. In his words, the TVA was to "fashion the future of a new America." The "real revolutionary" was the new machine "which might at last become as much of a liberating and regenerative agency as the dreamers of the early industrial revolution declared it would be." The Tennessee Valley Authority was to be marked by a complete "absence of politics" and decentralization into "factory-plus-farm villages" (1937: 83-95, passim). It would deny the iron laws of managerialism and bureaucratic revolution.

However, the TVA's own record has been a final reversal of these promises. Internally, it has developed technocratic structures, and its new towns display a company town psychology. By strip-mining and other such practices it has marred the landscape. Like its technological big sister, the Atomic Energy Commission, it is aligned economically and politically with parts of the military-industrial complex. If anything, the machine again became the real counterrevolutionary.

In *The Greening of America*, Charles Reich predicts a "transformation" beyond a "mere revolution such as the French or Russian." This new form of revolution offers answers to questions of identity and community, of history and politics. In the age of the computer and counterculture, Reich's rhetoric resembles Hutchinson's of four decades ago. For instance, "the machine itself has begun to do the work of revolution." And "prophets and philosophers have proposed these ways of life before, but only today's technology has made them possible" (Reich, 1970: 350-52).

Reich attributes to electronics and cybernetics the social *correlates* of a higher consciousness, participation in a shared community, and renewed contacts with the land. The trouble with the Reichean formulation of a revolutionary machinery and a new cultural emergence is that its manifestations are either illusory or ephemeral.

At bottom the counterculture is primarily an extension of the existing entertainment and leisure industries rather than a regeneration of the humane dimension. Reich cites the devotees of Woodstock and is silent on the Altamont tragedy. The record industry lets the counterculture have the prophetic lyrics and collects the profits and the real cultural power.

There is a pronounced tendency, however, for prophets and movements to resort to incantations to reassure themselves about their cherished illusions. The enthusiasts of the Tennessee Valley Authority a generation ago, as Harold Ickes observed sardonically in 1944, began to believe that they might breathe life into a new democracy merely by intoning "TVA, TVA, TVA." Similarly, the "greening of America" and like-minded counterculture scenarios impress one as nothing more than a chanting exercise for a new generation of Americans sent to their rendezvous with another electric destiny. Currently, the shaping of the future remains routed along past lines. We see technological patterns and organizational forms continuing the trend toward concentration and centralization of power and control in established institutions.

III

The writings of Reich and Toffler are merely the outer edge of a large body of literature forecasting another technological revolution and a new future. This revolution is preeminently one in communication, for as Norbert Wiener noted some years ago, "the present time is the age of communication and control." Modern engineering is communication engineering, for its major preoccupation is not the economy of energy "but the accurate reproduction of a signal" (Wiener, 1948: 39).

The first communications revolution was the innovation of printing, which mechanized the production of information, extended literacy, and enlarged the domain of empire. The second revolution occurred over the last century with the marriage, through electricity, of the capacity to simultaneously produce and transmit messages—a process that extends from the telephone and telegraph to television. Now, this third communications revolution involves the linkage of machines for information storage and retrieval with the telephone, television, and computer, producing new systems of "broadband" communication or "information utilities."

The revolutionary potential of these "improvements" in communication does not derive from the prosaic facts about them—more information sent faster and farther with greater fidelity. Instead, their attraction resides in the supposed capacity to transform the commonplace into the extraordinary: to create novel forms of human community, new standards of efficiency and progress, newer and more democratic forms of politics, and finally to usher a "new man" into history. The printing press, by extending literacy, not only taught people to read but was expected to eradicate ignorance, prejudice, and provincialism. Similarly, the telegraph and radio were seen as magnetic forces binding people into international networks of peace and understanding. Recently the "cybernetic revolution," by increasing available information by a quantum leap, promises to make "policy options . . . clearly defined, the probable outcomes of alternative measures accurately predicted and the feedback mechanism from society . . . so effective that man could at last bring his full intelligence to bear on resolving the central problems of society" (Westin, 1971: 1).

The basis of this third communications revolution, the marriage of the time-shared computer for both data analysis and information storage and retrieval to the telephone and television, is portrayed as the ultimate communications machine; it combines the speed and intimacy of dialogue, the memory of history, the variable output of sight and sound, the individuality of total information combined with totally free choice, the political awareness and control of a fully informed and participant electorate, and the analytic skill of advanced mathematics.

Despite the manifest failure of technology to resolve pressing social issues over the last century, contemporary intellectuals continue to see revolutionary potential in the latest technological gadgets that are pictured as a force *outside* history and politics. The future as it is previsioned is one in which cybernetic machines provide the dynamic of progressive change. More important, although certain groups—industrialists, technocrats, and scientists—are portrayed as the appointed guardians of the new technology, they are not ordinarily viewed as an elite usurping the power to make history and define reality. They are viewed as self-abnegating servants of power merely accommodating themselves to the truth and the future as determined by the inexorable advance of science and technology. In modern futurism *it is the machines that possess teleological insight*.

Moreover, the new communications technology is extended into virtually every domain of social life, invading even the family through home computer consoles for information, entertainment, education, and edification. And the public is invited to participate in a technical ritual of planning the future through World Games and electronic Delphic techniques as a rehearsal for the new stage of participatory democracy to be ushered in by communications technology.

Unfortunately, the vision of democracy by electricity has been with us since at least the telegraph and telephone and has been put forward by most writers about the future over the last century. James Russell Lowell, assessing the aftermath of the Civil War in the 1860s, felt that "the dream of Human Brotherhood seems to be coming true at last." He pinned this belief to the new form of the town meeting that technology could bring into existence:

> It has been said that our system of town meetings made our revolution possible, by educating the people in self-government. But this was at most of partial efficacy, while the newspapers and telegraph gather the whole nation into a vast town-meeting where everyone hears the affairs of the country discussed and where better judgment is pretty sure to make itself valid at last. No discovery is made that some mention of it does not sooner or later reach the ears of a majority of Americans. It is this constant mental and moral stimulus which gives them the alertness and vivacity, the wide-awakeness of temperament, characteristic of dwellers in great cities (Lowell, 1871: Vol. 5, p. 239).

Despite the faliure of town meetings, newspaper, telegraph, wireless, and television to create the conditions of a new Athens, contemporary advocates of technological liberation regularly describe a new postmodern age of instantaneous daily plebiscitory democracy through a computerized system of electronic voting and opinion and polling.

> Devise a mechanical means for nationwide voting daily and secretly by each adult citizen of Uncle Sam's family: then I assure you will Democracy be saved. . . . This is a simple mechanical problem involving but a fractional effort of that involved in distributing the daily mails to the nation. . . .Electrified voting . . . promises a household efficiency superior to any government of record, because it incorporates not only the speed of decision of the dictator . . . but additional advantages that can never be his (Fuller, 1963: 13-14).

But it is also obvious that the extraordinary demands made on the citizen by such a system would merely coopt him or her into the technical apparatus with only the illusion of control.

To participate in such a system the citizen of the future will have to undergo a continuing lifelong education in real time, the acquisition of new knowledge when it is needed in time to meet problems as they arise. Recognizing the implausibility of all this, Donald Michael has recommended a form of republicanism rather than direct democracy. He argues that specialists will have to mediate between the technology and the citizen and government. Such specialists will be retained by groups to represent them to the government. But given the engineered "complexity" of the new information systems, involvement of the public becomes a mere ritual of participation or overparticipation to legitimate rule by a new scientific elite. If either of these modes of citizen participation is seriously entertained as the way past the present crises in politics, then of only one thing may we be sure: no matter what form of government we live under in the future, *it will be called democracy*. In the writing on the future there is no consideration of the nature of the polity because, in fact, political community today is very near a total collapse by the rush upon it of the very values the new futurists represent: rationalization, centralization, and uniformity. Other writers, notably C. Wright Mills, at least recognized that the basic problem was the one of elitism. Although some futurist writers recognize that we are in a situation in which meritocratic elites replace the old plutocracy, they do not take the next step—the growth of technocratic elites presumes the atomization of society; the condition of their rule is the erosion of political and social community and the creation of a new monopoly of knowledge.

Many new futurists recognize that knowledge is power—they say it so often it perhaps has never occurred to them that first it needs to be meaningful and relevant knowledge—and that it can be monopolized like any other commodity. However, they rarely recognize that the phrase "monopoly of knowledge" has two interpretations. In the first, monopoly of knowledge simply means the control of factual information or data. Communications is crucial here because the development of more elaborate codes and storage facilities allows groups to control information and deny access to the uninitiated and disconnected. Moreover, competition for innovation in the speed of communication is spurred by the fact that if information flows at unequal rates, what is still the future for one group is already the past for another. The late Ithiel de Sola Pool illustrated this meaning of monopoly of knowledge and simultaneously painted a generous portrait of the new information systems in breaking this monopoly.

> The information facilities provided by the computer can . . . serve as a decentralizing instrument. They can make available to all parts of an organization the kinds of immediate and complete information that is today available only at the center. The power of top leadership today is very largely the power of their information monopoly. . . . A society with computerized information facilities can make its choice between centralization and decentralization, because it will have the mechanical capability of moving information either way (Westin, 1971: 248).

There is, however, a more stringent sense of the meaning of a monopoly of knowledge. When one speaks, let us say, of the monopoly of religious knowledge, of the institutional church, one is not referring to the control of particles of information. Instead, one is referring to control of the entire system of thought, or paradigm, that determines what it is that can be religiously factual, that determines what the standards are for assessing the truth of any elucidation of these facts, and that defines what it is that can be accounted for as knowledge. Modern computer enthusiasts may be willing to share their data with anybody. What they are not willing to relinquish as readily is the entire technocratic world view that determines what qualifies as an acceptable or valuable fact. What they monopolize is not the body of data itself but the approved, certified, sanctioned, official mode of thought—indeed, the definition of what it means to be reasonable. And this is possible because of a persistent confusion between information and knowledge.

Rarely in writing about the new communications technology is the relationship between information and knowledge ever adequately worked out, because it is not recognized as

substituted the mechanical coordination of buyer and seller, so the language of the telegraph displaced a fiduciary relationship between writer and reader with a coordinated one.

Similarly, the telegraph eliminated the correspondent who provided letters that announced an event, described it in detail, and analyzed its substance, and replaced him with the stringer who supplied the bare facts. As words were expensive on the telegraph, it separated the observer from the writer. Not only did writing for the telegraph have to be condensed to save money—telegraphic, in other words—but also from the marginal notes and anecdotes of the stringer the story had to be reconstituted at the end of the telegraphic line, a process that reaches high art with the news magazines, the story divorced from the story teller.

But as every constraint is also an opportunity, the telegraph altered literary style. In a well-known story, "cablese" influenced Hemingway's style, helping him to pare his prose to the bone, dispossessed of every adornment. Most correspondents chafed under its restrictiveness, but not Hemingway. "I had to quit being a correspondent," he told Lincoln Steffens later. "I was getting too fascinated by the lingo of the cable."[7] But the lingo of the cable provided the underlying structure for one of the most influential literary styles of the twentieth century.

There were other effects—some obvious, some subtle. If the telegraph made prose lean and unadorned and led to a journalism without the luxury of detail and analysis, it also brought an overwhelming crush of such prose to the newsroom. In the face of what was a real glut of occurrences, news judgment had to be routinized and the organization of the newsroom made factory-like. The reporter who produced the new prose moved into prominence in journalism by displacing the editor as the archetype of the journalist. The spareness of the prose and the sheer volume of it allowed news—indeed, forced news—to be treated like a commodity: something that could be transported, measured, reduced, and timed. In the wake of the telegraph, news was subject to all the procedures developed for handling agricultural commodities. It was subject to "rates, contracts, franchising, discounts and thefts.[8]

A second site for the investigation of the telegraph is the domain of empire. Again, it is best not to assault the problem as an overarching theory of imperialism but, rather, to examine specific cases and specific connections: the role of the telegraph in coordinating military, particularly naval, operations; the transition from colonialism, where power and authority rested with the domestic governor, to imperialism, where power and authority were reabsorbed by the imperial capital; the new forms of political correspondence that came about when the war correspondent was obliged to use the telegraph; and the rise of the first forms of international business that could be called multinational.

While the growth of empire and imperialism have been explained by virtually every possible factor, little attention has been paid to telegraphy in generating the ground conditions for the urban imperialism of the mid-nineteenth century and the international imperialism later in the century.[9] It is probably no accident that the words "empire" and "imperialism" entered the language in 1870, soon after the laying of the transatlantic cable. Although colonies could be held together with printing, correspondence, and sail, the hold, as the American experience shows, was always tenuous over great distance. Moreover, in colonial arrangements the margin had as much power as the center. Until the transatlantic cable, it was difficult to determine whether British colonial policy was being set in London or by colonial governors in the field—out of contact and out of control. It was the cable and telegraph, backed, of course, by sea power, that turned colonialism into imperialism: a system in which the center of an empire could dictate rather than merely respond to the margin.[10]

The critical change lay in the ability to secure investments. There was no heavy overseas investment until the control made possible by the cable. The innovation of the telegraph created, if not the absolute impetus for imperial expansion, then at least the wherewithal to make the expansion theoretically tenable. But it also created a tension between the capability to expand and the capacity to rule.

With the development of the railroad, steam power, the telegraph and cable, a coherent empire emerged based on a coherent system of communication. In that system the railroad may be taken as the overland extension of the steamer or vice versa, and the telegraph and cable stood as the coordinating, regulating device governing both.[11]

Although the newspaper and imperial offices are among the best sites at which to look for the effects of the telegraph, there are humbler locations of equal interest. It surely is more than an accident that many of the great nineteenth-century commercial empires were founded in the humble circumstances of the telegraph operator's shack. The case of Richard B. Sears of North Redwood, Minnesota, is instructive. One must not forget that Edison and Carnegie began the same way and that the genius of Jay Gould lay in his integration of the telegraph with the railroad. The significance of the telegraph in this regard is that it led to the selective control and transmission of information. The telegraph operator was able to monopolize knowledge, if only for a few moments, along a route; and this brought a selective advantage in trading and speculation. But it was this same control of information that gave the telegraph a central importance in the development of modern gambling and of the business of credit. Finally, it was central to the late nineteenth-century explosion in forms of merchandising, such as the mail-order house.[12]

In the balance of this essay I want to cut across some of these developments and describe how the telegraph altered the ways in which time and space were understood in ordinary human affairs and, in particular, to examine a changed form in which time entered practical consciousness. To demonstrate these changes I wish to concentrate on the developments of commodity markets and on the institutionalization of standard time. But first let me reiterate the basic argument.

The simplest and most important point about the telegraph is that it marked the decisive separation of "transportation" and "communication." Until the telegraph these words were synonymous. The telegraph ended that identity and allowed symbols to move independently of geography and independently of and faster than transport. I say decisive separation because there were premonitions earlier of what was to come, and there was, after all, pre-electric telegraphy—line-of-sight signaling devices.

Virtually any American city of any vintage has a telegraph hill or a beacon hill reminding us of such devices. They relied on shutters, flaps, disks, or arms operating as for semaphoric signaling at sea. They were optical rather than "writing at a distance" systems and the forerunners of microwave networks, which rely on relay stations on geographic high points for aerial transmissions.

Line-of-sight telegraphy came into practical use at the end of the eighteenth century. Its principal architect was a Frenchman, Claud Chappe, who persuaded the Committee of Public Instruction in post-Revolutionary France to approve a trial. Joseph Lakanal, one of its members, reported back to the committee on the outcome: "What brilliant destiny do science and the arts not reserve for a republic which by its immense population and the genius of its inhabitants, is called to become the nation to instruct Europe" (Wilson, 1976: 122).

The National Convention approved the adoption of the telegraph as a national utility and instructed the Committee of Public Safety to map routes. The major impetus to its development in France was the same as the one that led to the wave of canal and railroad building in America. The pre-electric telegraph would provide an answer to Montesquieu and other political theorists who thought France or the United States too big to be a republic. But even more, it provided a means whereby the departments that had replaced the provinces after the Revolution could be tied to and coordinated with the central authority (Wilson, 1976: 123).

The pre-electric telegraph was also a subject of experimentation in America. In 1800, a line-of-sight system was opened between Martha's Vineyard and Boston (Wilson, 1976: 210). Between 1807 and 1812, plans were laid for a telegraph to stretch from Maine to New Orleans. The first practical use of line-of-sight telegraphy was for the transmission of news of arriving ships, a practice begun long before 1837 (Thompson, 1947: 11). But even before line-of-sight devices had been developed, alterations in shipping patterns had led to the separation of information from cargo, and that had important consequences for international trade. I shall say more on this later.

Despite these reservations and qualifications, the telegraph provided the decisive and cumulative break of the identity of communication and transportation. The great theoretical significance of the technology lay not merely in the separation but also in the use of the telegraph as both a model of and a mechanism for control of the physical movement of things, specifically for the railroad. That is the fundamental discovery: not only can information move independently of and faster than physical entities, but it also can be a simulation of and control mechanism for what has been left behind. The discovery was first exploited in railroad dispatching in England in 1844 and in the United States in 1849. It was of particular use on the long stretches of single-track road in the American West, where accidents were a serious problem. Before the use of the telegraph to control switching, the Boston and Worcester Railroad, for one example, kept horses every five miles along the line, and they raced up and down the track so that their riders could warn engineers of impending collisions (Thompson, 1947: 205-206). By moving information faster than the rolling stock, the telegraph allowed for centralized control along many miles of track. Indeed, the operation of the telegraph in conjunction with the railroad allowed for an integrated system of transport and communication. The same principle realized in these mundane circumstances governs the development of all modern processes in electrical transmission and control from guided gun sights to simple servo mechanisms that open doors. The relationship of the telegraph and the railroad illustrates the basic notion of systems theory and the catch phrase that the "system is the solution," in that the integrated switched system is more important than any of its components.

The telegraph permitted the development, in the favorite metaphor of the day, of a thoroughly encephalated social nervous system in which signaling was divorced from musculature. It was the telegraph and the railroad—the actual, painful construction of an integrated system—that provided the entrance gate for the organic metaphors that dominated nineteenth-century thought. Although German romanticism

215

and idealism had their place, it is less to the world of ideas and more to the world of actual practice that we need to look when trying to figure out why the nineteenth century was obsessed with organicism.

The effect of the telegraph on ideology, on ordinary ideas, can be shown more graphically with two other examples drawn from the commodities markets and the development of standard time. The telegraph, like most innovations in communication down through the computer, had its first and most profound impact on the conduct of commerce, government, and the military. It was, in short, a producer good before it was a consumer good. The telegraph, as I said earlier, was used in its early months for the long-distance playing of chess. Its commercial significance was slow to be realized. But once that significance was determined, it was used to reorganize commerce; and from the patterns of usage in commerce came many of the telegraph's most profound consequences for ordinary thought. Among its first effects was the reorganization of commodity markets.

It was the normal expectation of early nineteenth century Americans that the price of a commodity would diverge from city to city so that the cost of wheat, corn, or whatever would be radically different in, say, Pittsburgh, Cincinnati, and St. Louis. This belief reflected the fact that before the telegraph, markets were independent of one another, or, more accurately, that the effect of one market on another was so gradually manifested as to be virtually unnoticed. In short, the prices of commodities were largely determined by local conditions of supply and demand. One of the leading historians of the markets has commented, "To be sure in all articles of trade the conditions at all sources of supply had their ultimate effect on distant values and yet even in these the communication was so slow that the conditions might change entirely before their effect could be felt" (Emery, 1896: 106).

Under such circumstances, the principal method of trading is called arbitrage: buying cheap and selling dear by moving goods around in space. That is, if prices are higher in St. Louis than in Cincinnati, it makes sense to buy in Cincinnati and resell in St. Louis, as long as the price differential is

216

greater than the cost of transportation between the two cities. If arbitrage is widely practiced between cities, prices should settle into an equilibrium whereby the difference in price is held to the difference in transportation cost. This result is, in turn, based on the assumption of classical economics of perfect information—that all buyers and sellers are aware of the options available in all relevant markets—a situation rarely approached in practice before the telegraph.

Throughout the United States, price divergence between markets declined during the nineteenth century. Arthur H. Cole computed the average annual and monthly price disparity for uniform groups of commodities during the period 1816-1842, that is, up to the eve of the telegraph. Over that period the average annual price disparity fell from 9.3 to 4.8; and the average monthly disparity, from 15.4 to 4.8 (Cole, 1938: 94-96, 103). The decline itself is testimony to improvements in communication brought about by canal and turnpike building. The steepness of the decline is probably masked somewhat because Cole grouped the prices for the periods 1816-1830 and 1830-1842, whereas it was late in the canal era and the beginnings of large-scale railroad building that the sharpest declines were felt.

Looked at from one side, the decline represents the gradual increase in the effective size of the market. Looked at from the other side, it represents a decline in spatially based speculative opportunities—opportunities, that is, to turn trade into profit by moving goods between distinct markets. In a sense the railroad and canal regionalized markets; the telegraph nationalized them.

The effect of the telegraph is a simple one: it evens out markets in space. The telegraph puts everyone in the same place for purposes of trade; it makes geography irrelevant. The telegraph brings the conditions of supply and demand in all markets to bear on the determination of a price. Except for the marginal exception here and there, it eliminates opportunities for arbitrage by realizing the classical assumption of perfect information.

But the significance of the telegraph does not lie solely in the decline of arbitrage; rather, the telegraph shifts speculation into another dimension. It shifts speculation from space to time, from arbitrage to futures. After the telegraph, commodity trading moved from trading between places to trading between times. The arbitrager trades Cincinnati for St. Louis; the futures trader sells August against October, this year against next. To put the matter somewhat differently, as the telegraph closed down spatial uncertainty in prices it opened up, because of improvements in communication, the uncertainty of time. It was not, then, mere historic accident that the Chicago Commodity Exchange, to this day the principal American futures market, opened in 1848, the same year the telegraph reached that city. In a certain sense the telegraph invented the future as a new zone of uncertainty and a new region of practical action.

Let me make a retreat from that conclusion about the effects of the telegraph on time because I have overdrawn the case. First, the opportunities for arbitrage are never completely eliminated. There are always imperfections in market information, even on the floor of a stock exchange: buyers and sellers who do not know of one another and the prices at which the others are willing to trade. We know this as well from ordinary experience at auctions, where someone always knows a buyer who will pay more than the auctioned price. Second, there was a hiatus between arbitrage and the futures market when time contracts dominated, and this was a development of some importance. An approximation of futures trading occurred as early as 1733, when the East India Company initiated the practice of trading warrants. The function of a warrant was to transfer ownership of goods without consummating their physical transfer. The warrant did not represent, as such, particular warehoused goods; they were merely endorsed from person to person. The use of warrants or time contracts evolved rapidly in the United States in the trading of agricultural staples. They evolved to meet new conditions of effective market size and, as importantly, their evolution was unrestrained by historic practice.

The critical condition governing the development of time contracts was also the separation of communication from transport. Increasingly, news of crop conditions reached the market before the commodity itself. For example, warrant trading advanced when cotton was shipped to England by sail while passengers and information moved by steamer. Based on news of the crop and on samples of the commodity, time contracts or "to-arrive" contracts were executed. These were used principally for transatlantic sales, but after the Mississippi Valley opened up to agricultural trade, they were widely used in Chicago in the 1840s (Baer and Woodruff, 1935: 3-5).

The telegraph started to change the use of time contracts, as well as arbitrage. By widely transmitting knowledge of prices and crop conditions, it drew markets and prices together. We do not have good before-and-after measures, but we do have evidence, cited earlier, for the long-run decline in price disparities among markets. Moreover, we have measures from Cincinnati in particular. In the 1820s Cincinnati lagged two years behind Eastern markets. That meant that it took two years for disturbances in the Eastern market structure to affect Cincinnati prices. By 1840 the lag was down to four months; and by 1857—and probably much earlier—the effect of Eastern markets on Cincinnati was instantaneous. But once space was, in the phrase of the day, annihilated, once everyone was in the same place for purposes of trade, time as a new region of experience, uncertainty, speculation, and exploration was opened up to the forces of commerce.

A back-door example of this inversion of space and time can be drawn from a later episode involving the effect of the telephone on the New York Stock Exchange. By 1894 the telephone had made information time identical in major cities. Buyers and sellers, wherever they were, knew current prices as quickly as traders did on the floor of the exchange. The information gap, then, between New York and Boston had been eliminated and business gravitated from New York to Boston brokerage firms. The New York exchange countered this movement by creating a thirty-second time advantage that ensured New York's superiority to Boston. The exchange ruled that telephones would not be allowed on the floor. Price information had to be relayed by messenger to an area off the floor of the exchange that had been set aside for telephones. This move destroyed the temporal identity of markets, and a thirty-second monopoly of knowledge was created that drew business back to New York (Emery, 1896: 139).

This movement of commodities out of space and into time had three other consequences of great importance in examining the effect of the telegraph. First, futures trading required the decontexualization of markets; or, to put it in a slightly different way, markets were made relatively unresponsive to local conditions of supply and demand. The telegraph removed markets from the particular context in which they were historically located and concentrated on them forces emanating from any place and any time. This was a redefinition from physical or geographic markets to spiritual ones. In a sense they were made more mysterious; they became everywhere markets and everytime markets and thus less apprehensible at the very moment they became more powerful.

Second, not only were distant and amorphous forces brought to bear on markets, but the commodity was sundered from its representations; that is, the development of futures trading depended on the ability to trade or circulate negotiable instruments independently of the actual physical movement of goods. The representation of the commodity became the warehouse receipts from grain elevators along the railroad line. These instruments were then traded independently of any movement of the actual goods. The buyer of such receipts never expected to take delivery; the seller of such receipts never expected to make delivery. There is the old joke, which is also a cautionary tale, of the futures trader who forgot what he was up to and ended up with forty tons of wheat on his suburban lawn; but it is merely a joke and a tale. The futures trader often sells before he buys, or buys and sells simultaneously. But the buying and selling is not of goods but of receipts. What is being traded is not money for commodities but time against price. In short, the warehouse receipt, which stands as a representation of the product, has no intrinsic relation to the real product.

But in order to trade receipts rather than goods, a third change was necessary. In futures trading products are not bought or sold by inspection of the actual product or a sample thereof. Rather, they are sold through a grading system. In order to lend itself to futures trading, a product has to be mixed, standardized, diluted in order to be reduced to a specific, though abstract, grade. With the coming of the telegraph, products could no longer be shipped in separate units as numerous as there were owners of grain. "The high volume sales required impersonalized standards. Buyers were no longer able personally to check every lot" (Chandler, 1977: 211). Consequently, not all products are traded on the futures market because some resist the attempt to reduce them to standardized categories of quality.

The development of the futures markets, in summary, depended on a number of specific changes in markets and the commodity system. It required that information move independently of and faster than products. It required that prices be made uniform in space and that markets be decontextualized. It required, as well, that commodities be separated from the receipts that represent them and that commodities be reduced to uniform grades.

These were, it should be quickly added, the conditions that underlay Marx's analysis of the commodity fetish. That concept, now used widely and often indiscriminately, was developed in the *Grundrisse* and *Das Kapital* during the late 1850s, when futures trading became the dominant arena for the establishment of agricultural values. In particular, Marx made the key elements in the commodity fetish the decontextualization of markets, the separation of use value from exchange value brought about by the decline in the representative function of the warehouse receipt, and the abstraction of the product out of real conditions of production by a grading system. In the *Grundrisse* he comments, "This locational movement—the bringing of the product to market which is a necessary condition of its circulation, except when the point of production is itself a market—could more precisely be regarded as the transformation of the product into a commodity" (Marx, 1973: 534).

Marx's reference is to what Walter Benjamin (1968) would later call the "loss of aura" in his parallel analysis of the effect of mechanical reproduction on the work of art. After the object is abstracted out of the real conditions of its production and use and is transported to distant markets, standardized and graded, and represented by fully contingent symbols, it is made available as a commodity. Its status as a commodity represents the sundering of a real, direct relationship between buyer and seller, separates use value from exchange value, deprives objects of any uniqueness (which must then be returned to the object via advertising), and, most important, masks to the buyer the real conditions of production. Further, the process of divorcing the receipt from the product can be thought of as part of a general social process initiated by the use of money and widely written about in contemporary semiotics; the progressive divorce of the signifier from the signified, a process in which the world of signifiers progressively overwhelms and moves independently of real material objects.

To summarize, the growth of communications in the nineteenth century had the practical effect of diminishing space as a differentiating criterion in human affairs. What Harold Innis called the "penetrative powers of the price system" was, in effect, the spread of a uniform price system throughout space so that for purposes of trade everyone was in the same place. The telegraph was the critical instrument in this spread. In commerce this meant the decontextualization of markets so that prices no longer depended on local factors of supply and demand but responded to national and international forces. The spread of the price system was part of the attempt to colonize space. The correlative to the penetration of the price system was what the composer Igor Stravinsky called the "statisticalization of mind": the transformation of the entire mental world into quantity, and the distribution of quantities in space so that the relationship between things and people becomes solely one of numbers. Statistics widens the market for everything and makes it more uniform and interdependent. The telegraph worked this same effect on the practical consciousness of time through the construction of standard time zones.

IV

Our sense of time and our activities in time are coordinated through a grid of time zones, a grid so fixed in our consciousness that it seems to be the natural form of time, at least until we change back and forth between standard and daylight saving time. But standard time in the United States is a relatively recent invention. It was introduced on November 18, 1883.

Until that date virtually every American community established its own time by marking that point when the sun reached its zenith as noon. It could be determined astronomically with exactitude; but any village could do it, for all practical purposes, by observing the shortest shadow on a sundial. Official local time in a community could be fixed, as since time immemorial, by a church or later by a courthouse, a jeweler, or later still the railroad stationmaster; and a bell or whistle could be rung or set off so that the local burghers could set their timepieces. In Kansas City a ball was dropped from the highest building at noon and was visible for miles around, a practice still carried out at the annual New Year's Eve festivities in New York City's Times Square (Corliss, 1952).

Not every town kept its own time; many set their clocks in accord with the county seat or some other nearby town of commercial or political importance. When the vast proportion of American habitats were, in Robert Wiebe's (1967) phrase, "island communities" with little intercourse with one another, the distinctiveness of local time caused little confusion and worry. But as the tentacles of commerce and politics spread out from the capitals, temporal chaos came with them. The chaos was sheerly physical. With every degree of longitude one moved westward, the sun reached its zenith four minutes later. That meant that when it was noon in Boston it was 11:48 a.m. in Albany; when it was noon in Atlanta it was 11:36 a.m. in New Orleans. Put differently, noon came a minute later for every quarter degree of longitude one moved westward, and this was a shorter distance as one moved north: in general thirteen miles equaled one minute of time.

223

The setting of clocks to astronomically local time or, at best, to county seat time led to a proliferation of time zones. Before standard time Michigan had twenty-seven time zones; Indiana, twenty-three; Wisconsin, thirty-nine; Illinois, twenty-seven. The clocks in New York, Boston, and Philadelphia, cities today on identical time, were several minutes apart (Corliss, 1952: 3). When it was 12:00 in Washington, D.C., it was 11:30 in Atlanta, 12:09 in Philadelphia, 12:12 in New York, 12:24 in Boston, and 12:41 in Eastport, Maine.

As the railroads spread across the continent, the variety of local times caused enormous confusion with scheduling, brought accidents as trains on different clocks collided, and led to much passenger irritation, as no one could easily figure when a train would arrive at another town. The railroads used fifty-eight local times keyed to the largest cities. Moreover, each railroad keyed its clocks to the time of a different city. The Pennsylvania Railroad keyed its time to that of Philadelphia, but Philadelphia's clocks were twelve minutes behind New York's and five minutes ahead of Baltimore's. The New York Central stuck to New York City time. The Baltimore and Ohio keyed its time to three cities: Baltimore; Columbus, Ohio; and Vincennes, Indiana (Bartky and Harrison, 1979: 46-53).

The solution, which was to establish standard time zones, had long attracted the interest of scholars. The pressure to establish such zones was felt more strongly in North America, which averaged eight hours of daylight from Newfoundland to western Alaska. Although standard time was established earlier in Europe, the practical pressure there was less. There is only a half-hour variance in sun time across England; and France, while larger, could be run on Paris time. But England, for purposes of empire, had long been interested in standard time. The control of time allows for the coordination of activity and, therefore, effective social control. In navigation, time was early fixed on English ships according to the clock of the Greenwich observatory; and no matter where a ship might be in the Atlantic, its chronometer always registered Greenwich time. Similarly, Irish time was regulated by a clock set each morning at Big Ben, carried by rail to Holyhead, ferried across the Irish sea to Kingstown (now Dun Laoghaire), and then carried again by rail to Dublin, where Irish clocks were coordinated with English time (Schivelbusch, 1978: 39).

And so it was no surprise when in 1870 a New Yorker, Charles Dowd, proposed a system of standard time zones that fixed Greenwich as zero degrees longitude and laid out the zones around the world with centers 15 degrees east and west from Greenwich. As 15 degrees equals one hour, the world was laid out in twenty-four zones one hour apart.

Dowd's plan was a wonderful example of crackpot realism. The lines were laid out with geometric exactness and ignored geography, topography, region, trade, or natural affinity. Maine and Florida were put in separate time zones. It is a wonderful example of the maxim that the grid is the geometry of empire. Dowd recommended the plan to the railroads, which adopted it provisionally and created an index out of it so that the traveler could convert railroad time to local time by adding or subtracting so many minutes to or from the railroad schedule.

For thirteen years the Dowd system was debated but never officially adopted by the General Time Convention. The railroads tried during that period to get Congress to adopt it as a uniform time system, but Congress would not and for an obvious reason: standard time offended people with deeply held religious sentiments. It violated the actual physical working of the natural order and denied the presence of a divinely ordained nature. But even here religious language was a vanishing mediator for political sentiments; standard time was widely known as Vanderbilt's time, and protest against it was part of the populist protest against the banks, the telegraph, and the railroad.

In 1881, the Philadelphia General Time Convention turned the problem over to William Frederick Allen, a young civil engineer; two years later he returned a plan. It was based on Dowd's scheme but with a crucial difference: it allowed for the adjustment of time zones for purposes of economy and ecology. In his scheme time boundaries could be shifted up to 100 miles away from the geometric lines in order to minimize disruption. Most important, he recommended that the railroads abandon the practice of providing a minute index and that they simply adopt standard time for regulating their schedules and allow communities and institutions to adjust to the new time in any manner they chose.

In the Allen plan the United States was divided into four time zones, with centers on the 75th, 90th, 105th, and 120th meridians: Philadelphia, St. Louis, Denver, and Reno were the approximate centers. The zones extended seven and a half degrees to either side of the center line. November 18, 1883, was selected as the date for the changeover from local to standard time, and an ambitious "educational" campaign was mounted to help citizens adjust to the new system. On that date Chicago, the railroad hub, was tied by telegraph to an observatory in Allegheny, Pennsylvania. When it reached one o'clock over the center of the Eastern time zone, the clocks were stopped at noon in Chicago and held for nine minutes and thirty-two seconds until the sun centered on the 90th meridian. Then they were started again, with the railroad system now integrated and coordinated through time.

The changeover was greeted by mass meetings, anger, and religious protest but to no avail. Railroad time had become standard time. It was not made official U.S. time until the emergency of World War I. But within a few months after the establishment of railroad time, the avalanche of switches to it by local communities was well under way. Strangely enough, the United States never did go to 24-hour time and thus retained some connection between the diurnal cycle of human activity and the cycle of the planets.

The boundaries of the time zones have been repeatedly adjusted since that time. In general they have been made to follow state borders, but there are a number of exceptions. The western edge of the Eastern time zone was once in eastern Ohio, but now it forms a jagged line along the Illinois-Indiana border. Boise, Idaho, was moved from Pacific to Mountain time, and recently twelve thousand square miles of Arizona was similarly moved. The reasons for such changes tell us much about America's purposes. One gets the distinct feeling, for example, that the television networks would prefer a country with three time zones: east, central, and west.

Standard time zones were established because in the eyes of some they were necessary. They were established, to return to the point of this chapter, because of the technological power of the telegraph. Time was sent via the telegraph wire; but today, thanks to technical improvements, it is sent via radio waves from the Naval observatory in Maryland. The telegraph could send time faster than a railroad car could move; and therefore it facilitated the temporal coordination and integration of the entire system. Once that was possible, the new definitions of time could be used by industry and government to control and coordinate activity across the country, infiltrate into the practical consciousness of ordinary men and women, and uproot older notions of rhythm and temporality.

The development of standard time zones served to overlay the world with a grid of time in the same way the surveyor's map laid a grid of space on old cities, the new territories of the West, or the seas. The time grid could then be used to control and coordinate activities within the grid of space.

V

When the ecological niche of space was filled, filled as an arena of commerce and control, attention was shifted to filling time, now defined as an aspect of space, a continuation of space in another dimension. As the spatial frontier was closed, time became the new frontier. Let me mention, in closing, two other dimensions of the temporal frontier.

An additional time zone to be penetrated once space was exhausted was sacred time, in particular the sabbath. The greatest invention of the ancient Hebrews was the idea of the sabbath, though I am using this word in a fully secular sense: the invention of a region free from control of the state and commerce where another dimension of life could be experienced and where altered forms of social relationship could occur. As such, the sabbath has always been a major resistance to state and market power. For purposes of communication, the effective penetration of the sabbath came in the 1880s with the invention of the Sunday newspaper. It was Hearst with his New York Sunday *World* who popularized the idea of Sunday newspaper reading and created, in fact, a market where none had existed before—a sabbath market. Since then the penetration of the sabbath has been one of the "frontiers" of commercial activity. Finally, when the frontier in space was officially closed in 1890, the "new frontier" became the night, and since then there has been a continuous spreading upward of commercial activity. Murray Melbin (1987) has attempted to characterize "night as a frontier." In terms of communication the steady expansion of commercial broadcasting into the night is one of the best examples. There were no 24-hour radio stations in Boston, for example, from 1918 through 1954; now half of the stations in Boston operate all night. Television has slowly expanded into the night at one end and at the other initiated operations earlier and earlier. Now, indeed, there are 24-hour television stations in major markets.

The notion of night as frontier, a new frontier of time that opens once space is filled, is a metaphor, but it is more than that. Melbin details some of the features common to the spatial and temporal frontiers: they both advance in stages; the population is more sparsely settled and homogeneous; there is solitude, an absence of social constraints, and less persecution; settlements are isolated; government is decentralized; lawlessness and violence as well as friendliness and helpfulness increase; new behavioral styles emerge. That is, the same dialectic between centralization and decentralization occurs on the temporal frontier as on the spatial frontier. On the one hand, communication is even more privatized at night. On the other hand, social constraints on communication are relaxed because the invasive hand of authority loosened.

The penetration of time, the use of time as a mechanism of control, the opening of time to commerce and politics has been radically extended by advances in computer technology. Time has been redefined as an ecological niche to be filled down to the microsecond, nanosecond, and picosecond—down to a level at which time can be pictured but not experienced. This process and the parallel reconstruction of practical consciousness and practical activity begins in those capacities of the telegraph which prefigure the computer. The telegraph constructed a simulacrum of complex systems, provided an analogue model of the railroad and a digital model of language. It coordinated and controlled activity in space, often behind the backs of those subject to it.

E. P. Thompson finds it ominous that the young Henry Ford should have created a watch with two dials: one for local time and another for railroad time. "Attention to time in labour depends in large degree upon the need for the synchronization of labour" (Thompson, 1967: 70). Modern conceptions of time have rooted into our consciousness so deeply that the scene of the worker receiving a watch at his retirement is grotesque and comic. He receives a watch when the need to tell time is ended. He receives a watch as a tribute to his learning the hardest lesson of the working man—to tell time.

As the watch coordinated the industrial factory; the telegraph via the grid of time coordinated the industrial nation. Today, computer time, computer space, and computer memory, notions we dimly understand, are reworking practical consciousness coordinating and controlling life in what we glibly call the postindustrial society. Indeed, the microcomputer is replacing the watch as the favored gift for the middle class retiree. In that new but unchanging custom we see the deeper relationship between technology and ideology.

Notes

1 See Chandler (1977), esp. Part II.
2 Among the most readable, accessible sources on the patent struggles is Josephson (1959).
3 See Wiener (1948: 38-44).
4 Whereas I have commented on the essentially religious metaphors that greeted the telegraph in the essays cited, Czitrom (1982) brings this material together in a systematic way.

5　By a vanishing mediator—a concept borrowed from Fredric Jameson—I mean a notion that serves as a bearer of change but that can disappear once that change is ratified in the reality of institutions. See Jameson (1974: 111-149).

6　See chapter 1. On changes in styles of journalism, see Sims (1979).

7　Steffens (1958: 834). For a memoir that discusses the art and adversity of writing for the cable, see Shirer (1976: 282 ff.).

8　The quotation is from an as yet unpublished manuscript by Douglas Birkhead of the University of Utah. Birkhead develops these themes in some detail.

9　On urban imperialism, see Schlesinger (1933) and Pred (1973).

10　Among the few studies on the telegraph and empire, the most distinguished is Fortner (1978); see also Field (1978: 644-68).

11　In making these remarks I am much indebted to the work of Fortner and Field.

12　On these matters there are useful suggestions in Boorstin (1973).

Works Cited

Adams, Henry (1931). *The Education of Henry Adams.* (Original edition, Massachusetts Historical Society, 1918). New York: Modern Library.

Andrews, William P. (1857). *Memoirs on the Euphrates Valley Route to India.* London: William Allen.

Arnold, Matthew (1954). "On the Modern Element in Literature" (1857). In John Bryson, ed., *The Poetry and Prose of Matthew Arnold* (pp. 269-283). Cambridge: Harvard University Press.

Axtell, James (1985). *The Invasion Within: The Contest of Cultures in Colonial North America.* New York: Oxford University Press.

Baer, Julius B., and George P. Woodruff (1935). *Commodity Exchanges.* New York: Harper and Bros.

Bailyn, Bernard (1986). *The Peopling of British North America: An Introduction.* New York: Alfred A. Knopf.

Bartky, Ian R., and Elizabeth Harrison (1979). "Standard and Daylight Saving Time." *Scientific American,* 240 (5), 46-53.

Barnes, Harry Elmer, ed. (1966). *An Introduction to the History of Sociology* (abridged ed.). Chicago: University of Chicago Press.

Beard, Charles A. (1914). *Contemporary American History.* New York: Macmillan.

Beard, Charles A., and Mary Beard (1940). *The Rise of American Civilization.* New York: Macmillan.

Bendix, Reinhard, and Guenther Roth (1971). "Sociology and the Distrust of Reason." In *Scholarship and Partisanship: Essays on Max Weber* (pp. 84-105). Berkeley: University of California Press.

Benjamin, Walter (1968). *Illuminations.* New York: Harcourt, Brace and World.

Benson, Lee (1951). "The Historical Background of Turner's Frontier Essay." *Agricultural History,* 25, 59-82.

Berger, Peter L. (1967). *The Sacred Canopy.* Garden City, NY: Doubleday.

Berger, Peter, and Thomas Luckmann (1966). *The Social Construction of Reality.* Garden City: NY: Doubleday.

Birkenhead, Earl of (1930). *The World in 2030 A. D.* New York: Brewer and Warren.

Boorstin, Daniel J. (1973). *The Americans: The Democratic Experience.* New York: Random House.

———(1974). *Democracy and Its Discontents.* New York: Random House.

Bourdieu, Pierre (1984). *Distinction: A Social Critique of the Judgment of Taste.* Cambridge, MA: Harvard University Press.

Briggs, Charles, and Augustus Maverick (1858). *The Story of the Telegraph and a History of the Great Atlantic Cable.* New York: Rudd and Carleton.

Brown, Dee (1966). *The Year of the Century 1876.* New York: Scribner.

Brzezinski, Zbigniew (1970). *Between Two Ages.* New York: Viking.

Burke, Kenneth (1957). *The Philosophy of Literary Form.* New York: Vintage Books.

Butterfield, Herbert A. (1973). *The Whig Interpretation of History.* Harmondsworth, England: Penguin Books.

Carey, James T. (1972). "Changing Courtship Patterns in the Popular Song." In R. Serge Denisoff and Richard Peterson, eds., *The Sounds of Social Change* (pp. 198-212). Chicago: Rand-McNally.

Carey, James W. (1969). "The Communications Revolution and the Professional Communicator." *The Sociological Review Monograph,* No. 13, 23-38.

———(1983). "The Origins of Radical Discourse on Communications in the United States." *Journal of Communication,* 33 (3), 311-13.

Carey, James W., and A. L. Kreiling (1974). "Popular Culture and Uses and Gratifications Research: Notes Toward an Accommodation." In J. G. Blumler and E. Katz, eds., *The Uses of Mass Communication: Current Perspectives on Gratifications Research* (pp. 225-48). Beverly Hills: Sage Publications.

Carey James W., and Norman Sims (1976). "The Telegraph and the News Report." Unpublished paper, University of Illinois.

Chandler, Alfred D. (1977). *The Visible Hand: The Managerial Revolution in American Business.* Cambridge, MA: Harvard University Press.

Clanchy, Michael (1979). *From Memory to Written Record: England, 1066-1307.* Cambridge: Harvard University Press.

Clarke, I. F. (1969). "The First Forecast of the Future." *Futures,* (4), 325-30.

Cole, Arthur H. (1938). *Wholesale Commodity Prices in the United States, 1700-1861.* Cambridge, MA: Harvard University Press.

Corliss, Carlton J. (1952). *The Day of Two Noons* (6th ed.). Washington, DC: Association of American Railroads.

Czitrom, Daniel Joseph (1982). *Media and the American Mind: From Morse to McLuhan.* Chapel Hill: University of North Carolina Press.

Dahl, Robert (1973). *Size and Democracy.* Palo Alto: Stanford University Press.

Dewey, John (1916). *Democracy and Education.* New York: Macmillan.

———(1927). *The Public and Its Problems.* New York: Henry Holt and Co.

———(1934). *Art as Experience.* New York: Minton, Balch.

———(1939). *Intelligence in the Modern World* (collected works). New York: Modern Library.

Donoghue, Denis (1987). *Reading America.* New York: Alfred A. Knopf.

Durkheim, Emile (1953). *Sociology and Philosophy*. New York: Free Press.

Emery, Henry Crosby (1896). *Speculation on the Stock and Produce Exchanges of the United States. Studies in History, Economics and Public Law* New York: Columbia University Press.

The Federalist (1961). Edited by Jacob E. Cooke. Cleveland: Meridan Books.

Field, James A. (1978). "American Imperialism: The Worst Chapter in Almost Any Book." *American Historical Review*, 83 (3), 644-83.

Fortner, Robert (1978). "Messiahs and Monopolists: A Cultural History of Canadian Communication Systems, 1846-1914." Ph.D. dissertation, University of Illinois.

Foucault, Michael (1979). *Discipline and Punish*. New York: Random House.

Fuller, R. Buckminster (1963). *No More Secondhand God and Other Writings*. Carbondale: Southern Illinois University Press.

Futures (1969). "Statement by President Nixon on Creating a National Goals Research Staff." 1 (5), 458-59.

Garvey, Michael Angelo (1852). *The Silent Revolution: Or the Future Effects of Steam and Electricity upon the Condition of Mankind*. London: William and Frederich G. Cash.

Geddes, Patrick (1917). *Ideas at War*. London: Williams and Norgate.

Geertz, Clifford (1973). *The Interpretation of Cultures*. New York: Basic Books.

———(1981). *Negara*. Princeton, NJ: Princeton University Press.

Giddens, Anthony (1979). *Central Problems in Social Theory*. Berkeley: University of California Press.

Goody, Jack, ed. (1968). *Literacy in Traditional Societies*. Cambridge: Cambridge University Press.

Gouldner, Alvin W. (1977). *The Dialectic of Ideology and Technology*. New York: Seabury Press.

Habermas, Jürgen (1984). *The Theory of Communicative Action*, Vol. 1. Boston: Beacon Press.

Hackworth, R., ed. (1972). *Plato's Phaedrus*. Cambridge: Cambridge University Press.

Hall, Stuart (1977). "The Hinterland of Science: Ideology and the Sociology of Knowledge." In Centre for Contemporary Cultural Studies, *On Ideology*. London: Hutchinson.

———(1982). "The Rediscovery of 'Ideology': The Return of the Repressed in Media Studies." In Michael Gurevitch, Tony Bennett, James Curran, and Janet Woollacott, eds., *Culture, Society and the Media*. London: Methuen.

Hayakawa, Samuel I. (1957). "Popular Songs vs. the Facts of Life." In Bernard Rosenberg and David Manning White, eds., *Mass Culture* (pp. 393-403). New York: Free Press.

Heaton, Herbert (1966). *The Economics of Empire*. The James Ford Bell Lecture, No. 3. Minneapolis: University of Minnesota.

Heidegger, Martin (1968). *Existence and Being*. Chicago: Henry

Regnery.

Hirsch, Fred (1976). *Social Limits to Growth*. Cambridge, MA: Harvard University Press.

Hoggart, Richard (1961). *The Uses of Literacy*. Boston: Beacon Press.

Hovland, Carl, I. Janis, and H. Kelley (1953). *Communication and Persuasion*. New Haven: Yale University Press.

Hutchinson, Paul (1937). "Revolution by Electricity." In Warren Bower, ed., *Directions* (pp. 83-100). New York: Lippincott.

Huxley, Aldous (1972). *Tomorrow and Tomorrow and Tomorrow and Other Essays*. New York: Perennial Library.

Innis, Harold A. (1930). *The Fur Trade in Canada*. New Haven: Yale University Press.

———(1950). *Empire and Communication*. Oxford: Oxford University Press.

———(1951). *The Bias of Communication*. Toronto: University of Toronto Press.

———(1952). *Changing Concepts of Time*. Toronto: University of Toronto Press.

———(1954). "Concept of Monopoly and Civilization." *Explorations*, No. 3.

———(1956). *Essays in Canadian Economic History*. Toronto: University of Toronto Press.

———(n.d.). *The Idea File* in the collection of the Thomas Fisher Library, University of Toronto.

Jameson, Fredric (1974). "The Vanishing Mediator." In *Working Papers in Cultural Studies*, Vol. 5 (pp. 111-49). Birmingham: Centre for Contemporary Cultural Studies.

Jefferson, Thomas (1854). *The Writings of Thomas Jefferson*, Vol. 8. Washington, DC: Daylor and Maury.

Josephson, Matthew (1959). *Edison: A Biography*. New York: Oxford University Press.

Kallen, Horace M. (1950). *Patterns of Progress*. New York: Columbia University Press.

Katz, Elihu (1959). "Mass Communication Research and the Study of Popular Culture: An Editorial Note on a Possible Future for this Journal." *Studies in Public Communication*, 2.

Katz, Elihu, and Paul Lazarsfeld (1955). *Personal Influence*. New York: Free Press.

Kornhauser, William (1959). *The Politics of Mass Society*. New York: Free Press.

Kropotkin, Petr (1913). *Fields, Factories and Workshops*. New York: Putnam.

Kuhn, Thomas S. (1962). *The Structure of Scientific Revolutions*. Chicago: University of Chicago Press.

———(1983). "Rationality and Theory Choice." *Journal of Philosophy*, 80 (10), 563-70.

Lazarsfeld, Paul, B. Berelson, and H. Gaudet (1948). *The People's Choice*. New York: Columbia University Press.

Leymore, Varda Langhold (1975). *Hidden Myth: Structure and Symbolism in Advertising*. London: Heinemann.

Lippmann, Walter (1922). *Public Opinion*. New York: Macmillan.

Lowell, James Russell (1871). *The Works of James Russell Lowell*. Standard Library Edition. Cambridge: Riverside Press.

MacDonald, Dwight (1962). *Against the American Grain*. New York: Random House.

Malinowski, Bronislaw (1962). *Sex, Culture and Myth*. New York: Harcourt, Brace and World.

Mandelbaum, Seymour J. (1965). *Boss Tweed's New York*. New York: John Wiley.

Mannheim, Karl (1965). *Ideology and Utopia*. New York: Harvest Books.

Matza, David (1964). *Delinquency and Drift*. New York: John Wiley.

Marx, Karl (1973). *Grundrisse: Foundations of the Critique of Political Economy*. New York: Vintage Books.

Marx, Leo (1964). *The Machine in the Garden*. New York: Oxford University Press.

Matthews, Fred H. (1977). *Quest for an American Sociology: Robert E. Park and the Chicago School*. Montreal: McGill-Queens University Press.

McLuhan, Marshall (1964). "Introduction." In Harold A. Innis, *The Bias of Communication*. Toronto: University of Toronto Press.

Melbin, Murray (1987). *Night as Frontier: Colonizing the World after Dark*. New York: Free Press.

Miller, Perry (1965). *The Life of the Mind in America*. New York: Harcourt, Brace and World.

Mills, C. Wright (1959). *The Power Elite*. New York: Oxford University Press.

———(1963). *Power, Politics and People* (Irving Louis Horowitz, ed.). New York: Ballantine.

Morley, David (1980). *The "Nationwide" Audience: Structure and Decoding*. London: British Film Institute.

———(1986). *Family Television: Cultural Power and Domestic Leisure*. London: Comedia Publishing Group.

Mumford, Lewis (1955). *The Human Prospect* (Harry T. Moore and Karl W. Deutsch, eds.). Boston: Beacon Press.

———(1959). "An Appraisal of Lewis Mumford's 'Technics and Civilization.'" *Daedalus*, 88.

———(1963). *Technics and Civilization*. New York: Harcourt Brace and World.

———(1967). *Technics and Human Development*. New York: Harcourt Brace Jovanovich.

———(1970). *The Pentagon of Power*. New York: Harcourt Brace Jovanovich.

Nevins, Allan (1971). "The Tradition of the Future." In Tom E. Kakonis and James C. Wilcox, eds., *Now and Tomorrow*. Lexington, MA: D. C. Heath.

Noble, David F. (1977). *America by Design: Science, Technology and the Rise of Corporate Capitalism*. New York: Alfred A. Knopf.

Park, Robert Ezra (1955). "News as a Form of Knowledge." In *Society* (pp. 71-88). New York: Free Press.

Pitkin, Hannah F. (1972). *Wittgenstein and Justice*. Berkeley: University of California Press.

Pocock, J. A. G. (1975). *The Machiavellian Moment*. Princeton, NJ: Princeton University Press.

Polak, Fred L. (1961). *The Image of the Future*. New York: Oceana.

Polsky, Ned (1967). *Hustlers, Beats and Others*. Chicago: Aldine.

Pred, Alan (1973). *Urban Growth and the Circulation of Information: The United States System of Cities, 1790-1840*. Cambridge, MA: Harvard University Press.

———(1980). *Urban Growth and City-Systems in the United Systems, 1840-1860*. Cambridge, MA: Harvard University Press.

Prime, Samuel Irnaeus (1875). *The Life of Samuel F. B. Morse. LL.D.* New York: Appleton.

Quandt, Jean (1970). *From the Small Town to the Great Community*. New Brunswick, NJ: Rutgers University Press.

Reich, Charles (1970). *The Greening of America*. New York: Random House.

Rorty, Richard (1979). *Philosophy and the Mirror of Nature*. Princeton, NJ: Princeton University Press.

———(1982). *Consequences of Pragmatism*. Minneapolis: University of Minnesota Press.

Ryle, Gilbert (1971). *The Concept of Mind*. New York: Barnes and Noble.

Sahlins, Marshall (1976). *Culture and Practical Reason*. Chicago: University of Chicago Press.

Sampson, Anthony (1974). *The Sovereign State of ITT*. Greenwich, CT: Fawcett Books.

Schivelbusch, Wolfgang (1978). "Railroad space and railroad time." *New German Critique*, No. 14 (Spring), 31-40.

———(1979). *The Railway Journey*. New York: Urizen.

Schlesinger, Arthur, Sr. (1933). *The Rise of the City, 1878-1898*. New York: Macmillan.

Schutz, Alfred (1967). *Collected Papers, Vol. 1. The Problem of Social Reality*. The Hague: Martinus Nijhoff.

———(1970). *On Phenomenology and Social Relations*. Chicago: University of Chicago Press.

Shils, Edward (1959). "Mass Society and Its Culture." In N. Jacobs, ed., *Culture for the Millions?* (pp. 1-27). Princeton: D. Van Nostrand.

Shirer, William I. (1976). *20th Century Journey: The Start: 1904-1930*. New York: Simon and Schuster.

Sims, Norman (1979). "The Chicago Style of Journalism." Ph.D. dissertation, University of Illinois.

Smith, Bruce James (1985). *Politics and Remembrance*. Princeton, NJ: Princeton University Press.

Steffens, Lincoln (1958). *The Autobiography of Lincoln Steffens*. New York: Harcourt, Brace and World.

Stephenson, William (1967). *The Play Theory of Mass Communication.* Chicago: University of Chicago Press.

Taylor, Charles (1975). *Hegel.* Cambridge: Cambridge University Press.

Thompson, E. P. (1967). "Time, Work-Discipline and Industrial Capitalism." *Past and Present,* No. 38, 56-97.

Thompson, Robert L. (1947). *Wiring a Continent.* Princeton, NJ: Princeton University Press.

Thoreau, Henry David (1957). *Walden.* Boston: Houghton Mifflin.

Toffler, Alvin (1971). *Future Shock.* New York: Bantam Books.

Trachtenberg, Alan (1965). *Brooklyn Bridge: Fact and Symbol.* New York: Oxford University Press.

Trilling, Lionel (1965). *Beyond Culture.* New York: Viking.

Turnbull, Colin (1972). *The Mountain People.* New York: Simon and Schuster.

Warshow, Robert (1964). *The Immediate Experience.* Garden City, NY: Anchor Books.

Weber, Max (1946). In H. Gerth and C. Wright Mills, eds., *From Max Weber: Essays in Sociology.* New York: Oxford University Press.

———(1947). *The Theory of Social and Economic Organization.* New York: Oxford University Press.

Wells, H. G. (1929). *The Way the World Is Going.* New York: Doubleday.

Westin, Alan F., ed. (1971). *Information Technology in a Democracy.* Cambridge: Harvard University Press.

White, Morton (1957). *Social Thought in America: The Revolt against Formalism.* Boston: Beacon Press.

Wiebe, Robert (1967). *The Search for Order, 1873-1920.* New York: Hill and Wang.

Wiener, Norbert (1948). *Cybernetics.* Cambridge: MIT Press.

Williams, Raymond (1958). *Culture and Society, 1780-1950.* New York: Columbia University Press.

———(1961). *The Long Revolution.* New York: Columbia University Press.

———(1966). *Communications.* London: Chatto and Windus.

———(1973). *The Country and the City.* London: Chatto and Windus.

Wills, Garry (1981). *Explaining America: The Federalist.* Garden City, NY: Doubleday.

Wilson, Geoffrey (1976). *The Old Telegraphs.* London: Phillimore.

Young, J. Z. (1951). *Doubt and Certainty in Science.* Oxford, England: Clarendon Press.

Index

INDEX

About the author

James W. Carey is the Dean of the College of Communications, University of Illinois at Urbana-Champaign. He held the George H. Gallup Chair at the University of Iowa from 1976-79. A former fellow of the National Endowment for the Humanities and the Gannett Center for Media Studies at Columbia University, Professor Carey is currently editor of the journal *Communication*. He recently edited *Media, Myths and Narratives* (Sage, 1988) and has published over seventy-five essays and reviews. He has been a visiting professor at Pennsylvania State University and the University of Georgia.